Gwennie's
DIARY

Gwennie's DIARY

A KIWI'S WORLD TOUR TO YORKSHIRE 1939-40

GWYNNE IRENE PEACOCK
Edited by ANTHONY DODSWORTH

FONTHILL

Learn more about Fonthill Media. Join our mailing list to find out about our latest titles and special offers at:
www.fonthillmedia.com

Fonthill Media Limited
www.fonthillmedia.com
office@fonthillmedia.com

First published in the United Kingdom 2014

British Library Cataloguing in Publication Data:
A catalogue record for this book is available from the British Library

ISBN 978-1-78155-268-1

Typeset in 10pt on 13pt Sabon LT Std
Printed and bound by CPI Group (UK) Ltd, Croydon, CR0 4YY

Contents

Introduction

On a cold winter's morning early in 2003 a postman struggled up the path of
a bungalow in Haugh Road, Rawmarsh, South Yorkshire to deliver a heavy,
rectangular parcel securely wrapped in several layers of thick brown paper. The
postmark showed it had been sent from New Zealand and, as it transpired, it
was to be the missing link in a story that stretched back over more than half
of the twentieth century. It was addressed to Malcolm and Noreen Brown and
when they tore away the wrapping they discovered a huge typewritten diary
that recorded the journey of a lifetime undertaken by Gwynne Irene Peacock
in 1939 and 1940. Gwynne, or Gwennie as she was known to all her English
family, was a distant relative of Malcolm's and he had met her just once. The
diary was extraordinary, particularly due to its great length, approximately
375,000 words covering just eighteen months of Gwennie's life, and to the
outstanding descriptive nature of its contents. The reason the diary ended up
in a mining village in Yorkshire, thousands of miles away from New Zealand,
literally the other side of the world, is a fascinating aspect of this story.

In 1939 Gwennie had set off from Auckland on a journey of discovery
to visit the relatives she had never met in the United Kingdom as well as to
complete a round-the-world trip. Her father, George, still had relations in
Northern Ireland while her mother, Susanna (*née* Turner), had left a large
family in Yorkshire many years before.

She sailed from Auckland Harbour on 14 February 1939 on board the
SS *Awatea* before transferring to the RMS *Orcades* for the long journey to
Europe. She made a number of stops in Australia before exploring Ceylon,
Aden and Egypt on the way to Villefranche in Southern France. She left the
ship there and set off by herself to travel across Europe at her own pace and

visited Italy, Switzerland, Germany, Holland, Belgium and France before crossing the Channel to England. She travelled to all corners of the British Isles using Rawmarsh near Rotherham in Yorkshire as her base. Her mother had left Rawmarsh for New Zealand about forty years before.

The declaration of war in September 1939 disrupted her plans and she had to adopt a less flexible approach for her return to New Zealand, travelling via Canada, mainland USA, Hawaii and Pago Pago. She eventually arrived home in July 1940.

There are two of the relatives Gwennie met in Rawmarsh still living there today over seventy years later, and Malcolm Brown's father was one of Gwennie's most constant companions while she was in Rawmarsh. Malcolm can remember the family talking about Gwennie a great deal when he was young, an intrepid lady who had travelled all the way across the world from New Zealand to visit her family in Rawmarsh. Malcolm's father, also Malcolm, was Gwennie's first cousin. The excitement of her visit is perhaps more difficult to understand in these days of widespread global travel and Skype, but back in the 1930s it was strange indeed for such direct contact to be made following a person's migration. There are memories of Gwennie writing copious notes on her adventures whenever she had a spare minute and then typing them up so that a copy could be sent back to her mother (who she often called 'little mother') and father in New Zealand. Fortunately she worked as a typist and so could complete her diary reports more quickly than most, however it is clear from her diary that she did find it onerous. She did seem to have a clear idea that this would be a journey of a lifetime, not to be repeated, and so recognised the need to record all her visits and activities in type as well as to help her parents 'see' what she was experiencing. She was a committed letter-writer (or typist) and once she returned to New Zealand she kept in touch with her English relatives and friends by typed letters every two or three months. She made sure she sent food parcels regularly to the family in England while the war lasted.

In 1993 Malcolm and Noreen finally achieved their ambition to visit Gwennie in New Zealand; she was in her eighties by this time and living in Henderson, a suburb of Auckland. They were collected at Auckland airport by Gwennie driving 'Oscar'—a pale green Austin four-seater. They remember vividly the journey back to Gwennie's home describing it politely as 'very lively' for Gwennie by then was an enthusiastic but erratic driver who would have been much better if there had been no other traffic on the roads! They found out later that Gwennie's neighbour, Nora, had tried to persuade Gwennie to get them a taxi instead (obviously knowing the shortcomings of her driving) but she would not hear of it. Safely delivered, but shaken, they got to know Gwennie and found her an energetic and charming host, quite small just like her mother and aunts had been. While talking about Rawmarsh, Gwennie rooted out of a cupboard the two volumes of her diary from 1939 and 1940 that covered her visit there and left them in the guest bedroom. Noreen can still remember sitting up half the night totally enthralled by the story the diary told. When they enthused about it to Gwennie in the morning she said she would make sure it was sent to them when she died. Malcolm and Noreen returned to England and over time forgot Gwennie's promise. Ten years later when Gwennie died, her neighbour, obviously on instructions from Gwennie, sent the diary to them.

Also living in Rawmarsh today, and in fact for his whole life, is John Turner, Gwennie's first cousin. John was a young boy growing up in Rawmarsh when Gwennie visited. He still remembers the excitement of her arrival at the railway station in Rotherham and recalled it clearly when Gwennie's account of the event was read to him. John's father, also John, was Gwennie's mother's brother. John and Susanna had grown up together in Netherfield Lane, Parkgate (a neighbouring settlement attached to Rawmarsh). Gwennie stayed with John's family for some of her time in Rawmarsh and brought him back presents from her travels around the country. He remembers her sending him a Maori boat carved with a piece of glass on her return to New Zealand. Like Malcolm, John grew up in a household where Gwennie was often mentioned and like Malcolm he too visited her in New Zealand when he retired. In January 2002 John and Betty, his wife, flew to Auckland via Singapore. By this time Gwennie was in her nineties but she was thrilled to welcome John once she realised he was actually the little boy she had met and loved over sixty years before. John and Betty found her alert and lively despite suffering from increased deafness; they still treasure the photographs they have of themselves with Gwennie. Sadly Gwennie was to die within a year of the meeting.

In all Gwennie's diary represents a monumental effort. To write 375,000 words in an eighteen-month period is amazing, but to write it first as rough notes and then type it all up while travelling round the world is truly incredible. She intended originally to type letters to her mother and father and send them along with carbon copies of her diary but eventually she settled on just sending them the copies of her diary pages. This is why there are comments in the diary typed specifically to her parents.

There is plenty of evidence that Gwennie had prepared for the journey for a long time, researching the places to visit in mainland Europe and especially the British Isles. She had obviously devoured E. V. Morton's books describing many of the attractions of Britain and frequently quotes from them at considerable length in her diary. She was fascinated by the wording on gravestones and memorials, which were obviously quoted extensively in Morton. These quotations have generally been left out of this edited version of her diary. She also had 'set-pieces' she wished to experience on her journey such as attending a service in St Peter's Basilica, Rome, having a flutter in the casino in Monte Carlo, walking through an English meadow ablaze with spring flowers, following in the footsteps of Burns and Scott and, perhaps more bizarrely, sleeping (if only for a few minutes) with the homeless in the crypt of St Martin's-in-the-Fields in Central London.

Gwennie clearly had a great love of literature and quoted extensively from the likes of Dickens, Scott and Burns and one feels these were memorised quotes rather than just copied from a book. While staying in her mother's birth village of Rawmarsh she took the opportunity to visit the impressive ruins of Conisbrough Castle less than five miles away. She was perhaps most excited by finding the little chapel or oratory in the keep 'where the noble Edith, mother of Athelstan, prayed during the burial of her son'. This relates directly to *Ivanhoe* written by Walter Scott, parts of which were based at Conisbrough. As usual she referred to the name of the place and discusses its possible origins. She seemed fascinated by words and accents throughout her journey and while in London spent time investigating Cockney rhyming slang at Billingsgate Fish Market. She even visited it at four in the morning! Her English teacher from Christchurch would surely have felt proud of implanting such interests in her pupil! She liked to record conversations as accurately as possible so she used unusual spellings to reflect the sound of what was being said. This is particularly noticeable when recording the banter of her Yorkshire family in Rawmarsh.

Gwennie grew up listening frequently to her mother's reminiscences of life in England and more specifically of life in Rawmarsh. There was a picture of Whitby Abbey, North Yorkshire, hanging up in her home in New Zealand and she was fascinated by the tales of her grandfather James Turner, and her grandmother Elizabeth. Her diary often mentions James and Elizabeth although they had died well before her visit. She was very interested in James's work as a coal miner and knew a great deal about Elizabeth's role in Rawmarsh as a midwife and nurse to her neighbours and friends. She apparently delivered all but two of her numerous grandchildren.

Gwennie was convinced she had gypsy blood and used this as an explanation of her need to 'wander'. Looking at the photograph of Gwennie's grandmother the gypsy link is certainly possible. In the diary she describes a memorable meeting with gypsies in Inverness where she sampled the delights of roasted hedgehog for dinner! Undeterred, when told she had eaten hedgehog, she asked for 'seconds'. She also describes a number of occasions when she visited a fortune-teller, again perhaps influenced by her belief in her gypsy origins.

Gwennie's family history is a story in itself, but briefly the Turner side of the family was closely linked with coal mining. Her great-grandfather, Samuel, and his family were living in Ilkeston, Derbyshire, at the time of the 1851 census, and at Greasley, Nottinghamshire, in 1861. By 1871 they had moved to Walsall Wood in the West Midlands, and Samuel (forty-eight) was working as a coal miner alongside his sons, Samuel (twenty-five), Henry (nineteen), John (sixteen) and James (fourteen). James was Gwennie's grandfather and by 1881 he had married Elizabeth and worked as a miner in Blackwell near Mansfield, Nottinghamshire. Ten years later James had moved to Netherfield Lane, Parkgate (beside Rawmarsh) and Susanna (Gwennie's mother) was part of the family that included then four sisters and two brothers. When Susanna finished school she went to Bradford with her older sister Eliza to work in service and Susanna became a companion for a sickly girl living in the city. The girl's parents were advised to move away from this damp and smoky area of England and moved to New Zealand. Susanna went with the family and eventually settled there. She married Captain George Peacock who was an important footwear supplier with links to the New Zealand Army. and Gwennie was apparently their only child. Gwennie was born in May 1908 in Christchurch and probably went to school there. Subsequently the family moved to Auckland and Gwennie lived at home with her mother and father while working as a typist in a firm that may have had links to coach building.

Gwennie's time in Rawmarsh was spent at the heart of Susanna's family and she knew it was very important to convey to her mother all she saw and heard. She had an old address book of her mother's with the names of people to visit and was building on her mother's memories from forty years before. She regularly wrote how much she wished that her mother was with her to meet all these people again and to be re-united with her brothers and sisters. Gwennie swapped around where she stayed, moving from one uncle and aunt to another and back again. When she first saw her Auntie Lizzie at Rotherham Station she could not get over how similar she was to her mother. She revelled in her place in a large, extended family perhaps particularly because she was an only child. She loved going around with her male cousins, sharing secrets with her girl cousins and chatting deep into the night with her aunts and uncles. She was loved from the moment she met the family and this she fully reciprocated. Her avid search for presents for every single one of her relatives and new friends at Christmas 1939 is one small sign of her appreciation. Despite being treated by all her relatives she made sure she helped out whenever she could with house cleaning and cooking. Her wonderment at the rituals of Monday washing days suggests things were rather different in New Zealand. She certainly felt that some aspects of life in Yorkshire were old-fashioned compared to her homeland, for example she was amazed at all the ornaments and brasses in people's homes. In New Zealand she felt all these had been done away with because it was so time-consuming to keep them clean.

It is interesting to read Gwennie's diary and use it to provide clues to her personality and her aspirations. First impressions from the diary might suggest the creator was in her early twenties rather than in fact in her early thirties. She was clearly energetic, independent and had a real talent for getting on well with people she met. She was not sophisticated in many senses but was certainly well educated and could cope impressively with dining in the Savoy and in the Waldorf in London, and 'playing the tables' in Monte Carlo. She had studied foreign languages and indeed in Germany caused considerable surprise at being 'English' and yet able to understand German. She practised using an escalator when she first got to Australia to make sure she would not be 'shown up' in Europe or North America later in the trip. She was not rich but obviously there was considerable expense involved in such an extended global holiday. One can imagine her and her parents saving up, perhaps for years, to enable her to go. She does mention several times an Auntie Mollie who makes the journey to Europe with her and, once separated, sends her cheques. She was certainly not extravagant, recoiling at the prices charged in many of the clothes shops she entered. On the ships she travelled third-class and that meant sharing sleeping accommodation sometimes with three other people. She stayed in hostels in many places and occasionally bed and breakfasts. She travelled a great deal by train and bus in Britain and was always keen to hitch a lift when possible whether it was a smart Rolls-Royce, a motor-bike or a small saloon on its last legs (or tyres). She played golf in New Zealand and belonged to a tennis club which suggests a certain social status at that time, but her wardrobe was limited and throughout the entire trip she was excited about the fur coat she had bought specially for travelling. If one compares the photograph of her with her relatives without the fur coat and the photograph of her with a relative wearing the fur coat she almost seems a different person. She looks so much more confident and self-assured in the coat. She was upset by poverty wherever she came across it, be it in a village near Kandy in Ceylon, queuing for a show in Glasgow or walking the sidewalks in New York, but upset even more by people begging or busking for money. She felt something should be done so that no one was so poor that they needed to do that.

Many times in her diary Gwennie refers to herself as English but occasionally she becomes aware of this and reminds herself she is really a 'colonial' and not English at all. Despite this she was clearly proud to be a Kiwi and born in New Zealand. In her diary she occasionally uses words common in New Zealand but unknown in England, generally these words are of Maori origin. She saw things to criticise in the way of life followed in England but also much to admire particularly when compared to the 'continentals' of France, Germany and Italy. She was amazed how well the wives of Yorkshire look after their husbands as well as their working and unmarried daughters. She was astounded that women in England 'spring-cleaned' the house in preparation for Christmas and did most of the decorating in the home rather than the men. She enjoyed the company of both men and women, perhaps equally, but on occasions liked to get away to be by herself. In general she was overwhelmingly positive about herself, her life and her trip but just a few times she seems to get depressed recognising that she might well be on her only trip of a lifetime and that it would soon be over. She must have looked forward to this trip for such a long time, probably several years, planned it very carefully and then wondered what life would be like for her when it was finished.

Her attitude to other nationalities is interesting, she was far from bowled over by the Germans *en masse*, being quite rude about them on occasions, and was highly suspicious of how friendly the French music hall shows were towards the English, recognising it as a by-product of the increasing tension in Europe as war approached. Her most vitriolic comment was saved for men in New York. 'The heat is terrific and I mentally divest myself of woollen underclothes. Every man we pass mentally divests me of them too. Never had that feeling about men in any country in the world!' What saw her through all the highs and few lows of the trip was her delightful sense of humour, she laughed with people, she laughed about people and she laughed at herself. She loved dogs, she loved variety shows and she was an avid collector of recipes. She had been well brought up by her mother for her Yorkshire puddings met with full approval amongst her Yorkshire relatives!

Right at the beginning of the diary Gwennie explains that she had a 'Private Diary No. 2' in which she recorded all of her indiscretions. She had a toy owl that she referred to as the 'chaperone'. He was unpacked from the bottom of her case when she arrived in Yorkshire. She drew a little cartoon owl in her diary occasionally to represent the 'chaperone'. He is shown with both eyes wide open when Gwennie's behaviour has been beyond reproach for the day, one eye is shown closed when her day includes some minor dubious behaviour and both eyes are shown closed when she feels her behaviour has been beyond the pale. It seems likely that the behaviour she was most conscious about was her relationships with men. It is important to remember that copies of her main diary were being sent home to her parents. She did enjoy the company of a number of men on her journey across the world and perhaps the 'chaperone' with closed eyes reflects the times she went beyond a bit of flirting. She certainly gloats a little about being the first one of the 'girls' party to be picked up in the ballroom at Blackpool and by a handsome serviceman too. Just before she left Yorkshire for the last time L., a Scotsman, arrived to spend a last bit of time with her. They walked across the fields to Wentworth where the village, 'turns out to see L. in his kilt'. (Gwennie quite often hides the names of people she encountered on her travels using just initials to refer to them). John Turner, Gwennie's cousin, remembers L. in his kilt and thought him large and rather stern at the time.

Later in the trip she met Jim, a Mountie, in Regina on the Canadian Prairies and was almost instantly taken off to an afternoon show at the cinema, in this case to watch Walt Disney cartoons that Jim clearly loved. At times Gwennie does seem to hint that her status as a single woman into her early thirties was something she was conscious of but the completion of her trip plainly overtook all other considerations. She eventually married Tom Vivian in New Zealand in 1947. He was considerably older than she was and after he died in the 1960s Gwennie was a widow for the rest of her life, a period of well over thirty years.

Perhaps the most fascinating aspect of Gwennie's description of her global adventure is that it all took place initially in the deepening shadow of world war and then for almost the whole of the first year of the war itself. She must have had friends and family warning her off in New Zealand early in 1939 as the international situation deteriorated, but she was single-minded and determined to set out on her dream journey. She often refers to her inner, strongly held, belief that she would be safe. She seemed to know that nothing in the war could disrupt her 'grand tour'. Perhaps it was the gypsy blood she believed ran in her veins, foreseeing the future. As she travelled across the world between March and May 1939 the possibility of war was a persistent topic of conversation and some of the boat passengers from New Zealand intended to return straight away from Europe to avoid what they saw as inevitable. Gwennie avoided the subject when she could, but in Italy there seemed to have been soldiers mobilising everywhere and in Germany attitudes were even more threatening. A German youth hosteller confessed to Gwennie that she thought all the English were silly and degenerate even though she had never met any. A young 'serious, bullet-headed giant' of a German was also surprised she spoke some German and said 'The English they spik no German … but soon they all spik German'. While staying with a family in Baden she was advised not to go to England but to return home and when the father of the family said 'When I come to New Zealand perhaps you will show me your country?' Gwennie recorded in her diary that she assured him she would and 'sent up a fervent prayer that he might come in peace and not waving his swastika in a fanatical desire to rescue New Zealand from the clutches of the English'. When Gwennie visited Paris she wrote how strange it was that all the French music halls were putting on peace numbers with a great waving of flags and Rule Britannias. She continues:

Methinks it is overdone. It is hoped we never have to ally ourselves to France. They'll be a mill-stone round our neck—they are not stable. Their sudden love of the English seems too artificial. One feels they laugh at us even while they wave our flags.

Her keen perception of the situation shows that she had an impressive understanding of the way people thought.

On arrival in London Gwennie wrote of, 'A longer more lasting love (of England) that comes from association—after all I am English in spite of saying 'Ja, ja' by mistake to the bus driver'. While in Surrey she helped an emigrant from Budapest and recalled having met a Jewish mother and child on the Continent desperately fleeing their homeland to join up with the woman's husband who had already reached America. While in Westminster Abbey she stood by the Unknown Soldier's Grave and prayed, 'That there would be no more war—even as I pray I know it is coming.' Madame Tussaud's was one of Gwennie's 'must visit' destinations and she noted, surely with great amusement having seen him in person in Italy, 'Mussolini away for repairs or renovations'. On her journeys round the country she was impressed by Britain's attempts to prepare for war but worried they will be far behind Germany. In August 1939 on a visit to Invergordon in Northern Scotland she saw 'Battleships and seaplanes swooping about' and realised the sounds of war were getting louder. She went on to visit a lighthouse near John O'Groats and was advised to put her notebook away 'In case they think I'm a German spy'. As the end of August approached she hurried back to Yorkshire stopping with acquaintances in Richmond. 'Both Mr. and Mrs. W. are air-raid wardens. Realise for the first time how organised England is'. She was back 'at home' in Rawmarsh with her family when war was declared. She wrote:

> The Prime Minister's speech came through. It is a sad speech but determined. My heart aches for the man—he has put up such a fight for peace. Has a man ever humiliated himself or his nation so much in an effort to preserve peace? And with it all war has come and we must face it as best we can.

From this time the diary reflects the effects of the war, and especially the blackout, but without dwelling on them. Gwennie risked sea journeys to and from Ireland despite the threat of submarines and similarly when she finally left to sail across the Atlantic and Pacific back home to Auckland. Strangely it was very close to home where she was most in danger. The final leg of the journey from Hawaii to New Zealand was obviously to be completed by sea. The boat, the *Niagara*, which made the journey immediately before the one Gwennie was booked on, was sunk by a mine as it left Auckland harbour. Gwennie returned safely to Auckland in July 1940 and never travelled so far again. She kept in touch by regular typed letters with many of the people she met on her trip and saw a few of them again when they visited New Zealand.

The diary is an evocative record of an amazing adventure and now, over seventy years later, is finally in print. One suspects Gwennie always hoped that it would eventually be read by a much wider audience. It vividly recalls a bygone age at a time of global danger, but above all is testament to an engaging Kiwi whose energy, humour and positive spirit still shine on after seventy years and into a new millennium. It has the feel of records in the Mass Observation archives but also of a travelogue in the style of Fyfe Robertson, Alan Whicker or even Michael Palin. Editing the diary to produce an abridged version has been a real pleasure but also a concern because by necessity it has involved choosing over 250,000 words to leave out. Obviously much of interest has had to be cut from the final draft but what remains hopefully provides a true reflection of Gwennie's personality and her global adventures. Gwennie's punctuation and spelling has been retained and her original text changed as little as possible in editing. Certainly in editing the diary I have travelled the world at Gwennie's side and learned to love and admire her through this record of her feelings and beliefs and of a world long disappeared.

It was as Chairman of the Rawmarsh and Parkgate Local History Group that I first met Malcolm Brown and John Turner and it has been wonderful to talk to both of them and their wives about Gwennie. I must thank Malcolm, Noreen, John and Betty for all the help and encouragement they have given me. I must also gratefully acknowledge the help I have received from contacts in New Zealand in collecting information on Gwennie and in particular Bridget Simpson at Auckland Central Library, Matthew Gray of the *Western Leader* newspaper in Auckland and Noelle McCarthy and Jim Mora at Radio New Zealand. Sue Judd, who knew Gwennie in Auckland for many years, has kindly shared her memories of Gwennie. Jane, my wife, has spent a great deal of time checking my editing and for this I am truly grateful. Thanks are also due to Alan Sutton and all at Fonthill Media for ensuring that Gwennie's diary is finally in print.

THIS IS THE DIARY
OF ONE
GWYNNE IRENE PEACOCK

Height—5 ft 2 ins.
Weight—7 stone 6 lbs. (For the benefit of American readers 104 lbs).
Distinguishing marks—Gold filling in front tooth (the only bit of gold she's likely to have when she returns home).

Travelling the world under the benign protection of the great British Empire as represented by His Excellency Viscount Galway.

Read if you will, but remember it is primarily written for her own reference. Laugh at her faults, forgive her indiscretions (which anyway are not here, but recorded in Private Diary No. 2) and live with her on her trip which is going to be fun all the way.

February 1939

Auckland, Sydney, Hobart, Melbourne, Fremantle, Perth.

Sailed by S.S. *AWATEA* from Auckland this day 14ᵗʰ February 1939, Gwynne Irene Peacock, two suitcases, one portable typewriter, a camera and a travelling rug (from the best staff of the best firm in the world).

I shall never forget that send-off. The dear faces of Daddy and Mother and the friends on the wharf. All the good wishes and the flowers, telegrams and presents. I have to run down the gangway to get Kathleen's flowers just as they are pulling it up. I stand by the rail and wave and wave. I am conscious of dropping flowers and always they are put back into my arms. Someone has given me their place by the rail—I see the dear ones on the wharf until the very last. There is exhaustion in a farewell. I turn a little wearily. The man standing at my side has flowers in his arms. Strange to farewell a man with flowers—and then I realise that they're my flowers, still more roses, more lilies. It is a moment worth recording this very first meeting after I left Auckland. His was the first face that I looked at on a basis of equality, not as hostess towards guest, superior to inferior or vice versa, or as man or woman but as fellow traveller to fellow traveller. His pleasant voice assures me that giving up his position on the rail was no hardship—he was only passing through—there was no one to see him off. And then I realised that at other ports I should be like that. But I liked this first face that I saw—it belonged to F.L. an American surely from his accent, but no he is Canadian. As I say American do his eyebrows raise a trifle quizzically and a half smile play over his face as if to say 'My <u>dear</u> lady…?' Is there a measure of superiority then in being a Canadian as against an American?

After that such a rapid succession of things. I want to dwell on Rangi growing hazier in the distance, Auckland under its summer sky drifting away but we were queued up to be told our places for dinner! It was a lovely dinner and afterwards a walk on deck, a hauling out of suitcases and a falling over of other people's belongings. A confused recollection of a marvellous day and so to bed.

15 February 1939

Up bright and early, a shower and then up on deck feeling slightly the worse for wear. No roll or pitch; but vibration. Stomachs were not made to be 'shook'. Yellow-faced figures droop pathetically in deck chairs, shrouded in rugs, and gaze weakly up at a deck-hand washing the ceiling. I do myself. An Australian bicycle agent is a dear and brings me water biscuits and an apple. He has travelled extensively and knows places, not by having learned about them but by having seen them. Renewed my acquaintance with F.L. Asked him if, when American children learnt elocution, they learn American or English. He said they just don't learn elocution at all. He and 'the man from Boston' who sits on our table drink 'tomato juice' (to rhyme with potato) and eat their lettuce. Managed a good lunch and to the pictures in the evening. Lily Pons in something or other. It came to an unfortunate end—they'd left the latter half in Auckland. Bed—thankfully.

17 February 1939

This morning up at fiveish, packed, breakfasted and up on deck to see the Harbour and the Bridge. I could hardly believe I was really in Sydney. Then one thing happened after another. No longer were we of the Awatea. It is strange how our instinct takes us as quickly as possible to a new home when the old is lost to us. Ticket handed to Orient man, taxi to the 'Orcades'[1], cabin claimed and then out to town just as easy as that. Lunch with F.C. at the Prince's and then to Koala Park. The wee bears drooping in the heat in the forks or trees— a mother wallaby with a baby in her pouch—and an Aborigine boomerang thrower (it didn't boomerang when I threw it but just sailed gleefully into the air over the fence into the wallaby run). Back to Sydney and then the adventure of finding the bus back to the ship. Walked dozens of streets to find a policeman (where is the vice in Sydney?) and finally found one who told me wrong. Eventually back at Woolloomooloo and the 'Orcades'.

18 February 1939

Up early and just dying to 'go places and see things'. Over the bridge and back I walked, the harbour lying like a picture before me. Later to the shops. Up and down escalators. Bracing myself firmly at the top I muttered 'People are looking at you, you silly ass, be quick'. A desperate plunge and I fell back into the arms of an astonished floor walker, who nevertheless recovered sufficiently to replace me on the step. A breathless, relentless journey down, praying it would not ever come to the end, and then a desperate jump. Shot straight into, well not quite the arms of, a portly gentleman and fled blindly to find myself in the men's underclothing looking soulfully at socks and suspenders. Back to practise again—no escalator in the world is going to get the better of me. And then the afternoon. A stroke of luck. God certainly looks after fools and tourists. Found there was an excursion to Pinchgut, the little fortified island which I had noticed on the way in. To Macquarie Quay and instinct led me to a smartly-dressed little group of people one of which, with the air of a mother hen, was rounding up the others. Without another thought I marched up to her with my ten shilling note and announced that I'd come to go to Pinchgut. An astonished expression passed over her face and I realised I had gate-crashed into a private party. I felt like my New Zealand 3*d* bit must have felt when I offered it to the Sydney bus conductor, and made a hurried explanation. Instantly all was well. I was introduced all round, made welcome in every possible manner and pressed to join the party. (The 3*d* bit I must explain wasn't so lucky. It was handed back with a superior 'That's not worth a tin of fish Missie').

Such a delightful day. Launch over to Pinchgut, everything explained. Later a hunt for a ladies' lounge. Can it be that Sydney people are so modest? The lift man stuttered and stumbled and finally left me on the top floor without a word. I gazed about at discreetly shut doors, and after passing it six times, finally located it camouflaged as the 'Retiring Room'. Back to the ship and too weary to do 'owt'.

23 February 1939

At sea again and a day to tackle the stern realities of life, such as letters and diary, and a spot of washing. The cabins are all equipped with gadgets that blow air in and are beautifully cool. Played deck tennis. The most polite thing would be to say I was out of practice. So far wonderfully calm in spite of life-boat practice. Had orders to rush up to B deck No. 9 section with life belt. After much enquiring of the way finally found B deck and was assisted into the contraption by 'The Sergeant', one of the Brisbane to Hobart crowd.

Down went the life-boat and in jumped the cooks in their tall white hats to man the oars. Why the cooks? A shouting of orders, a clanging of chains, confusion and a tense atmosphere amongst the crowd. Would we have to get into the life-boats? The girl next to me whispers 'That's a nice cook, the third one from the end. I'm sitting there'. Then we were calmly told it was all over. 'The Sergeant' extricated me from the life belt and we carted the blessed thing downstairs again! Poor Aunt Molly (who is with me). Overwhelmingly the lowering of those lifeboats brought back to her the memory of that other wreck years ago. All its horror in the dark night. How little we know what it would be like. So must those of the Titanic have laughed at their life-boat drill. Laughed with the laughing waves, while all was calm...

Into Hobart later in the day and it was sunny. The warm smell of apples everywhere. 32,000 cases of fruit taken on board, some say 23,000. I suppose an odd thousand or two is neither here nor there. At any rate we had apple pie for dinner. Perhaps it's 22,999 now. A good companion, Auntie Molly. Our little adventures and all our little jokes will tie us together for many a year to come. Back up the gangway we went to type letters and do accounts. I found the 2/6d I was out. This commercial training doesn't give one much peace.

27 February 1939

Melbourne—a bigger Christchurch, as Auckland is a little Sydney. The Yarra, yellow and swollen from recent rains, and still raining. To the State Parliament Building and the Aquarium before the Fitzroy Gardens under a cleared sky. A garden city this Melbourne, beautifully planned and the leafy spaces jealously guarded, not rakish as her sister city Sydney, but a stout, comfortable matron beautifully clad to enhance her natural comeliness and her few short-comings. Then to Capt. Cook's Cottage. This was built at Gt. Ayton, Yorks. by the parents of Captain Cook and removed to Melbourne as a memorial. Stone floors in large blocks, a time-worn 'dresser', a cane-bottomed chair and drop leaf-table. The fireplace just a grate on the floor and above a hole in the ceiling. An absurdly wee room off the living room. Surely it must be considerably reduced in size. It would be sheer impossibility to place Father and Mother Cook, the Captain and no doubt other little Cooks into it? Perhaps it was the early influence of these tiny rooms that bred that later desire to sail the seas of discovery.

A quaint little soul on board who confided that all her life she's wanted to get married but hadn't just managed it. A man who also seemed to have taken a fancy to me to the extent of popping up suddenly each time I turned a corner or came out of the dining room or cabin. Introduced the two and suggested that the stars looked wonderful from the top deck. Off they went, so I'm hoping for the best.

March 1939

*Cocos Islands, Colombo, Kandy, Aden, Suez, Heliopolis, Cairo, Giza,
Stromboli, Naples, Pompeii, Villefranche, Nice, Monte Carlo*

5 March 1939

I make the acquaintance of dear old Mr. W, a hard-headed Yorkshire farmer
of sound common sense. A councillor, but with a vast sense of humour, and a
shrewd understanding of human nature. He very seldom commits himself in
any way but his 'Oh aye' has a wealth of thought behind it.

In Fremantle we say hello to the First and Last shop in Australia and
then by train to Perth. Old Mr. W. elects to come with Auntie Molly and I.
Still another garden city—Perth on the River Swan—I remember that from
school. A go-ahead town this. No wonder our bus and tram services don't
pay. Bus conductoresses over here. A curly blond with a green cap and a buff
uniform, a flash of white teeth as she smiles and a flash of crimson nails as
she hands you the ticket. Mr. W. and I to the Observatory at the top of which
is a truly worthwhile view of Perth. Blue ranges in the distance and a happy
wide-spread town following a shining river. Hundreds of steps to go up before
you saw it. Thought I'd be killing Mr. W. but he did it in half the time I did
and carried all my parcels into the bargain. Who said the British race 'Ain't
what it used to be?' Later, back in town I got separated from the others and
asked the way from an old lady. 'I thought when I saw you, you were from the
country' she beamed. A hasty look in the first mirror. From the country, and
me in my smartest frock! They might have farewelled us at Fremantle, I don't
know, I was fast asleep. Not blasé yet, just tired, and all respectable Christian
folks should be in bed at 12! We're in for a busy nine days before Columbo.
Goodbye Australia. I've loved every minute of your sunshine and rain.

9 March 1939

No more comings and goings at ports. Faces become familiar and great fun with games, especially deck golf. The knitting women firmly established in a corner of the lounge from which vantage point both staircases are visible. A thousand scandals knit themselves into jumpers and cardigans. 'And my dear I saw her coming out of his cabin at half past two in the morning'. 'They went up there directly after dinner and I'll swear they didn't come down until midnight'. 'Her daughter didn't die, she committed suicide, and a minister's wife too!' The dear old souls are thoroughly enjoying their trip and I have an insane desire to give them something to gossip about. My cabin mates are Jenny and Mrs. S. The latter a kindly woman from Scotland who gives me good advice and tucks me up at night. Heard a peculiar thumping in the early hours. On making enquiries of the steward found it was caused by a particularly stout lady doing her exercises. His description was vivid. I can see her in a four berth cabin, just fitting into the floor space in the centre, on her back, kicking—one, two, three, four—until one morning, so the stewardess reports, bang went the seat of her pyjamas.

I just love breakfast on board. Stewed figs, brains and bacon, brown roll and marmalade. The meals are really good but they can't make salads. Did I record afternoon tea? Someone will be killed in the rush one of these days. Hung delicately back the first few days, and then diffidently joined the scrum. Got swept headlong in and, to my embarrassment, found myself one of the first ones in.

13 March 1939

Passed the Cocos Islands at 10.15. Coconut palms against the sky and a green lagoon contrasting with the blue blue sea. Four white yachts growing larger as they come from the distance to the side of the ship. A barrel-like box is taken from the ship containing letters and presents for inhabitants. A bottle is handed over too amid cheers and they sail away again, bending to the wind. It is on these islands that the Emden was beached after her action with the Australian cruiser Sydney. There are twenty-four small islands forming a roughly broken circle nearly approaching the horse shoe shape common to coral atolls. The Eastern Telegraph Co. leases one of the islands, named Direction Island, from the owners, the Clunies-Rose family, and has erected a cable station. Here are marooned about ten employees for about a year at a time and every three months supplies are sent from Singapore. No mention about the said supplies containing anything in a bottle, so no doubt the visit of the 'Orcades' was welcome. We passed the Equator today but the Orient

Line does not encourage celebrations. Father Neptune on the menu was all we heard about it. The swimming bath tactfully emptied for repairs. But it is still the Equator and I'm not a bit too hot. Someday when I'm rich I'm going to find an island for sale right on the line and revel forever in the heat.

15 March 1939

Such a rushing over breakfast, passports to be visa-ed and tickets to be bought for the launch to go ashore. Rushed round getting in everyone's way all to no purpose and then discovered old Mr. W. had fixed everything up for us. Poor Auntie Molly not well enough to go ashore. Feel rather mean dashing off so full of fitness and leaving her but no doubt in England in the cold my turn will come for staying behind.

A clear day and a fierce sun, catamarans with red sails, lean brown natives and sparkling white launches. It would seem as if this Colombo is a land of contrasts. Dirt there is, and squalor, but where there is cleanliness it is a cleanliness very seldom seen in a 'white' country. Laundry work goes from the ship to be returned spotless in a few hours. Out of the launch, a fleeting glimpse of the bazaars, of topee-ed men in rickshaws, of lean bodies straining at the shafts, of white hotels and white-clad policemen in shorts and then on our way in the car to Kandy. A smooth road lined with jacaranda trees—white bungalows with blue shutters set in a coconut grove—cane tables and chairs on cool white verandas. Native houses with thatched roofs and walls of unbaked bricks. A calm-faced mother, her baby on her hip, black hair parted smoothly, golden earrings flashing in the sun. A lean and hungry dog with an undocked tail sniffing round a lean and hungry man lying asleep outside a hut. Everything is lean in Ceylon. The oxen patiently pulling thatch-covered waggons. The men paddling in the rice field, brown as the earth which they till. The women sitting and selling yellow cakes or sweetmeats in green leaves.

Everyone has something to sell, be it a coconut or a pineapple, half a dozen peanuts in a grubby little hand or a bright flower for luck and at every village the small brown boys with the appealing smile and the lustrous eyes murmur 'Baksheesh lady—penny Sir—money—money'. A man loading coconut fibre into a primitive cart, his oxen placid in the sun. A plucking at your arm 'You come this way lady. I show you temple'—a voice in the other ear 'no this way lady—this way'. There is an old man gazing at me now, shrivelled and old with a few grey hairs on his chin and red betel-stained teeth. His body is shrouded with a swathed garment of dirty red. He props himself up against a hut. It would seem that he was dead but for the vital life in his eyes. A busy little village. Open-fronted shops displaying their goods all to the fore. Meat dangling in the heat. Bright cotton goods hanging around a man sewing a white garment on a machine. Red flowers, great bunches of yellow bananas. A woman cooking on a brazier with children clustered around her.

And then Kandy. Dinner at the Hotel in a large airy room. The lake lazily laps a low stone parapet and from somewhere the tiny tinkle of a native instrument. Everything in the hotel is cool, wide and airy and outside in the streets and in the shops, small, hot and congested. It is in the Temple of the Tooth where we make contact with the East. We slip round a corner and there a white robed woman on her knees before a little shrine, swaying. The benign face of Buddha looks down—it was then we realised the age old significance of the temple. We would have lingered almost overcome by the heavy scent of the freesia-like temple flowers but a lean brown body comes in dragging a sack of grain which he pours out on the stone floor, evidently an offering to the temple and its priests. Outside the beggars besiege us, pitiful objects with stumps of arms and legs bound in dirty rags. A man with so little of him left that one would wonder how he lived. The more one gives the thicker they come. From being held with elbow bent and hand outstretched their arms extend up to your very face. I must confess to panic. I was not afraid of the poor souls themselves but we're being made so germ conscious. Old Mr. W. waves his stick and shoos them off. I feel horribly guilty, what right have we, clean, well fed and free from caste restrictions, to shoo them away? I threw my last coin to a skeleton hand that touched my dress as we passed. The mob had fastened itself on to someone else.

And then as if to dispel the memory of that confusion and poverty we walk in the Gardens. The air is heavy with the wonderful perfume of nutmeg trees. An avenue of palms bright green against a blue sky. A workman fetched me a flower—a bright bougainvillea. I smile and take out my purse but strangely enough he is gone, softly padding down the path with a basket balanced on his head and his hand on his hip. We're out of the Gardens and back along the smooth road through the tropical night. Raucous hand-blown horns blow in different keys. The crowd in the car begin to sing—John Brown's Body, Tipperary and Killarney. Killarney, in that Buddhist country where little temples stand out against the sky! It is not the first time I have longed for the time when I shall travel on my own. It is impossible to carry parcels to the boat. They are snatched out of your hand by lean brown hands. Brown faces bobbing, smiling, always smiling and always hoping for the tossed coin. The bright lighted ship draws nearer and Colombo has gone. A bright blue electric sign is all that remains 'Ceylon for good tea'.

16 March 1939

Up early and washed while the laundry was still comparatively cool. Rather disquieting rumours of the European situation. War talk prevalent. Several passengers announce their intention of landing in England and booking their passage straight back again. The Minister's wife announces complacently that she'll be alright as she'll be met by the clergy! upon which little Mrs. F. hastens to announce that her uncle was a Bishop. I leave the little group to resurrect ecclesiastical relations from comfortable graves and flop into a deck chair. Games start again with great enthusiasm on the part of those who boarded at Colombo. More talk of war. The 'Orcades' is fitted to carry a good many guns in case of war. Some are almost sick with wondering. They all want to die at home if it comes to dying. Strangely enough something doesn't seem to register with me. All I can see is my trip to the end. If the war comes it may, it will add to experience but I'm set on a course and some sixth sense tells me I'll see it through. I wonder if I could accept Death with the same fatalistic attitude?

But who talks or thinks of Death? The first shock of the war rumour is forgotten and we're all making fancy dresses for the dance at night. Myself a London paper boy in Mr. W.'s cap and old shirt and slacks with a bundle of papers and sucking an orange. Unfortunately orange didn't last long enough or I started with atmosphere too early. Consumed a huge grapefruit and three Jaffa oranges before the judging.

21 March 1939

And Aden. It is said they haven't had rain for seven years! Precipitous craggy hills silhouetted against the sky, brown and barren with beaches of yellow sand. Everything dry and sharply defined. Arabs, Jews, Somalis, Indians and Negroes lounge in the streets. Tethered goats bleat sleepily adding to the indescribable odour of the streets. Camels draw rough native carts and gaze with a supercilious air on the mere tourist! One gets the impression that the whole town slept until the boat arrived. The ultimate memory of Aden will be masses and masses of underclothes. Brassieres, scanties, nightgowns and slips in a confused mass, turned over and over by the eager greedy fingers of tourists. A smiling Arab, the latest in a white shirt dangling free out of his blue skirt, his red fez with its tassel at a slightly rakish angle. A stout respectable British matron, well-corseted and costumed, her feet swelling slightly in the heat. The smiling face comes closer 'Scanties, lady, you look very nice in these'. She backs away 'No' she mutters faintly and, clutching her gloves and umbrella tightly as if for moral support, she makes for the door. Dignity is hard to maintain in Aden. Even at the door the bobbing red cap follows 'Scanties, lady'. 'No' she almost shrieks and turns into the road to face yet another eager black hand 'Cigar, lady, cheap. So help me God only 4/6 a box'. Four of us go into one of the side streets narrow, grubby its little dark overflowing shops spilling half their content into the street. I would have loved to penetrate further but the smell of goat drove the others back. Goats tethered at every corner to be milked as one desires to drink. A quick run in a taxi to the reservoirs and when we come back the streets are quiet and we fly back to the ship in a panic in the nick of time. Cabin parties in the evening, a traipsing along corridors with armfuls of underclothes, bargains to compare and gloat over. No greater 'gloater' than myself. Poor Mr. T. has bought a pair of boy's pyjamas for his nephew whom he has never seen only to find on his return to the boat a photographof the said nephew who is over six foot!

22 March 1939

We're in the Red Sea and trying hard to imagine it opening up to let the Israelites through. Ships passing in the night and the day. People coming and people going. Shoals of big fish leap out the water and flocks of birds in the air. Not so warm now. Idled about and as Mr. W. wrote in his diary 'Did nowt but gossiped'. A lazy day. Diary and letter writing with an effort in a haze of cigar smoke. Pictures at night George Formby in 'I See Ice'.

25 March 1939

Cairo today! In the tender to Suez and bought mother's camel skin bag on the boat. Then the long trek of 75 cars across the desert winding like beetles along the bitumen road. There's an incongruity about a bitumen road across the desert and still more so about the line of whitened oil drums down each side. No piles of sand hills, clean and white as I'd always dreamed but rather a dirty desert, the sand a sort of hard stony stuff. We did not drive through the desert, we flew. Not a word did the driver say but sat as steady as a rock and just looked and drove. Up and up went the speedometer until it registered 90 kilometres. We whizzed past cars and missed oncoming vehicles by inches. We hooted until the very insistence of our hooting gained us a right of way past the other cars. No time to take photographs but little gems whizz past. A group of black-robed figures driving a flock of black goats standing out clearly against the yellow sand. A deserted palace of some Sheik rising up against the skyline, a small lonely little mosque—a road-makers' camp. On and on, stopping only at Cook's Rest House until Heliopolis. Heliopolis, City of the Sun, full of the British building barracks. Aeroplanes overhead and notices 'Beware of gunfire and bombings'. One imagines the roar of a thousand cannon and the fortissimo of bursting bombs, and then another sign 'No hooting after 11 p.m. and before 7 a.m!

The streets gradually merge into Cairo. It is just the Cairo we see in pictures but how little those pictures convey. Always the blue sky with glistening white minarets sharply defined. Large modern buildings side by side with Egyptian architecture without any incongruity. Even the cheaper types of buildings are striking and pretentious. The streets hung with flags in honour of the marriage of Farouk. We pass through busy streets, past camels and donkey-drawn carts, street vendors and a side-show man with his show on his back. The women dressed in black with veils of open net, seemingly only a conventional remnant of the old time customs. A vendor of yellow cakes, his wares on his head, his long white shirt floating in the breeze, stops to gaze at a cinema advertisement. Is he too worshipping Norma Shearer? Large modern flats and everywhere Corbusier architecture (rather like a boat with sun decks). To the Museum of Antiquities to see the relics of the tomb of Tutankhamen. Poor little Tutankhamen of 1350 B.C. Married at 16, dead at 28. Such a fuss for one small life. Three coffins, the first one, and the mask, being of gold. There is something very human and very pathetic about this boy of 16. There is an oppressive atmosphere about relics and a headache and a feeling of sickness made me welcome the fresh air outside. To lunch at the Victoria Hotel. Egyptian waiters in long white—shall we say shirts, with maroon belts and the red fez. A conventional lunch but delicious hors d'oeuvres, macaroni cheese, roast beef and vegetables, sponge pudding with fruit sauce.

Then the lovely run to Giza and Mena House past Egyptian homes set amidst cotton and rice fields, all irrigated. Double-decker trams in Hobart, rickshaws in Colombo and now camels in Cairo! I hold tight and put up a prayer to Allah as 'Whiskey and Soda' gets up—a benign animal who looks thoroughly bored as no doubt he was. The Dragonman, in his long white robe, followed cheerfully behind. Away we went and I found to my amazement that I could really ride a camel, so I indiscreetly dug it in the ribs and growled 'Giddap'. Giving something between a squeal and a grunt it jerked suddenly forward. Faster and faster we went and one by one we passed the long camel column. I could see out of the corner of my eye the white-robed owner kick up his heels and follow us at a run, waving and shouting. But I had no time to worry about him. My hat slid to the back of my head, my camera went bumpety-bump at my side and my dress felt as if it would soon be up round my neck. I clung to everything I could find, the saddle and tufty bits of hair. Assuredly I couldn't fall on such a broad back. I glimpsed the Pyramids ahead, they at least I knew—but past them out into the stony desert, what was there? But Whiskey and Soda knew his destination and slowed down with a lolloping stride. I sat in dread lest he should decide to sit. I dared not move lest he should take it for a sign, but there he stood until a white-robed figure tore into view followed by the camel procession. At command Whiskey and Soda lowered himself gently and investigated my foot with a moist snuffle. I slithered off. His face wore a supercilious expression as he turned and gazed. Finally he blew a large bubble, drew it in again, closed his eyes and dismissed me from his mind forever.

There were the Pyramids looking just as they always do in pictures. I should like to see them at night, alone and deserted, silent under the moon in a clear sky. They have nothing to do with curious tourists. It was an impressive scene, the Pyramids rising to the skyline, at their foot the camels and the drivers, black-robed and white-robed with the red fez. The Sphinx gazes as she has gazed in thousands of pictures. She has the body of a lion for strength and a human head for wisdom. One wonders how she lost her nose! Back to Giza on a milder donkey at an even pace and wave to Auntie Mollie in a donkey cart. Then to the Nile to drink tea on a house-boat anchored beside a promenade. We eat little sticky cakes and dry currant buns. The tea is delicious and a sense of placidity and well-being steals over one. We are driven to Mouski then and to a perfume shop. An exquisite place with Egyptian furnishings. But then one realises in the scented breeze that the small phial is 10/- and there is nothing under. So I bowed myself out, softly and regretfully. Oh! so different is the Jewish Jewellery and general cheapjack bazaars. They grab you by the arm and edge you into the shop, have you draped with silk and hung with bracelets before you can think, their brown eyes admiring, adoring and when you don't buy a look of resignation and a shrug. Somehow I have sympathy with the Jews. I seem to feel the significance of their fatalistic attitude, their little 'It's just too bad' shrug and their ready smile. A little repartee and it sets their eyes dancing and their tongue quick with a ready wit. A quick joke that sets them laughing and then out before they realise. We leave for Port Said by train and have dinner. At nine we come alongside the canal and then on board and bed.

28 March 1939

This was one of the most thrilling parts of being on board ship. We went down into the engine room. I have never seen such huge masses of machinery and steel platforms. And the furnace! We even had to look at it through smoked glass. Then at night we passed Stromboli. It was a pitch black night with an angry sea and Stromboli loomed up blacker and angrier than it all, belching fire from her peak. Time and again it shot up like a gigantic firework display and then sank to a dull grumbling glow. Even as we waited breathless Stromboli spoke again. A crimson curtain spread itself in the air—and there are people who live on one side of the mountain while the molten lava pours down the other! It was the 29th when we crept to bed. Somehow we felt smaller and almost afraid.

29 March 1939

And Naples. Dear dirty Naples, so lovely in the sun but, like the coquette, she is a draggled old woman in the wet. But even on a clod grey morning the charm is there—Vesuvius smoking in front and the white palace on the hillside. The sun would have put a sparkle into the sea but nothing could put a smile on to the faces of people. All day we saw but one smile and that on the face of a young lad. But it was a weary half-hearted attempt. Poor drab souls in clothes that one labelled as 'jumble sale', so ill-sorted that they defy description. A freezing day and the tail-end of their winter but all their shoes were thin and 'flip-floppy' and the children without stockings. The women seemed apathetic, pulling their coats round them perpetually, vainly seeking from the thin worn material a protection it could not give. Every second women seemed a prospective mother and one hoped that, before the little new being was called upon to face the world, nature would have provided the warmth that Mussolini seemed unable to give. But we cannot altogether blame Il Duce. They have been poor for a long time. Poor in everything but their lovely land and their summer sun. Five of us hired a car to drive to Pompeii. We went down the historic Via di Roma and then through all the little everyday streets. Little narrow alleys deep in mud, grey-looking washing hanging across the street. Everything black or grey, even the sky. Everywhere are soldiers and police and everywhere the writing on the wall 'Duce a noi' (The Duce for us). A group of young lads about 14 are marching in uniform and their poor drab mothers weep over them as they say Goodbye. It may be that the process of re-generation is slow but to me it was a sad sad place.

And then Pompeii. I feel a delicious little tingle run up my spine when I realise that I've actually been there. A popular pleasure resort for the Romans and then came the eruption and the earthquake and it was destroyed. There was utter deadness here that I did not feel even at the Pyramids. Perhaps the more so because of those little poignant evidences of daily life that are everywhere. The oven where they made their bread and the very lava-encrusted loaves taken out. A beautiful home with the paintings still upon the walls and an inner courtyard kept fresh with palms and flowers. The men were taken aside to be shown something not for the more refined feminine eye. Per medium of a husband and wife we discover this to be a chamber of rather lewd paintings. There is a little delicacy left even on the Continent. Then we ladies were given a veiled hint to proceed round the corner while the men were herded off in another direction. We did so and sure enough there was a sheltered little spot amongst the ruins! We all got the giggles, it seemed so utterly incongruous and indeed more than a slight sacrilege in such a place. Then to the Museum to see the lava-encrusted figures, the dog straining at its leash and the woman shielding her face. The epic of Pompeii suddenly ceased to be history and became tragedy. I wanted to go back to Pompeii when all the others were gone. The irresistible desire to see things alone is always with me. It is far easier to people this place with Romans than to try to imagine modern Italy as it was in those days. For Pompeii died suddenly in full power. There was no decadence, no gradual melting into new fashions and new manners. There were ghosts that walk under Nero's Arch and if I were there alone, perhaps at night when the sky and moon were clear, I would see them.

A ride then round Naples in a phaeton and a last look at the soldiers in their green cloaks asleep on the park seats, at the little donkey carts full of firewood or lettuces, always with someone asleep on the load. The smallest of the children often wear a black pinafore that is done up behind when there are any fastenings on. All these things one sees in the streets of Naples and then back to the boat.

30 March 1939

And we berth at Villefranche. Such a gay pretty hill town with little coloured boats bobbing on the water, friendly cafes outside the shops and narrow streets winding up amongst the hills to houses perched in every available spot. Terracotta houses with red shutters and cream houses with blue shutters. France held out its arms to us and smiled when Italy wept. We saw a funeral—such a one as I've never seen before—a coal-black hearse and the horses black-coated with terrifying-looking holes for the eyes and bobbing black plumage. It proceeded at a slow and stately pace—I wanted to follow it to learn who had left this lovely world when Spring was calling. Then by bus to Nice. The same gay insouciance, smiles under black berets, the children plump and immaculate in knickerbockers and pinafores. And the hats! I'm having a French hat to come back with so watch out. As we've heard the one colour here is black with dark stockings. The people are friendly. They smile at us with their carmined lips and tilt their little hats over cheeky curls. There are beautiful shops in Nice—lingerie worth a fortune and furs! Perhaps they are bought by those who win at the Casino. Champagne at an outdoor café. Can't you imagine dapper Frenchmen in black berets sipping black coffee and playing cards? We drank our coffee black too, delicious as only the French can make it, and with it ate French pastry, a great square thick with cream and squashy with jam. Brioche is always on the table. A little French woman at the same table expressed horror and surprise that we had never had brioche. With many gestures she gave me the recipe in staccato French.

Then back to the ship to get into evening dress for Monte Carlo. Monte Carlo—not so much a sight as an experience. The brilliantly lighted Casino with the rectangular sweep of gardens in front, green with palms and misty with the blue of violas. I was so excited that it seemed as though my very breath would stop. My mind seemed to stop working and when it started again it was to repeat foolishly over and over again 'This is where he broke the Bank'. Inside there was a speaking quietness, broken only by the monotonous call of croupiers and the chatter of chips as he raked them in. We had our little flutter on roulette but lost as I lose at everything. Had the excitement of putting on for everyone as I was the only one of the party who could speak French. Got such a thrill out of leaning over and murmuring 'Trente deux'. An effeminate man bedecked with bracelets and rings played with a casual air that was too studied and further back in the more expensive rooms was the strangest figure of all—The Woman in Red. Her stockings, shoes, frock and hat were a bright red matched only in vividness by the red of her lips. Her face was dead white with jet black hair swathed in a peculiar fashion over her temple. Her movements were jerky but her eyes were fixed as if hypnotised on the roulette wheel. Her long red gloves raked at the chips like claws—she was losing steadily. Suddenly she rose. Her heels clattered along the beautiful inlaid wood floor. She made straight for the bar and swallowed something quickly and then sat down to drink steadily. We drank our Gin and French and realised that here was money such as we of New Zealand had never seen before. The Woman in Red was sagging, her mouth was loose and her eyes heavy—she was half under the table now. We left them reluctantly—it seemed that we had had a glimpse and that's all, just enough to make us feel raw Colonials!

31 March 1939

And just a scramble. The goodbyes that I hated saying and had meant to convey so tactfully and sincerely, hastily, almost casually, dispatched. Somehow I'm on the tender and they're waving to me from the ship. In the early morning light it all seems so dim and unreal. I can hear Auntie Molly say 'Look after yourself dear' and dear old Mr. W.'s 'If tha gets into any bother or lose tha money send me a cable'. I feel as though I were leaving home again and so I am. The boat grows dim quickly in the early light. I stop at the Maritima Hotel and sleep till late afternoon. An ecstatic little dance before the long wardrobe mirror from sheer exuberance of spirits and out in the rain to explore. Instinct led me to a restaurant and I eat the famous French snails, and liked them! Just like an unsalted cockle. To the theatre at night with the little lady from the hotel—a real French variety with plenty of custard tart humour and much expanse of leg. A skit on the English tourist with his guide book and don't we deserve it!

April 1939

Toulon, Nice, Le Lavandou, Cannes, Genoa, Pisa, Rome, Venice, Milan, Lugano, Saint Gotthard Pass, St. Moritz, Lucerne, Interlaken, Grindelwald, Geneva, Basle, Baden, Heidelberg, Mainz

1 April 1939

Mon Dieu! How I love the Riviera. Ever since I've been such a little girl I've longed to sit up in bed and ring for petit dejeuner and it arrived just as I've always imagined it arriving per medium of a white-coated waiter, delicious black coffee and hot milk, a crisp roll, butter and jam. Boarded a big P.L.M. bus for a lovely run from Toulon to Nice, all for 9/-. It is so easy to travel in France. I've been Madame-ed and Mademoiselle-ed through the Riviera as quietly and pleasantly as possible. Everywhere they smile and I smile and with my bit of French and the dictionary I seem to get what I want and where I want. The bus route runs practically round the sea front like a scenic drive. The Mediterranean is traditionally blue. Magnificent villas, colourful with wisteria-covered arches and long palm avenues, stretch down to the sea. Then the farmhouses. Whole families working in the fields and a woman getting water from a stone well. Queer grey fowl, rather like species one sees at the zoo, wander round every farmhouse. Lunch we had at Le Lavandou, a little fishing town on a harbour of polished silver. On and on past the red rocks, past Corniche D'Or and into the exclusive Cannes. How shall I describe Cannes? She is even more beautiful than the coquette that is Nice—her harbour full of fishing boats, her great hotels looking through rows of palms to the sea. In one shop some of the loveliest furs I've ever seen and the dearest little hats. On the bus again and the smart little French woman who had travelled beside me all the way gave me a little poke and smiled, nodded to a couple of lovers in front. 'You see it not in England, no?' I hastily disclaimed any such spectacle in any English bus. But then they weren't your half-ashamed lovers in England, but warm-hearted and French. His black eyes adoring, her red mouth provocative! and their kisses as frequent and sound as they felt inclined. And I can safely say that we two were the only ones in the bus who gave them even a cursory glance.

How can I dispose of the rest of that glorious road by saying 'and so to Nice' but I must. Such a lot of things are imprinted on my mind. Gay restaurants with dance floors on the roof, old castles and churches with spires outlined against the sky, factories for bottling olives. A little brasserie and, doubtless for the edification of the tourist, 'snack bar' written underneath.

3 April 1939

To Cook's to buy tourist lira for Italy. Goodbye to smiling, welcoming France and the train at 1.22 to Genoa. The efficient Cook's put the wrong platform number on my ticket and my goodbye to Nice was not accompanied by any degree of dignity. At the border the train seems suddenly to fill with men in uniform. We were in Italy. Stern-looking Customs officials demanded that you produce all your money to be counted and entered on a form and then they say something like 'Any jewellery, perfumery or radio?' I wasn't quite sure what he said but I replied 'No' on principle. After saying 'No radio' in a surprised tone of voice, off he went. And that was that! But he did have a face like Mussolini. Then the lovely ride from Nice to Genoa, the start of the Italian Riviera—another marvellous scenic drive round the seafront. All the hills marked off into squares and triangles with gardens terraced for carnation growing or vineyards. One imagines the flowers going to Covent Garden in the early morning with the dew still on them. I shall see that too. A crowd of working lads got in in black berets. They spread out a coat and played cards, flicking their cards and their lira deftly. True to tradition, one of the lads in the middle of his card playing burst into a selection from 'Il Trovatore'. At Genoa, one seized my bag and, signing to me to follow, raced up hundreds of steps with it out of the station. A little breathlessly I caught up to him as he reached the top and, almost before I could thank him, he was off again to re-board the train. I hastily pressed some cigarettes on him—and his voluble thanks continued all the way down the first flight. He looked like, and acted, as if those cigarettes were gold. First to the Hotel Vittoria and then food. Being in Italy I tussled with spaghetti. It was not until the end of the meal I learned to wind it neatly round the fork. I just had to suck it in and hope for the best. I'd been warned that Italian wine is stronger than French, and so it is. I'll leave you to stagger up to bed.

4 April 1939

There are palaces in Genoa but one would never know it. There are high formidable stone walls facing the street, that gives the city a grim look but it is behind them that beauty lies. Through doorways one catches glimpses of gardens, the loveliness of which takes one's breath away. I consult the map and locate the Museum. I shot smartly up some stairs past a minor Mussolini resplendent in rows of medals, past a soldier at attention, and through doors at the top. I stood for a moment and turned at the touch of my arm. The minor Mussolini placed himself between me and the inner room with a firm 'Signorina?' I'd gone wrong somewhere, the soldier was coming forward too. What had I done? 'Musee' I enquired anxiously. The minor Mussolini appeared to stutter indignantly. They held a conference and the soldier, slowly, carefully and loudly enunciated 'No mees. Tees, it is not the Musee, these it is the Royal Palace!' I fled.

How can I describe the narrow streets in Genoa, not six feet wide. Here people live, not squalidly but cleanly and humanly, shopping at the tiny shops in other narrow streets. There is no sign of dirt here as in Naples, no haggling over price. Here is the true Italian, laughter-loving, opera-singing. A pair of black eyes laugh at me from beneath a rakish beret. A man is sitting on the steps of a shop in an old paved street playing his concertina and a little girl dances with her skirts outstretched.

I get the train by the skin of my teeth. My watch stopped at a quarter to three but the Signorina, aided and abetted by two loudly vociferating porters, was pushed in bag and baggage to land breathless on the lap of a man who might have been my own brother. Never have I seen a nose so like my own. The despised nose with the bump is Italian. Somehow I feel very much at home. Opposite sits a little individual for all the world like Franz Schubert. Short and stout he sits with one hand on his knee and the other reflectively under his chin. Instinctively one wonders what mighty symphony is finding birth within him and then suddenly he grunted, heaved a deep sigh and finally snored happily! I caught the eye of a woman with red cherries in her hat, and we both giggle. The man with the nose, with a broad smile and many nods in our direction, leaned forward and poked the sleeping one. He awoke suddenly, grabbed his hat and made for the door. That started the ball rolling. 'Inglese?' Ah, the man with the nose could speak English. His name was Signor Gambardella and he'd been to Cambridge. He travelled in marble and in a few days would go to Bombay. The Italians, he said, would have to go to war if England didn't take the duty off cotton goods into India and Africa. The Italians were poor, they must trade. 'We are great friends with the Germans' he said and obviously waited for more but I didn't pursue it further. Instead I spoke of how I liked Italy and the graciousness of the Italian people. I mentioned how I had found the people of Naples so sad and poor. He laughed and the woman with the cherries in her hat, snorted. 'Naples' he said derisively, 'we call them natives, we tell them they're not European'. There is no sleeping of soldiers in the streets here, no mud in the side streets.

5 April 1939

This morning in Pisa I paid my two lira and went up the Tower. I can hardly realise that I'm really at the Leaning Tower, and that it really does lean! I don't think at school I ever really believed it did. Up and up stone steps to the very top. There are no rails round the galleries. Presumably if Italians wish to commit suicide off such a sacred place they are welcome to do so. But the view! Far in the distance the Pisan Mountains and the Leghorn Hills and to the fore Pisa and the winding Arno. Next the Cathedral and then the Baptistry but it is at the Campo Santo that I could have lingered for days. It would take a lifetime to study the intricacies of the paintings here. It is said the earth in the cloister was brought from Calvary. And then we walked back down the long Via Roma. The big fair man spoke very bad German, so we tried a little French and a little Italian. He must be, I concluded, a Swiss. Like myself he was not a devotee of art. His had been a busy life but like myself he was surprised at the emotion these things of beauty aroused in us. All this and more I learnt as we walked along, gesticulating, pointing, a word here in French, a phrase there in Italian and sometimes German. It was very tiring. And then as we neared my lovely little church of Maria della Spina, I stopped and breathed 'Isn't it lovely?' The big fair man stopped dead. He was not looking at the church but at me. 'My God' he said 'Are you English, so am I!'

Time—time—I'm still longing for Pisa and I'm on the electric train for Rome. The porter, whom my modest tip has inspired to guard my bag with his life, chatted volubly. 'I like the English' he volunteered. 'The girls are pretty—like you Signorina'. Just then a German girl passed—a typical product of the Hitler regime—really hefty with blonde hair like straw and a freckled face as innocent of powder as her hair was of perm. The versatile Italian face registered disgust. 'Gross' (fat) he said and pointing to me brought his hands to about one inch apart and sighed 'Ah' in ecstasy. Fortunately the train came. My limited Italian was not sufficient to cope with moments like those. At one of the little stations a group of soldiers were boarding the train—rather a different type to the Neopolitans, one of them with a concertina. Thick green uniforms, good stout boots and packs, no shoddiness here. Their superior officers in black as immaculate and disciplined as the English. It seems there will be no weak spots in equipment or organisation. It all looks as purposeful and strong as Mussolini's face. But can they turn those excitable little men of Naples into strong hard fighters? At Rome, where all roads lead, about 6.30.

8 April 1939

A soft day such as Rome knows in Spring. Met at breakfast an American journalist, one Effie Ross, who tramps Rome as I do but with a more purposeful air. There is an old Englishman here too and his sister. I notice that they have their own little pot of Hartley's marmalade! To the Piazza Populo so early that the sweepers are still about and then to the Foro Mussolini. Here there are stadiums, swimming baths fit for a race of young giants. It is all calculated to inspire in the breasts of young Italians a great patriotic fervour. A little man sitting on the side in a black swim suit, and surprisingly enough a black beret, sunned himself lazily. 'There was always sun in Italy' he said. 'Neither Hitler nor Chamberlain could take away from us the sun and the blue skies'. I hastily assured him that Chamberlain had no such designs on his country but he shook he head mournfully. All the world was against Italy. There are thousands of Germans in Italy. They come in organised parties of hundreds each wearing cockades in their hats or distinctive uniforms. They are all big, fat and fair and are accompanied by a loud-voiced guide. The Italians hate them because they leave no money. The German people themselves pay their Government. The Italian Government pay the Italian hotelkeepers who keep them at a very reduced rate, so that no money passes between Germany and Italy, but a huge debt is being paid off! The Italians may have a holiday in Germany but they work, each according to his trade while there. A young American stared and said 'Gosh!' and thanked God he was American. I thought how much splendour I would give up for freedom. How much more I would enjoy a swim in the old Mangaotaki River[2], with my bit of a tent on the banks, than be marched black-skirted and white-bloused to the Mussolini baths. And then felt furious with myself because I was just being smug.

Next to the Catacombs of St. Sebastiano. A party just going through and I found myself by the side of a little brown monk in a brown habit and girdle with his hair shaven except for a ring all round. Our little guide showed us two boarded-up tunnels that, he said, had once held the bodies of Peter and Paul. I could feel a smile spreading all over my face in spite of myself, for on his head, covering the shaven part, the little monk had a brown hat an exact replica of the 'beanie' I had on!

9 April 1939

Today I have seen all the pageantry of Rome. I had a black veil. I had to have it to enter the great church of St. Peter's at Easter time. I left at 7.30 and there were thousands pouring into the Square but I had a ticket to get inside. I know I should have given mine up to those whose Faith made the day one of supreme importance but I just couldn't—I wanted to see the great church come to life. About 9.30 there was a stir that grew to a rumble as the crowd moved. Down the centre aisle were soldiers with rifles and fixed bayonets in glorious uniforms. There was a great clapping and a shouting, people leapt into the air shouting 'Alle Papa, Alle Papa'. The Pope passed about four feet from where I was standing borne high on the shoulders of men in red in the sedia gestatoria[3]. He lifted his hand frequently to bless with first and second fingers the crowd beneath him. He sat perfectly still and poised a thin ascetic man with pince-nez, a huge ring on the outstretched finger which I afterwards noted was encased in a rich glove. No one, not even those of us who are not of the Faith, could remain unmoved. The Mass lasted till 12.30.

In the evening to the cinema to see Deanna Durbin in 'The Certain Age', all in Italian. You never heard such a clatter. All her speaking parts were synchronised in Italian but she alone could sing! So perforce it was in English—sorry Effie, American.

10 April 1939

Today I must see all the rest of Rome! The sheer impossibility of it is crushing. First the Colosseum and then the Forum Romanum. On to the Palatine and then back to the Piazza Venezia. Noticed that a crowd was collected. All eyes were fixed on the square building that was Mussolini's offices. All eyes on a balcony, all traffic had stopped. There, waving his arms, his head thrown back, was Mussolini. The short, strong and stumpy figure that we know so well. I trembled to think that while I had been vegetating in the ruins, dwelling on the vanished Caesars, I had nearly missed the Emperor in all but name of modern Rome. He spoke for but a few minutes, but excitedly, and as he then turned to go inside a great roar went up from the crowd. Every face glowed. He was their deliverer, his was the right to command, the right of a builder of a nation. A new God to supercede [*sic*] Jupiter—the God Mussolini!

14 April 1939

I'm actually in Venice giving little squeals of delight every time I look out of the window on to the Grand Canal. There is no traffic in Venice, just a broad path and then the Canal. It is easy to find a hotel in Venice, in fact it would be hard to avoid one. From out of the long line of porters who met the train there sprang an extra handsome one who could manage a little English. I embrace him (metaphorically of course) and in a matter of mere seconds I was whisked out of the melee [*sic*] of clambering porters, excited women and voluble men into a gondola. I could see my fellow passengers being bundled into motor-boats and I thanked God that I was not as others are! The Pensione is a dear little place kept by Germans. I find nearly everyone knows a little German, at least in Italy, so I get on quite well. There are blue skies and soft still air. Pigeons are hopping about to be fed. Sailors laugh and joke round the little wine shop and a message boy, with a basket on his head, bursts suddenly into one of the lesser known airs from the Barber of Seville. To St. Mark's Square—'tis said it looked just as it does now seven centuries ago. It is like a big intimate courtyard bounded by lovely arcades. There are palaces in Venice, the palaces that children dream about. They have spires and towers and glitter with gold. One still expects to see a fairy princess come out to feed the thousands of pigeons fluttering almost into one's very eyes. They are poor the people of Venice, desperately poor. Work is scarce, so much so that having once obtained it, wage conditions are of no consequence as long as it keeps the body together. But there is spirit that keeps them singing in the summer sun and living, loving, laughing through the soft warm days. At little stalls souvenirs were being sold, little gondolier badges and a very popular one of Mussolini and Hitler! Monsieur H. bought one and, with a grand gesture, threw it far into the Canal.

Signor de S. offered to take me out from the Pensione in the afternoon and Frau. W. the proprietor told me he was really a Count who had fallen on hard times. I'm afraid I laughed for are they not all Counts whom English girls meet in golden Venice? But it was true she said, he had lost his money when his big new shop was destroyed in a storm. 'And so' she finished complacently 'he goes to the wars to try to get killed for the honour of the house. He goes to the Abyssinian war but nothing happens, soon he goes to the Spanish war, if nothing happens there he go to the war with the English—the big war'. It was not till she had gone that the significance of her last words dawned on me, and to give the good woman her due, I don't think that at the moment she connected me with the English. Venice is a city of paradoxes. There is a shrine at every corner and a cat on every roof. There is perfume from flowers placed tenderly before a shrine and round the corner a latrine taking up three quarters of the path! It seems that even Mussolini has forgotten Venice. The one time splendour of the walls of its houses had faded.

15 April 1939

We go ashore at Burano to see lace being made. In a lace school the girls all sit in rows on hard chairs, their feet resting on the rung of the chair in front. The design is done on paper and the cotton worked over it. The older ones looked as if they had worked their very lives into the beautiful work, their backs were rounded and their eyes red-rimmed and weak. The young ones quick and deft but with a frequent straightening up and a quick sigh. The old, old woman in charge moved about amongst them, her hands in front of her busily knitting a black stocking. It is lovely stuff but I will never buy hand-made lace again. I could not look at it without seeing those poor weak eyes. Outside in the village children played round a well. A woman with a wee baby came and begged for a cent. They seem so very poor these lace-makers. A woman washes clothes in a tub outside her door and two young boys splash round in the canal with toy swords and bayonets. At Torcello we visit the Museum and the Cathedral and then back by boat to Murano, here is the glass factory. A spot of liquid glass, a blow and lo! we have a vase. Girls are painting intricate designs. I did not think there was so much hand-work done in the world. We had lunch, Signore de S. and I. He wanted to write, he said he was going to the Spanish war in a fortnight. He told me the tale of the lost money and of the family honour. It was necessary that he should die, to live would be a disgrace. When I heard no more he would be gone.

16 April 1939

In Milan and I go to Cook's but they're not very interested in third class travellers and looked unutterably bored with my enquiries as to where to go and reduced fares in Switzerland, so I took myself off to the Swiss consul. Did I get help from the Swiss! I've enough pamphlets and information to sink a ship. Do you know you can get a rail ticket for eight days to go practically anywhere in Switzerland, including steamboats on the Lakes, for £2.10.0?

Certainly I have become rusticated in Venice. I still feel bewildered in Milan. It is the traffic. There are big cars in plenty and fashion. 'Tis said other towns produce and Milan collects and sells. After dinner to the Teatro Scala. One dresses to go to the Opera for coats are not allowed inside. And the opera is La Traviata. Where should one hear Verdi but in Italy and where in Italy but in Milan where the great chandeliers blaze with Victorian richness. The house is full as it is every night but why do things begin so late in Italy? The Opera at 9 to finish at 12.30.

I had my last look at Milan from the tower of the Duomo. It was a clear day and the view magnificent. Through the telescope the Alps were wonderfully close. 'Ah Signorina you are lucky one can see the Matterhorn'.

18 April 1939

There can be nothing more simply lovely than Lugano in the early morning. The women getting their butter, eggs and cheese ready to sell at the stalls in the streets. The little furnicular buzzing to and from the station. I bought a suede hat—a Swiss suede hat and found to my disgust it was made in England! Lake steamers are gliding across the water scarcely disturbing its placid depths and there are little sailing boats. There are lovely walks round the lake side—leafy promenades. It is on the run from Lugano to Zurich that we go through the Saint Gotthard Pass at 6,936 feet. How shall I, who has hardly ever seen snow, describe that tunnel and gorge? It was wet, the hills lost in angry clouds, white merging into grey above and into vivid green below. And then the snow came fluttering down so delicately, just sprinkling the green. It looked so harmless so fairy-like. But then it came blindingly, it piled up on the ground, soft and white all-enveloping. It seemed to stifle all sound, all action. The air is fresh and keen. It is placid and lovely country. There are green fields that stretch flat without a bump until the next range is reached, every inch is cultivated and families work side by side. Pink and white blossom everywhere and green mingled with the pink where the leaves are starting to come. And as we pass scenery that I have come thousands of miles to see the man in the corner seat slept solidly. He opened one eye and I ventured to say that we were at St. Gotthard but he just said 'Ja, ja' and went off again. I shared a roll and a piece of cheese I bought in Lugano with a little French woman in the same carriage. She had a little black hat with a cyclamen feather which bobbed whenever she laughed or spoke. We bit into our rolls simultaneously. I saw a peculiar look pass over her face and then I knew. It wasn't cheese I had bought—it was soap! We laughed until the little cyclamen feather quivered and shook.

22 April 1939

There is a pale pink glow on the snow as the sun rises. I was barely awake when I left St. Moritz, a day was just dawning. Lake Zurich was a dream, motionless, dark rushes along the water's edge. Beguiled myself by reading the notices on the train. I know them all in three languages now. 'Nicht rauchen' is easy but 'Bitte nicht in den Wagen zu Spucken' did puzzle me for a while. It simply wasn't in the dictionary. I asked a kindly peasant woman with her basket full of chickens and she shook with delight. I pointed out that if I didn't know what I hadn't to do, maybe I'd do it. And she shook again. 'Nein, nein' she gasped. At length I got out of her it merely meant 'Don't spit'. A motherly soul with a son of about 15, she suggested I stay the night at a hostel for young girls. Poor soul! She was an Austrian refugee trying to follow her husband to New York. He was a Jew and had escaped early. She was travelling from country to country working as she went with her boy, spending five months here, five months there to qualify for passports. Next month she would join her man in New York and she was struggling to learn a little English. She was so tired of waiting in strange countries. The boy he liked it. He nodded vigorously, his shining round face looking the picture of health. Vienna was her town. 'It is beautiful' I said. Her eyes filled with tears as she answered 'Vienna <u>was</u> beautiful but everyone is sad now and frightened'. She had left all her people to follow her man to New York. It was a big undertaking for a stout, middle-aged housewife called Rosa.

Rather fun at the Hostel that night. About 12 in the room—French, Swiss, Dutch, German and English, although which nationality snored I couldn't really be certain, but it wasn't the English because she was awake! But they were all jolly girls, all nicely dressed and on holiday.

24 April 1939

Stopped with the Schenck family in Lucerne after asking a policeman for help to find a bed for the night. His sister kept a pensione. I learned that Swiss policemen have big feet too. Frau Schenck and numerous offspring welcomed me loudly. She carried my case into Mama's room. It was Mama's feather bed she said in thick guttural German and laughed because I spoke my German like a 'lady'. I joined them in the kitchen. At the bottom of my case I found some chewing gum! Cigarettes I saw would be useless for Herr Schenck with his huge lidded Swiss pipe. Frau Schenck turned over the gum curiously. Neither she nor the children had ever seen it. What did one do with it? I gathered the children onto a line and explained. Did they know where America was? 'Ja' came a chorus. Well American children chewed gum. Illumination grew on the eldest boy's face. He knew his cinemas. He grabbed a piece and chewed vigorously and then pulled it out. Herr Schenck removed his pipe and sent out a loud guffaw into the room and the children scrambled for the rest. There was chewing gum on chairs, on the plain wooden table, Frau Schenck found some in her hair. They laughed until everyone was weak. Somehow the 'kinder' were got off to bed, each retrieving his gum and rolling it carefully into a ball for tomorrow. I got a soft gummy kiss from each.

Up at an absurd hour and, with the blessing of the Schenck family on my head, to the train for Interaken. It is a lovely run down through the land along a chain of lakes. The little train just trickled along. There was a dear little girl sitting opposite who was dying to practise her English. In May she goes to a finishing school in England to learn properly. She already speaks Swiss, German and French. We shared an orange and giggled at a man with a long black beard. With a sort of final triumphant burst the train rushed importantly into Interlaken. Followed the crowd rather vaguely and then found I'd joined a day trip to the Grindelwald glacier. It was Fate doubtless. It is a lovely Switzerland at the foot of the Alps—luscious country and Grindelwald a valley favoured by the Gods. We walked along rugged paths to a little cow shed where we saw the long horn used to call the cattle. I begged to try it and the big Swiss in the Tyrolean hat, which I strongly suspect he put on for our benefit, (although he did have the white stockings too) obligingly showed me how. But the cattle didn't come. A weird unearthly sound issued from the far end of the horn and a quietly-browsing cow suddenly kicked up his heels and fled! We followed a mountain track that grew steeper and steeper to the base of the great Grindelwald glacier—a great white mass of snow and ice bearing slowly down. At one point it had been presumably hollowed out and we entered with boards underfoot. It was like being in an icy cavern, the home of the Snow Queen. It was so coldly blue. At a chalet we drank milk and ate bread and cheese. We came back down through the valley and the hills. The Germans sang vigorously under their leader. Occasionally they 'Heiled'. I had an uneasy feeling that somehow I was traitorous to England just being there so I breathed the first verse of God Save The King in the hopes that it would have the same effect as the Lord's Prayer on the devil!

It was dark when we got to Interlaken. The Germans metaphorically goose-stepped away into the darkness, all I could see was fields. 'Wo ist Interlaken?' I asked the station master. He explained the town was some 20 minutes away. So I walked and found the Hotel Huchen.

27 April 1939

In Geneva in a hostel similar to the one in Montreux and shared a room with another girl. She spoke only French of a provincial type that I seemed to be wholly unfamiliar with but all girls are the same and we got on nicely. We both put in a few curlers and compared face cream. It is strange that my first impressions of Geneva should be happy holidayers with armfuls of flowers when it should have been international conferences and the League of Nations. I went to the wonderful League of Nations building, it is truly the most beautiful of modern art. Spacious marble rooms, delicately coloured with flooring of polished rubber. Pictures of great modern artists all symbolic of the freedom of mankind from war and disease. At the end of the tour to a neat little cinema to see a film on the fight against disease. Even if the League should fail in its fight for peace it has the eternal battle of disease and for that alone it is worth all the effort. We walked round to another park to see the statues of the great Protestant leaders such as Calvin, Knox and Cromwell. In those days religion caused wars. Now there is very little religion but there are still wars.

Trains seem home to me now—towns come and towns go but one always finally comes back to a train. It seems months since I 'fussed' over anything. We've reached Basle. Now I have in my purse French money for Strasbourg,

Belgian money for Brussels, German money and Dutch. I seem to be getting fat! Caught sight of my face in a shop window and it looked like a full moon!

30 April 1939

Baden was an agreeable surprise, it is only an hour and a half from Strasbourg. Now Baden is a friendly little place embosomed among the hills. It has only 10,000 inhabitants and possibly as many tourists. One would think the whole of Germany came to Baden to take the waters—in fact these Nazis while scorning the good things of life in one breath partake of them gluttonously in the next. It is strange how each country is definitely, well—that country. One could never call Baden anything but German for all its quaint beauty. It is clean and controlled and so many things are 'verboten' just as I had always read. However as it happened I hadn't the slightest desire to do those 'verboten' things so it didn't matter much. Found a little place to stay up the Lichtenthaler Strasse and was invited to go with Herr.S. [*sic*] and his good Frau for a run in the car. Our little hostess beamed and whispered to me hurriedly that they were beyond reproach and good Nazis, it would be quite alright for me to go. Herr.S. and his cigar filled the front seat completely but they were a jolly couple full of the new regime. I promised to read, mark and learn everything about the New Order as I went. Herr.S. looked at me from under bushy brows. 'You're not afraid to go to England just now' he said. 'Maybe you'll go home soon, no?' I assured him I didn't want to go home for ages, I'd only just started, and he shook his head and said the German equivalent to 'Ts, ts. ts'. For hours it seemed we drove through the little towns and villages of the northern part of the Black Forest. We got back late—very late. I thanked Herr. S. and his good Frau. She shook my hand vigorously. 'You are a good girl' she said in her limited English. 'Your German it is good'. I almost expected her to say 'You would make a good Nazi' and kidnap me forthwith. Herr. S. smiled without guile. 'When I come to New Zealand perhaps you will show me your country?' I assured him I would and sent up a fervent prayer that he might come in peace and not waving his swastika in a fanatical desire to rescue New Zealand from the clutches of the English. That seems to be the big idea here at present. Still I am grateful to Herr.S. whatever may happen in the future.

29 April 1939

I crept out of Baden apologetically. It is a place to spend a season in not just a day. It was still morning when I got to Heidelberg. We had passed through a pleasant district. Huge trees that looked like walnut trees shade the roads and it is said that tobacco is grown in this district. Somehow it seemed more like France than Germany. There is one little part of it which anyone even looking English is immediately ushered, with great ceremony, towards. Our guide, a voluble, bullet-headed but efficient if slightly mechanical, guide shoved me forward so that I might miss none of it. It is called the English Palace. It is the final piece of the building erected in 1601 for Mary Stuart, the daughter of our own James I, and grand-daughter of Mary, Queen of Scots. Mary's grand-daughter it would seem was more fortunate than Mary herself. We are joined here by a fantastic party in tam-o-shanter hats with a feather in and green cloaks. Wondering for a minute if they were a pageant and found them to be only a German tourist crowd. They marched—positively marched—up to the Castle singing lustily. They were so solemn—even when the big barrel in the cellar was shown to us there arose not a smile—even a surreptitious licking of the lips would have been human. They eyed it stolidly. But the others were better, many a joke was made of the capacity of the present company compared with the 200,000 bottles of wine that could be contained in the cask.

I saw serious bullet-headed, albeit young, giants all over the town. One retrieved my map which blew away on to a 'verboten' stretch of grass. 'You're English' he said 'and you spik German'. His surprise was unmistakable. Said rather lamely that I just liked to speak other languages—it helps contact and enables one to get about. But he shook his head. 'The English they spik no German, mostly they say we speak their English. But soon they all spik German. You come from New Zealand. Auckland, Wellington or the odder island?' 'Maybe I meet you there some day, eh?' I hoped not and hurried on. There are too many Germans wanting to meet me in New Zealand and what's more they know a lot about us. A whole lot more than we know about Germany. It's a pity I don't like beer for the very word Heidelberg conjures up great foaming handles. I drank a sparkling Moselle with my cheese sandwich. Have learnt not to rely on butter or meat—both seem remarkably scarce. Off to Mainz, which is venerable, and found the youth hostel. They may be youth hostels in Germany but they are not confined to youth—there was many a woman of nearly 40. But they were tough—hikers and cyclists, some in pairs but mostly in parties. But all the rules and regulations! A long list hangs on the wall in every room. The girls were rather nice but hardly any used any make-up. They 'borrowed' my powder delightedly, scorned my lipstick but just put it on to try. Gave me the impression they thought I wasn't bad for an English girl. One confessed she had previously thought all English were silly and degenerate—but she'd never met any. All marshalled off to bed at 10. It was fun going to bed in the upper bunk. A covert look at German undies revealed no frills but one would hardly expect hikers to go in for pink ribbons. A good healthy wash at night and a vigorous brushing of teeth seems the general rule and not a perm among the lot! Wrote out the words of the Horst Wessel Song (the Nazi National Anthem).

May 1939

Amsterdam, Volendam, Brussels, Paris, Versailles, Fontainebleau, Dieppe, London, Haslemere, Southsea, Portsmouth, Winchester, Brockenhurst, Lyndhurst, Ringwood, Wimborne, Salisbury, Amesbury, Stonehenge, Wilton, Dorchester, Tolpuddle, Honiton, Exeter, Princetown, Widecombe, Torquay, Plymouth, Polperro, Penzance, St Ives, Land's End, Mousehole, Bodmin, Tintagel, Bideford, Appledore, Clovelly, Barnstaple, Epsom, London—St James Park, Admiralty, Buckingham Palace, Whitehall, Cenotaph, Caledonian Market, Petticoat Lane, British Museum, Westminster Abbey, Scotland Yard, Hampstead Heath, Kenwood, Chelsea, Oxford Street, Piccadilly Circus, Kew Gardens. Northolt, Stokenchurch, Oxford, Henley, Stoke Poges.

1 May 1939

Somehow May has such a peculiar sound. It sounds unfamiliar like the dawn of a new era. Doesn't Europe always wait for riots on May Day? But there are no riots in Amsterdam—just a drip of water in the canal and the clatter of clogs as men go to work. On to a boat and drift up the Canal to Volendam. Dear little cobbled streets here and rows and rows of tiny toy houses. The people all in national dress, the women in black peaked caps and black full skirts and bodices and the girls the same. Some bonny little girls with stout hands knitted socks. They wore scarves with bobs on and tiny clogs. The little boys wear velvet pants, jerseys and round caps. It was washing day in toy-town and the women bent over big tubs outside, spreading the clothing out to dry on the freshly scrubbed stones—big red shirts that the men wear well tucked into their pantaloons and brightly coloured hankies. Met Frau Plett here—a widow with a family of eight! The good Frau is amazed that I should have come from New Zealand. She is afraid to go to Amsterdam but the girl knows about New Zealand. Their church sent a missionary there for the Maoris! A long time ago? She shook her black-capped head—it was but two years ago. I ponder on this amazing fact. I didn't know, even the Maoris need missionaries. I'll admit we're heathens but it's purely apathy not lack of opportunity to worship. And on to pass the tulips. Great red patches alongside great yellow and purple patches. Piles of brilliant blossoms ready to be used as manure! It is said the season has been bad from the point of view of selling the flowers. They are so unbelievably brilliant. Back to Amsterdam and the rain again. Amsterdam with narrow canals hugged closely down to the water's edge by seven storied houses leaning crazily but she is not Venice. She does not laugh and flirt. She is a comely maiden with a gentle placid smile. The canals speak of trade and the flat drip of rain. But with it all the streets are beautiful.

4 May 1939

And my birthday. Today I see Brussels and Paris. Brussels is a big city. I never realised that it held 900,000 souls. There are lovely boulevards surrounding the city and near the Bois de La Cambre I found the Edith Cavell monument. It is a poignant monument with a winged angel and a female figure indicating the carving in the low stone—'A Edith Cavell/ A Marie Depage/ 1915. Passant dis-le a tes enfants. Ils les ont tuees.' (Passer-by! Tell your children. They killed them.) Brussels is rather a bewildering city but one thing stands out alone as something not to be forgotten—the beautiful Palais de Justice. On rising ground it commands the whole of the city. One is not conscious of poverty but just of depression, except in the café where a gay cosmopolitan crowd gathers, but they are not Brussels. Out to the site of the Battle of Waterloo and there is a good smell of cow in the air, a smell of the earth. Then into the silence comes the 'zoom' of an aeroplane. It is strange how one's thoughts turn not to Waterloo, in 1815, but to 1914. The men dig stolidly on in the fields. The Belgians are a strange people. Their history seems to have bred in them a dogged spirit, an apathy as if they would say, 'If a war comes and we are wiped out we will gather up the remains and plod on again as we have done before'. One can imagine no soldiers here. It seems that they would wait to be defended and if no defence came they would bend to the yoke. Time alone will show.

I caught the train to Paris. Oh dear, if only I didn't always have to say goodbye—but there's a jolly crowd in the train and they were all proud to meet someone from New Zealand. I must share their meal—they might never meet a New Zealander again. I assured them we were plentiful but they shook their heads. They impressed on me that in Paris I must be careful, there were pickpockets! and I was going alone—I was in grave danger. It is very, very late when we got to Paris but my companions insist on coming to the Hostel for Young Ladies with me. They explain at length to the directoress just who I am and then, wreathed in smiles, they depart. The dears!

5 May 1939

It's Paris, Paris in the spring. Nothing could be more lovely. I have seen Notre Dame. It is mysteriously dim except for the light from the three great rose windows. I like Notre Dame. For all its history it is a friendly church. It was lit by a thousand candles and people were in prayer. Up hundreds of stone steps to the tower, the same tower up which raced the hunchback. Below is the sparkling Seine and its seven bridges. Paris at last! I meditated deliciously and then a voice from behind me said 'Eh by gum, this is summat like a view!' The English hit me like a pistol shot. It came from a shock-headed youth of about 20, grinning broadly, evidently quite unaware of my presence. He was from Sheffield too and enjoying Paris to the full. Then to Sainte-Chapelle. One forgives the Palais de Justice. If a city produced nothing but one Sainte-Chapelle one would forgive it anything. It is an exquisite little Gothic jewel built by St. Louis as a shrine for the Crown of Thorns. It has glorious stained glass. Walked a leisurely and delightful way back to the hostel.

But if Paris itself is interesting so is the hostel. It is full of English women, mostly governesses who have come over to France in their youth. They become attached to families, live their lives in a narrow groove. They never go back to England and yet they never become French. They are more English than your English woman—they cling to customs of 20 years ago. Told of all my doings to the dear souls on my table. Little Miss. H, who minds two children daily, is a cheerful but timid little soul who speaks of 'not being allowed to do this or that'. Not allowed at 60! And then Miss. M—all that an English governess is portrayed to be—prim 'Cranfordish' and really making an effort to be sociable. Immaculate—it seems as if her daily life is made up of walking on a chalk line—anything to the left or right is wrong. At night to the Folies Bergere! Miss. H. told me how to get there and what seats to take, but suggested tactfully it would be best not to mention it to Miss.M. Mrs. M. came with me—a traveller like myself, she admitted her life had been dull while the estimable Mr. M. lived but now he had gone; poor dear! She sighed dutifully and said she had no idea before he went that the world was such a beautiful place. I am glad that the Folies lived up to their reputation. That the girls, except for a fig leaf, were as they were born. Beautiful girls they were and not too thin! They made one horribly conscious of being too short in the legs, too broad in the hips. (Which reminds me when I left home I was too bony). The chief girl comedians took off Mussolini perfectly—a vivacious couple with a bit of English to help things along. A coster does the Lambeth Walk and, on being dragged off, is replaced by the latest Parisian dance. To the café afterwards and coffee. We dance; at 2.30 whisper that perhaps we'd better go home and Mrs. M. agrees reluctantly that perhaps we had. Rang up the night porter, gave him a tip for his trouble, and squeaked up the stairs to bed.

6 May 1939

Up early. Mrs. M. not visible. Peeped in her door, saw a pink slumber net hiding curlers and heard heavy breathing so came out quietly. Slipped down to the Place des Ternes to buy toothpaste. Immediately I spoke a voice shrieked 'Marie, Marie!' and Marie came pattering down from upstairs. She was kept specifically for English customers. She knew enough English to produce my Gibbs in exactly the same tin as I have at home but with all the writing on it in French. Then to Montmartre—to Sacre Cœur, that holy pile on top of a wicked hill. The Metro is a real blessing to wanderers in Paris. You descend, go up to the ticket window and say 'un' (the more like a grunt it is the better) and pay 1.30F. One could stay down all day for that being whizzed about the whole of Paris underground but immediately one mounts the steps and sees the light of day, it is another 1.30 to go back. Wandered through the little streets and saw an exquisitely dressed woman enter a bakery. She is in immaculate black with a tricky little hat forward on her head. She wears long white kid gloves. A minute after she comes out grasping firmly by its middle half a yard of loaf with a wee bit of paper only where she held it. That is the trouble with buying eatables in France. There is never enough paper. One's purchase is always open to the enquiring gaze of the public long before home is reached. Found Maxims in the Rue Royal, outside mahogany-coloured wood with gold decorations. There are no prices up outside Maxims, the few café tables outside are empty, no one seems to come or go except with huge cases of bottles! One feels that it waits for the night.

To the Palace of Versailles and then into the little town of Versailles to find something to eat. Found a shop with a horse's head over the door, which indicated that they sold horse meat. Curiosity fought with a natural abhorrence—an old horse and cart clattered by, I decided I just couldn't do it. Tonight we have seen many nightclubs. All the dancing is just the usual slow fox-trots with a good sprinkling of the rumba. The French are wonderful dancers, the girls neat and precision itself on the quick steps, and the men lithe. There are old, old women in tiny shoes with stilt heels, their hair lacquered into shape in a thousand ringlets. Their frocks were cut cleverly to hide scraggy necks and scrawny arms. It is the early hours again when we get home.

9 May 1939

I was up at 3.30! I met people coming home as I was going out. To the Halles, that great meat market that Emile Zola called the stomach of Paris. Does Paris really eat all those thousands and thousands of carcasses? I don't want to see meat for a long, long time. There are already little old French women hurrying about with their baskets, marketing to the best possible advantage. There are flowers with the dew still on them and vegetables with just one day to live. Big barrels of pickled herrings—and through it all a quick French wit. The old women with their shawls over their heads and their white aprons are as quick as the pert girls with their shining curls. Out to Fontainebleau, then to the Casino with Miss. H. to meet Maurice Chevalier. I have always liked Maurice and never more so than now in Paris. Here he is at home. Just the same smile, the same' cheek' and, in spite of his 50 years, he brings the house down. He struts, hat over one eye. He addresses the English (cheers), he addresses the French (cheers) and he sings (the very house rocks). Somehow the rest of the show is good but one just waits for Maurice again. Must admit he's the one and only actor I've ever had the slightest desire to chase backstage after. Think I'd better leave Paris if it's going to take me like that!

Strange how all the French music halls are putting on 'peace' numbers with a great waving of flags and Rule Britannias. Methinks it is overdone. It is hoped we never have to ally to France. They'll be a millstone round our neck—they are not stable. Their sudden love of the English seems too artificial. One feels they laugh at us even while they wave our flags.

10 May 1939

There was such a bustle to say goodbye to all those little ladies at the hostel. They are looking so wistful for after all they are English. Train to Dieppe and on to the boat, such a little boat, not much more than a ferry. Tips in England heavy. I'll be glad when I get rid of my luggage. Only a few hours and we're there. I sit with fur coat and rug as if going to the South Pole. And then cliffs, not the white cliffs of Dover but really England. Through Customs and on to the train. Third class in England most comfortable with upholstered seats. They seem so infinitely superior these English people, but it's third class. Where do the ordinary people travel—perhaps they stay at home. After the Continent it appears as if everyone talks in whispers and shuts up suddenly immediately a stranger approaches. Surely I have not grown like the Continentals in so short a time but then I must remember I'm not English either. But the scenery! Fields of buttercups and primroses in pale yellow lumps, bluebells smiling like a summer sky. It's all true, the joy of an English spring.

But we're near London. I know we are because of all the chimney pots, thousands of them. What a crash there would be if there were an earthquake! It goes for miles this London. At Victoria Station no one asks if they can help as they would on the Continent. All those one has been speaking to immediately become secretive as if you wished to follow them home. But the Cockney porter's a real delight. He trundles me along to Ebury Court , advises me to go to 'Me and My Girl' and leaves with a cheerful 'Thanks, Loidy'. Dinner and then make the acquaintance of the little Irish maid whom I found snivelling into the making of my bed. Poor little soul, she has only been at the hotel three months. She works for 17/6d per week and her keep. Fourteen rooms to do a day and the stairs like climbing to heaven. Often she is working to 12 and up at 7. But she's dying for her week's holiday when she'll spend £5 (all she's saved) and go home.

11 May 1939

The Very First English Breakfast. Tea, porridge, bacon and eggs, Toast and marmalade! Dead silence in the breakfast room. Onto the bus for New Zealand House and such a lovely pile of letters. Then to buy a haversack in Petticoat Lane and be warned by the little Jew about the dangers of London. When I first went into the shop he is speaking German but he wouldn't admit to it again! Made the acquaintance of the lions in Trafalgar Square and peered up at Nelson. It is so much smaller than I thought. I thought of the Place Concorde and then said firmly if rudely 'Shut up!' There shall be no comparisons. There is a love at first sight, but there is also a longer more lasting love that comes from association—after all I am English in spite of saying 'Ja, ja' to the bus driver. Tea at Lyons Corner House, the 'Nippies' are certainly smart, and proud of it. Must remember to leave a tip. Always forget—not meanness just absent-minded.

12 May 1939

I can hardly believe this is London. I feel I should be sight-seeing and instead I'm rushing around buying things. Bought a little stove and some meths plus a cup and provisions for the youth hostels. Over a cup of coffee a dear soul warns me about being a lone girl in the big city of London. When she heard I'd been to Paris she shook her head as if it were indeed a wonder I'd got out alive. Passed down Fleet Street and then away by the train with haversack and no luggage, starting on a great adventure. Away through beautiful Surrey. All that I had ever read about—green luscious pastures, yellow with buttercups, roadside blue with bluebells, lanes through leafy lands and lazy streams winding round, trailing branches in their waters. It is all so quiet. Off the train spontaneously at Haslemere, a bit commercialised one can see but still lovely. A little German emigrant at the station, poor little girl shaking like a leaf and a group of not very understanding Haselmerians trying to make her understand that Mrs Patterson couldn't meet her at the station but she was to take the bus and they'd meet her there. She hadn't slept for three days having come from Budapest and not a word of English did she know. Thought hard things of Mrs Patterson who couldn't get herself or anyone else to the station. The little soul waved pathetically to me as I went up in the bus to the centre of town. Found a little place to stay, down a path with a lovely garden. Such a pretty place and so English. Copper jugs shone on a shelf, a hot water bottle was in bed—a blue china one. I'm terrified of it falling out and breaking.

13 May 1939

Decided to go to Southsea and Portsmouth. At Portsmouth the Victory and at Southsea sailors and their girls. Decide, goodness knows why, to stay at the Y.W.C.A., an admirable institution which kept me waiting for half an hour before deigning to appear and then couldn't do enough for me! Breakfast and then to the Isle of Wight. Took the train to Sandown and then to the famous Cowes. There are yachts on the harbour just enough to give an idea of the 'season'. Every quaint little shop is under 'Royal Patronage'. Later to Portsmouth to see the Victory. It looks so strange anchored at Portsmouth— one's first impression is of piles of wood. How these galleons must have blazed! A party just going over her so tramped the decks that made history—saw the spot where the disobedient hero died. At night to Southsea where there are lights all along the promenade, festoons of them, and the piers stretch far out to sea. On these piers are trick mirrors before which jolly Jack Tars and girls in excessively short skirts stand with arms around each other's waists and laugh. There are dance halls and old time gadgets for amusement. There was even 'What The Butler Saw'. Frankly I have always wondered exactly what did the butler see. Now I know. Merely a woman in W.B.s and white embroidered drawers fastening up her stockings. She is a product of 30 years ago and even in the intimacy of her boudoir was discreetly covered, more so than the average girl of today is on the street in summer! At the Clarence pier is a big wheel and there are fountains playing with coloured lights. It is quite light up till about nine!

16 May 1939

Up really early full of beans, albeit wet. Paddled to the bus in Winchester to go to Brockenhurst. At the church are the graves of New Zealand soldiers. The sexton, E.C. Jemray is a personality. His family have been sextons for a hundred years. He has a peculiar and enviable gift. Robins, blue tits and sparrows all come and feed from his hand. They perch on his shoulder, whisper secrets into his ear and pull at his hair. His wee daughter, aged 4, is just the same. On the graves of the New Zealand soldiers are wreaths and lovely flowers. He says they are kept there by a Brockenhurst woman quite voluntarily. We have much to thank her for. Set off to walk to Lyndhurst, 11 miles through the New Forest. Quite alone on the road for a long way and I deviated many times following little tracks. Aroused from a reverie by a friendly voice 'Would I like a lift?' A set of golf clubs are removed from the front seat on to an indignant and aristocratic chow dog at the back. The driver, a woman about 50, has the heftiest pair of shoes I've ever seen, an old tweed hat and ruddy cheeks. Learned she spent last winter in Switzerland and intensely dislikes people who hike in 'shorts', from which I gathered that my modest skirt had earned me the ride. Dropped near Burley and walked on. A Walls ice-cream man with his 'Stop me and buy one' sign, buzzed past.

Had a cup of coffee at a little shop and there, sitting by the fire, was a real English farmer with his pint in one hand and his pipe in the other. He was huge and ruddy, complete with leggings and corduroy trousers. He laughed a laugh that went right up the chimney at my pleasure in the mantelpiece decorations—polished brass medallions which he used to have on his cart horses. He made me nearly stand on my head to look at the hams smoking up the chimney. Various irons hung about to pull out and hang kettles on. We sat for an hour baking by the fire and discussing farm conditions. Like New Zealand they can't get men for farm work. When he was a boy they worked. Nowadays all they want to do is sit on their (umph umph splutter) in picture shows. But on the whole he was a tolerant old soul and well he might be. He had just acquired another farm. New Zealand land he said was richer than theirs. And did we have a very difficult time avoiding snakes! Shares my opinion that modern diseases are caused by artificial manures. Got up reluctantly from the oak seat, out into the wind to tackle the other eight miles. Men are hoeing in the fields and wave a greeting. 'How far are you walking, Miss?' 'Hey Jock, the young lady's walked from Brockenhurst'. Jock pushes his cap back and stares, and finally emits 'Where for? Ringwood! I'd rather be hoeing spuds, eh George!'

A few more miles and a long stop to locate a cuckoo. A voice from behind, an 'Oxford' voice. 'Excuse me but would you like a lift?' A fearsome figure in helmet and goggles mounted on a snorting, exploding monster. The goggles removed, a little natural beauty came into view, a friendly freckled face. So I climbed on the back of the motor bike and we snorted off. I heard no more cuckoos. Climbed shakily down at the Ringwood station. Goggles put his foot on the starter, the freckled face beamed, and my thanks were lost in the exhaust. Arrived finally at Wimborne and the Coach and Horses, no youth hostel here. Slept the sleep of the just.

18 May 1939

Yesterday at Salisbury and the lovely spire that rose up from the smooth lawns, surely the most beautiful in the world. One must stop for a moment to gaze down the entire length of the nave, the best view in the whole church. The windows have, strangely enough, plain glass, some architect having the idea of making the church as light as possible. Today still cold but not so wet. Up very, very early and on the road by half past seven to Stonehenge, no half past six due to having read my watch wrongly. A glorious walk out through Amesbury, about ten miles. The Salisbury Plain is glorious. It rolls like a well-kept lawn far into the distance, looking like a patchwork quilt with boundaries of live hedges. And after Amesbury—a long white road leading to the mystery of Stonehenge. They saw me coming long before I saw them and greeted me cheerily, the two men in the ticket office. The Irish one picked me for a New Zealander. They offered me a cup of tea and insisted on adding a huge cheese sandwich. We argued about the possibilities of the war and Mr Chamberlain, about the relative merits of jellied eels and shrimps for supper and then went over the road to look at the stones. Really so little is known about this particular pile of stones. Nowadays it is completely disassociated with the Druids. These great stones stand out so strangely here on the Plain. From a mile back one can see them. Just lately it is said an old road underneath the present fields was discovered from the air, showing the way the stones were brought—one being dropped in the river on the way. The Irish guide even brought a hammer and got me a chip as a souvenir. Full of real Irish blarney which was cut short by the arrival of a car load of tourists. They needed the conveniences. The 'Ladies' away across the field stands out as clearly as Stonehenge itself. A long path leading to it, straight for about 50 yards then forking into two, running parallel a few yards between, one marked 'Ladies' the other 'Gentlemen'. They both met again at the little house! I left and back by the long road, the two guides waving vigorously. Stonehenge growing smaller and smaller. Another thing seen that I'd dreamed about.

The bus to Wilton and at the carpet factory, 'No', most definitely no, no one could see through. Large parties had come and been turned away. Only this morning boy scouts had come and been refused. I 'tse, tse—ed' sympathetically. But would I like to see a large carpet just completed for the Bank of England? Assuredly I would and I was led upstairs. I just stood and gazed. Woven to a special design incorporating the Prince of Wales' feathers, it measured 43 feet by 28 feet, and all made by hand. I trod on it cautiously and apologetically and sank into its soft springy depth. 'Would you like to see where it was made?' So in the end I saw it all, the huge looms, the girls seated in front with the different coloured wools making carpets which wear a lifetime. Did they get to New Zealand? Then a pained reply 'No, not these ones, only the machine-made ones!' I thanked him and said that I quite understood that people were not shown round the factory. With this perfect understanding we parted.

19 May 1939

Up at daybreak with a lot to do. A shivering bus to Dorchester and then on to Tolpuddle. Nearby there are Puddletown, Afpuddle, Turner's Puddle and Bryant's Puddle; so close together that surely so many puddles would form a lake! It is at Tolpuddle that the first trade union was formed. It is from here that the six men concerned in its forming were transported to Tasmania. Their descendants still live in Tolpuddle for after serving a short time in Tasmania they were all brought home again! There is a memorial arch erected to one of the men, James Hammett. On the village green is the tree under which they held their first meeting. The little village school bell was tinkling and a small girl who hitched up her little white pants as she ran, scampered past. Decided that the world with all its faults was better for the little girl with the white bloomers than for James Hammett, which proves conclusively that we have progressed! Offered a lift to Exeter and asked did I mind if they speeded. I didn't. We flew to Exeter, we went so fast that the tail end of The George in Little Mudbury seemed to merge into the beginning of The Dog and Pheasant at Great Puddleton. The rain poured down, the wig-wags on the windscreen worked overtime. We chased through Honiton and so Dorset melted into Devonshire.

Booked in at the G.F.S. because it was the first place I saw. Exeter is such a conservative place and rightly so for it is old. But the markets! All the fresh dewiness of England is here. Great basins of Devon cream and pigs' trotters all cold, clean and jellied. Hogs pudding and the home-made sweets man with huge humbugs. Lettuce as crisp as when it was picked, and warm brown eggs alongside golden butter. Found that I have a market instinct. Cathedrals vanish from my mind and I long for a basket to fill. Traffic very dense in the narrow High Street and the people provincially conservative. Exclusive little shops and their prices denote a monied district.

20 May 1939

A finer day but still cold. Heavens preserve me from ever being an elderly lady such as one meets at G.F.S.[4]'s. Either continually depressed or purposefully cheerful. Out first thing to find a bus excursion to Dartmoor Prison. Find out to my intense disappointment that we only look at it from a distance. All the way from Mary Tavy Dartmoor is visible. At Princetown we see it properly.

See it with a shudder, the Moor is bleak and cold. It is drizzling with a fine relentless wetting rain. In the distance the tors look formidable, like jailers. A warden lounges negligently at the entrance, too negligently, somehow I had expected to see six at least with fixed bayonets. Then I remembered, he was merely keeping people out! No doubt he found it easy enough. Great blocks of buildings round about and quarries where prisoners work under supervision. And so back to Exeter through Widecombe and the lovely Dart Valley. There are treasures in Exeter Cathedral from the moment one enters the Close, there is an all-pervading atmosphere of sweetness and sanctity, of a mellow peacefulness. Inside everything shrouded because of the alterations. Bishops tucked up for the night and Crusaders ghostly in shrouds. There is a Bishop's Throne 59 feet high and put together without a single nail. Stood for a long while looking down the nave—it is strange to think that so little time ago I knew nothing of all this. It reminds one of the Continental cathedrals. Then train to Torquay. Torquay is bright at night, it has boulevards, trippers and beaches but all these coastal pleasure resorts have a similarity.

22 May 1939

Good British bacon and egg and then to Plymouth Hoe. A big air display on. Bombers swoop down filling the air with a great droning sound. Crowds sit on the stone wall and strain their necks upwards. Plymouth is very beautiful where she is beautiful and very dirty where she is dirty. Ragged little urchins as one would expect from the slums of Glasgow. Small, pale, thin boys with tousled heads and beggar-like appealing eyes—surely not embryo Devon men! Talk to a young couple—they're driving a delightful little old wreck of a baby car—not much money but having a lot of fun. Make me a sporting offer to take me with them through to Penzance for a very moderate sum—no get there, no pay. We stopped at Polperro to eat Cornish Pasty. He who has never eaten Cornish pasty has never had a meal! It was a huge pasty and contained a whole dinner, peas, potatoes, meat, carrots and rich gravy. At Polperro men sat about mending nets on the rocks. It seemed as if the houses were built right into the sea. To live in one would be to hear the waves lap against the walls as if in a boat. But they are people of the sea—they crowd together as if frightened of the land. Washing was hung out on poles through the windows.

It is a strange land this Cornwall, sometimes bleak, sometimes luscious. Fishing boats are tied up alongside little wharves and nets hung up to dry. The people talked together. But what did they say? They were 'furriners' alright. And then Penzance, the little car tootling along in fine style. Staying with Mrs Rogers, a friend of Mrs Thompson, and that night to go walking on the Prom, meeting the Thompsons' friends and relations. To have pointed out the swimming baths, the gardens and the gas works! Everyone walks on the Prom and eat chips. Light until 10 and did we go to bed when we got back? No! We sat down to a supper of pickles and cheese saffron cake, heavy cake and Cornish cream at 11 o' clock. A lovely warm fire—bed at 2—a great day.

23 May 1939

Why is it that English eggs have always such rich yellow yolks? Bus in the dewy morning to St Ives to mutter to myself all through the narrow streets 'When I was going to St Ives I met a man with seven wives etc'. The houses here are of grey stone with women in aprons at the doors. Here artists come to live at Harry's Court and paint Land's End. Here in olden days the smugglers gathered and here today the Salvation Army holds full sway! Bang goes the drum, clash go the cymbals, 'Come on sing up. Let her go!' There are notices to show where the water comes up to in a storm. And to prove that storms do come is the Wreck. St Ives' people are proud of their wreck. Out then to Land's End, past delightful little Cornish villages. Past queer little Cornish crosses in stone and rhododendrons, a mass of pink blossom. In the little villages people leaned against the grey stone walls, men smoking their pipes and women nursing their babies, those dark almost alien men and women. When they spoke one could not tell what they said—their's [sic] was a language jealously guarded. They take a delight in the fact that you cannot understand them. Land's End, and I clamber with the bus driver to the very tip, or as near the very tip as I dare go. The ground covered with pink and white anemones and heather. Far in the distance, like some enchanted land, are the Scilly Isles. The steady chug of the lobster boats is heard fighting against the cruel sea. They are pulling in now, they have seen a thin white cloud approaching. We had been in the 'Films, teas, postcards' shop for no more than ten minutes when it came. The wind and the rain beating mercilessly on the end of England as though it would beat it all away. But those rocks have stood for a long time. Round the coast through St. Just, that old deserted town where tin mines once flourished and 750 men once worked—now only 120. Nothing more dreary than a deserted town. Back to Penzance to gather stones on the beach. It is said there are semi-precious stones in them.

To Mousehole but St. Michael's Mount unfortunately not open to the public as the family 'at home'. And then hurried out of Penzance. A friend of Mr. T.'s, a traveller, is 'travelling' to Barnstaple and if I can be ready immediately he'll take me. The first stop is Bodmin. While the Traveller displayed his wares (wares sounds much more important than ladies' stockings!) I wandered amongst the bluebells in the woods; a cuckoo mocked from the trees. Again at Wadebridge. Ate a Cornish pasty and sat on a seat with two ladies. Who should one be but the cousin of Miss Elizabeth Loe of the British Drama League. Back to her house to see through a real dream place. We went on to Tintagel—not to sell stockings, for who in that rugged headland would hold a stock of anything so flimsy? There were stockings on the line of one of the little grey slate-covered houses but they were stout knitted ones. What strange old ruins are here. It is so easy to picture King Arthur and his followers riding to battle in the cause of lovely ladies in distress. It was very late when we got to Bideford. The Traveller took me to Miss Mules and then disappeared amidst my sincere thanks. Miss Mules showed me to my room—a quaint Victorian room with a huge bed and under the wooden washstand the 'conveniences' stood. On the hearth shells, souvenirs and a defunct tortoise (or was he alive and sleeping!). Followed Miss Mules to show me the bathroom and then crept up the stairs again. Groped round a long time to find the switch. Rang a bell by mistake and held my breath but no one heard. Finally tripped over my haversack and located some matches in the pocket. There was light and discovered the reason for no switch. It was gas! Turned it on full and it blob-blobbed, scaring me out of my wits. Pulled down the blind which was secured by a cord wound round a hook at the side. It had no spring, it fell with a resounding smack on my head. Into the big bed and pulled the canopy curtains. They swung together in a cloud of dust. Perhaps they hadn't been drawn for centuries. Horrified I drew them back again and lay still listening, but for all my noise the house still slept. And before long so did I.

24 May 1939

Awoke to find old Queen Vic staring at me in a disapproving manner from the opposite wall. Couldn't find anything I'd done wrong to warrant a look like that. Bacon and egg, toast and marmalade for the beginning of another day. I've just realised the Derby is tomorrow. Somehow I must be in London by tomorrow. But that's tomorrow. Today it's Bideford where Charles Kingsley dreamt his Westward Ho! Out to Appledore where Devon people say 'Goodnight' with an upward lilt and the very babes eat fish and chips at all hours. A woman with a fat friendly face and smiling eyes offered me a chip and we walked to the sea-wall. I shared chips with her baby. Yes her husband fished, they all fished here. Her baby would fish when he grew up. It was like that. Our feet resounded on the little cobbled narrow street as we walked back past the old inn. Out to Clovelly. It is quaint but everyone knows it. A party of tourists—I don't wish to criticise I'm just a tourist myself—but I thank the Lord I am not as they are. As I climbed up that steep street I wanted to belong to these places, to live here and to know them. (No doubt to be bored in time by their narrowness and parochialism, but one must realise all to be complete).

The little donkeys and their carts, and those with little saddles on their backs with baskets on either side, blinked at me lazily, glad that I preferred to walk.

Bus to Barnstaple and, cursing the Derby, fell on the train in the nick of time assisted by two porters who threw in my haversack, camera and bluebells after me. Managed to meet quite calmly the surprised, and slightly pained, look of the individual in the corner with the grey striped trousers and the pince-nez, put on my hat and settled down. Arrived at a scandalous hour and slept at Mrs Davies' on the floor.

25 May 1939

On to a train at 9.50 and out to Tattenham to plunge into the Derby. Ran straight into Ruth, the youth hosteller from St. Ives, so we joined forces and pushed through the crowd. A gorgeous day—cloudless. It seemed almost a miracle. 'Daisy—daisy' yelled the merry-go-round. 'Tell yer fortune dearie, you've a long life'. We went into the grand-daughter of Gypsy Lee. Got a pretty good fortune because I hadn't anything smaller than 2/-. Ruth's 1/6d only brought her a mere journey and a present. A few steps further and a notice outside a little cream caravan announced that the original Gypsy Lee would oblige clients. Anyone who could prove she wasn't Gypsy Lee would get £200. The sun grew hotter and hotter. At last England had summer and me with two blouses and a jumper on. 'Come this way—only famous striptease act in London'. I stood and gazed when the view changed suddenly to a big white placard 'Flee from the Wrath to Come' it warned and we fled! I remembered the warnings about my purse and clung tighter. 'Excuse me lidy but yer dropped this', a cheerful little 'arry in his muffler and cap smiled at me quizzically and returned a glove. 'Yer may as well 'ave it, it ain't no use to no-one else yer know'. 'Jellied eels!' I yelled excitedly above the racket, and off we raced. There they were traditionally smothered with vinegar, pepper and salt, and as much bread as one wished. Say what you like, jellied eels are a meal for the gods, and if the gods refuse them it's their loss. We stood under the big umbrella and ate them out of a little basin.

We took our stand by the rails—gazed at the more fortunate ones on top of the buses and decided we were better off. ''Ave a peanut, dear', so we 'ad a peanut. We also 'ad an orange, a piece of chocolate and a huge chunk of coconut. The stout lady that provided the supplies really didn't look as though she'd ever get up again so to stretch our legs we fetched her tea. 'Four to one, Blue Peter. We're betting on the Derby. 'Bet with Samuel in safety and with security'. But Blue Peter had no interest for me. I staked on Mauna Kea and with a fatalistic sinking, pressed against the rails, not from choice but because, being the fortunate possessor of a vantage point, I had the weight of those behind. It's nearly time now. With our united efforts the stout lady rises. An aeroplane advertising cigarettes drones through the air 'A timely tip, Blue Peter'. The crowd pressed still forward. 'Flee from the Wrath to Come' joined by 'Hell is ever Present' fought their way for a better view dropping their boards as they ran. They're coming—they're rounding the corners, a thunder of hooves and Mauna Kea somewhere in the rabble. A bit of real Derby mud in my eye and I saw them to the finish—Blue Peter, Fox Cub and Heliopolis'. So much for Mauna Kea. The men on an old-fashioned wagonette nearby lowered their glasses and took off their lavender gloves. They drank solemnly from a bottle of Hock but whether to recover from the shock of loss or to celebrate a win, I don't know. The ladies climbed down as gracefully as possible, which wasn't very graceful, and stopped the first Lyon's man to buy ice cream. The bookies rubbed off the derby for another year and shouted 'Ladies and gentlemen we're betting on the Caterham Stakes'. We struggled over the course, past the jellied eels, caught a bus to Epsom and then into London. Stayed at Warwick House.

26 May 1939

Out to town to see a rehearsal of the Irish Guards for Trooping the Colour. The green leafiness of St. James Park is ahead; it is strange to find it here so close to the hub of London. To the North of the Parade is the Admiralty. Somehow it is not the great quadrangular pile that thrills me, it is the knowledge of the life that pulsates within. The wireless aerials above are in touch with all British warships even in far distant seas. Straight through the Park on its western side is Buckingham Palace! It is just like the other palaces I have seen. Perhaps I am childish but I would have loved it to be like those gorgeous Eastern palaces. But there are sentries outside in two funny little boxes. They are like little toy soldiers; suddenly to my amazement, they pop out, goose step a few yards each way and return to the little boxes. This happens at regular intervals—just like little figures wound up. I gazed at the impassive face of the sentry and suddenly the absurdity of the whole thing got the better of me. I broke into a huge grin and fled before I disgraced myself further by laughing at the age old tradition of the Great British Nation. Out onto Whitehall at the Cenotaph. It is a lovely simple monument and a fitting one somehow now I am in England and of the English again. This simple monument to so great a sacrifice is far more suitable than the great Victor Emmanuel monument in Rome to one man. It is our way and it is well.

Out to the Caledonian Market to see it at its best. I love markets. Couldn't drag Auntie Mollie[5] away from the old silver stalls. She has a teapot complex as I have for produce. People loaded up with vegetables for the weekend and I longed to be loaded up too. Lost Auntie but found her amongst the teapots. Crooned over cameos that I didn't really like but they were so cheap! Bought a coral ring. It satisfied my desire to buy without damage to my purse and subsequent regret. Poked about amid old medals, signet rings and lodge regalia. A huge daub of green and yellow mystery marked 'Constable'—enough to make the poor man turn over in his grave. Six o' clock and they all pack up. Wrap up their thousand and one articles in newspaper and cart them away. That was Friday. Saturday is the Jewish Holy Day and then they spring up again on Petticoat Lane on Sunday morning. There is nothing lovely about markets after six. The vegetable stalls leave their mess behind, small boys shy rotten apples at each other. The last of the little donkey carts trail away and Auntie and I do likewise, Auntie holding her nose. A decayed orange whizzes past our cheek—a stray from small boys. A barefooted youngster trails us pushing a bunch of onions under our noses, 'Only a penny, lady', but the ladies hurry on.

At night to see 'Me and My Gal' at the Victoria with Stanley Lupino. Believe it's been running for two years! A real London comedy and appreciated by the Londoners or rather the Cockneys. Which raises an interesting point. How can people see the humour of themselves? If they know they're funny why don't they change? Came to the conclusion they're proud of being as they are. On the other hand we appreciate jokes about the 'Raw Colonials' but in our own hearts don't really think we're like that one bit. Walked home through Pimlico humming the 'Lambeth Walk' all the way.

28 May 1939

To Petticoat Lane on a Sunday morning. Set off first for St. Paul's but Petticoat Lane won. A cheerful rabble here. At first boxes and boxes of stockings and Sam the Stocking King slaps his knee—'2/6d ladies, and I'll tell you what I'll do. I'll add another—five pairs for half a crown. Even suppose they are a fraud, could you go wrong with buying five pairs at 2/6d? But they're not frauds. I'm Sam, I am. Sam the Stocking King—been 25 years on the one stand. Thank you lady—and another—and another. Now I'll tell you what I'll do...' I pass on. Chocolates next. Not one man but two, keeping up a running patter, poking chocolate into a bag. 'Thank you, lady—taking it home for the kids—no kids? You've been lucky haven't you?' '21 pieces for 6/6d'—the original Moe clattered a tea set together in a bowl. 'All English China. Others 'll sell you Japanese but not Moe. Moe never took you down'. Into the jellied eels again but resisted temptation. The tea urn doing a roaring trade, everything clean enough. The men's underclothes fascinated me, that is the seller. 'They're cheap I'm telling you. I'm not asking you to believe. I'm letting you see. As sure as my right arm's part of my body I'm telling you, as one white man to another, they're cheap...' 'Oh they're cheap right enough but Bert don't like pajamas'. 'A 'andbag, Lidy, real skin as it might be yer own'... but propelled from behind by three blind men singing 'Rock of Ages' I was swept past. Reached the carrots and cheese and marketed to my intense satisfaction.

Trailed wearily to Aldgate Underground. Was the change to the British Museum too great? I went in hearing an echo of 'I'm Sam, I am. I'll tell you what I'll do..' But the mood soon left me. We have been brought up knowing of the big Reading Room which contains more than 4,000,000 books. Here is the historic Magna Carta and quite near a mortgage on which appears the signature of Shakespeare. The first edition of Robinson Crusoe is here too and the diary of Captain Scott with its last words faintly pencilled. Saw the Elgin Marbles. A wild rumour going round that they had been spoilt through some new-fangled cleaning but the lustre and delicate shading is just as I have always imagined them to be. Lost in the collection of Indian metalwork when the bell went. Wandered out feeling vaguely uncertain—I must come back. To the service at Westminster Abbey and stood by the Unknown Warrior's Grave, where a lovely wreath was placed, and prayed that there would be no more war—even as I pray I know it is coming. Strolled along the Embankment and down a narrow street is Scotland Yard. Now I can always imagine where detectives return with important news. Where telephone lines pulsate with information that will catch and hang a man for murder done in the wilds of Tibet! I gazed with awe—may as well admit it, I love detective stories—lurid ones! Big Ben booms—I realise I'm tired.

29 May 1939

Didn't sleep very well—think I'm overdoing it a bit. But whether I'm tired or not there's the Horse Parade in Regent's Park. Bitterly cold in the mornings in London even on sunny days. Now I know why Londoners who have money start the day in the afternoon. I shouldn't ever appear till two. But the horses! Great beautiful beasts all decorated, combed and shining. Leave Auntie Mollie to go to Hampstead Heath. Where else should one go indeed on Whit Monday? Never so surprised as at the size of it. A big crowd but they're scattered over the Heath and the whole great green 'lung' of London, a beautiful park. Through the Fairground first where the fun would be at night. As at the Derby I only saw one Pearlie, but noticed a peculiar type of London woman, pale, thin and wearing a long frock or coat—very flat-chested as a rule and nearly always married with a young baby—a lusty youngster who takes all her strength. Walked round the Heath past Leg-of-Mutton Pond. Little model boats sailing round, the trees alive with birds. It all seems so big and open. Hawthorn trees make patches of white and the beeches are in flower. Could only find one convenience and had to wait in a queue. Then it was an old-fashioned one—in a place like Hampstead Heath! Walked up past Jack Straw's Castle and the Old Bull and Bush. Round here were the homes of Keats, Galsworthy and Romney.

Next to Kenwood and then walked down Highgate Hill to the Underground, past lovely homes behind grey stone walls. A beautiful part of London—the glimpse of St. Paul's and the City from Kenwood should not be missed. Past Dick Whittington's stone which says 'Sir Richard Whittington, thrice Lord Mayor of London'. So it was here he walked with his cat.

30 May 1939

Started with washing and shopping. The only yards in Chelsea are about two inches square and in London things want washing every day! Never have I been so grubby—absolutely black in fact. Then to Oxford Street to buy a hat. Soon located Peter Robinson's, Marshall and Snelgrove's and Selfridge's. A peculiar thing—Selfridge's has no name up anywhere, just a lot of flags flying. One is supposed to know! Dresses much cheaper than New Zealand, and furs! A good silver fox for £10 and a quite presentable, wearable one for £5. The guinea shops with little summer frocks—smartly made, all for £1.1s.0. Met Aussie and Mrs Cooke at Piccadilly Circus for morning coffee at the little Monseigneur café at ten and to the Newsreel Theatre till lunch time. Funny little theatres these, showing only newsreels but so handy to pop into with an hour to spare. Lunch at the Regent Palace Hotel, which in spite of its smart appearance is still owned by J. Lyon's & Co. An excellent meal and feeling at peace with the world, to Kew Gardens. It may be just past lilac time but it's rhododendron time. It is a truly lordly park with lovely avenues and sheltered walks. There are little temples hidden away and a slender Chinese pagoda. There is a beautiful Palm House with a wonderful collection of alpine plants, orchids and water lilies.

Home through Hammersmith—the bus conductor says stridently ''ammersmiff!'—to dress in one's best to dine at the Savoy. It was Aussie's idea, I couldn't help it. Dinner was a leisurely, stately thing with wonderful service. There were red roses as decoration in a bowl nearby. I admired them tremendously. The waiter bowed. 'Madame likes them—perhaps Madame would like some—if so..' What could Aussie do although he protests it was his idea to buy me some. So the waiter returns with three red rose buds at 2/6d each. After, a toss up where we should go, and the old Palladium comes up. Just what I needed a real laugh at an old-fashioned vaudeville show. Clever acrobatic acts and trapeze artists and another 'tourist' sketch, I can always appreciate those. Supper in Soho just for fun. Where I don't know, we just dived in. It was Italian and the coffee exquisite.

31 May 1939

Out by car to see the old inns of Buckinghamshire, explore Oxford and safely home. Aeroplanes drone overhead, huge bombers from the 'drome at Northolt. There are other 'holidayeers'—tandems pass mostly for two but one was even built for three. Through Beaconsfield and High Wycombe to Stokenchurch. Here there is a young girl driving her geese to the pond, she has a scarf round her head and her face is rich with youth and health. They are fat white geese that waddle indignantly. Drink at a little pub—a fascinating drink called Perry which is like cider but made of pears. And then Oxford. There are two distinct cities at Oxford living side by side intermingled, but as far apart as the poles. One is the tranquil dignified life of the University and the other the bustling vigorous life of the city. We were in the High! It was really that fact and not the Perry which made me utter little squeals of ecstatic delight. High is the street that leads through the Colleges right to the Magdalen. Spent a long time in New College. Sometimes there are places where one feels one belongs better than others. There is wisteria and a profusion of Canterbury Bells. The newness of New College dated to nearly six centuries ago! In Trinity on the noticeboard we read 'Gentlemen are reminded that 'Swarrie' parties to which more than fifteen persons are invited may not be held in the College in the College Colony or at Saville House unless special permission has been given by the Dean. Permission should be asked for before invitations are issued'. Socially an excellent piece of advice. There are things I've forgotten, things I might never remember, but everything has left its mark. It has registered a peace into which I can return at some far distant date.

Back via Henley and at Slough we get a 'ticket' for having a worn tyre but get out of it by buying a ticket for the Traffic Cops' dance. There are highwaymen in England yet. To Stoke Poges in the dusk, it is here that Gray wrote his Elegy and he is buried in the churchyard. There was a mighty droning in the sky. I looked up 'Isn't it marvellous' I remarked casually 'how they can fly in those big bombers in such perfect formation?' Mr. Ness' mighty laugh roared delightfully. There was only one bomber up! I had seen inside too many inns of old England alright! Home to a huge supper with bread in long French rolls and so to bed.

June 1939

London—Westminster Abbey, Madame Tussaud's, Limehouse, Hyde Park Corner. Staines, Somerdale, Bath, Glastonbury, Wells, Cheddar Gorge. London—Acton, Chelsea, Soho, Tate Gallery, Drury Lane, Bank of England, Pudding Lane, St Paul's Cathedral. Windsor, Chertsey, Greenwich, Aldershot. London—Embankment, St Martin's-in-the-Fields, Covent Garden, Billingsgate, Shepherd's Market, Bond Street, Big Ben, Houses of Parliament, Albert Hall, Kensington High Street, Oxford Street. Leicester, Rotherham, Rawmarsh, Greasbrough, Wentworth, Parkgate

1 June 1939

Straight to Westminster Abbey to prowl undisturbed. Somehow I like always to go back to origins however dim they may be. One's first impression is of overcrowded corners behind tombs, and monuments are dim. Many beautiful things are hidden altogether. It is in the South Transept that everybody lingers for it is Poets' Corner. Mostly they are only monuments, the actual bodies being buried elsewhere. Sometimes fame came too late. Chaucer is buried here ironically enough not because he was a poet but because at the time of his death he was Clerk of Works at Westminster. There are the graves of Browning, Tennyson and Rudyard Kipling. The ashes of Thomas Hardy are here but his heart is buried at Stinsford. Perhaps I am lacking in sentiment but I'd just as soon my heart went with the rest. The Chapel of King Henry VII is sheer beauty, the stone almost seems as if it would sway in a breeze. In one of the little chapels off the main one is buried Oliver Cromwell, his mother and sister, but it is said that their bodies were exhumed after the Restoration and, in view of the devastation of beauty for which he was responsible, I should hope so. The Chapel of Edward the Confessor is impressive because one enters it up steps. It is here against the stone screen that the Coronation Chair is placed. Underneath it is the Stone of Scone. It is attached to the chair by a sort of clamp. Maybe they are afraid the Scots will steal it back again! Roamed in the Cloisters for a while and found by accident the Chapter House! To think I might have missed that floor. It is of beautiful mosaics nearly rivalling the mosque in Cairo. In the Crypt below are ornaments of the Abbey. Was rushed out of here as it wasn't supposed to be open!

It was good to get in the open air again. Felt that I couldn't take in Westminster Cathedral so soon. Decided on Madame Tussaud's and made a terrible mistake. Knew all about the policeman and programme seller and smiled in a superior manner at a poor woman who spoke to a wax attendant. Paused in front of the Death of General Gordon and bumped against a Chelsea Pensioner in his red coat. The poor old soul was half leaning on the rails in a way the very old have. He didn't even move, and giving a hasty look round, I gave him a poke. Sure enough he was wax! I swallowed my apology and hoped no one had heard! One's first impression of Madame Tussaud's are peculiar. I nearly went away again because it was so crowded and then, looking again, found that the crowd were figures, only about six people wandered about. They certainly haven't flattered Mrs Simpson. Mussolini away for repairs or renovations. It seems undignified. I would have liked to renew acquaintance with the bombastic little figure in Piazza Vittorio Emanuele. A big case contained an effective tableau—'The Murder of The Princes in The Tower'. Their murderer stalks in the gloom. I thought of their tomb in the Abbey—it was so real. Suddenly a voice, almost in my ear said clearly 'What has been done can be done again!' I spun round and nearly knocked over a woman quietly dressed in black. She turned on me a pair of eyes narrowed in intensity. 'Don't you think so?' she added suddenly. I muttered a hesitant 'Yes' and moved on putting several people between us, and then was a victim of sudden remorse. What had that scared 'yes' done, would it fan the flame of a desire to murder her own children? Would she perhaps seek to enter the Royal Household and smother the Princesses? And in that frame of mind I entered the Chamber of Horrors. Charlie Peace is the hero here, his ugly face seems to dominate the place. Definitely disliked Death Masks but all the same would sleep here willingly for £10.

Dined with Aussie at the Waldorf—faultless service. On the spur of the moment took a car to Limehouse. Have often wondered where Limehouse was. It is just a street lying in between the Grand Union Canal and the river. Rather fascinated in the Canal because it runs right round North London, traverses the Midlands and eventually unites the Thames with the Mersey at Liverpool. How I would love to 'barge' round England. Aussie thinks I've barged into things too much as it is. Aussie didn't see anything queer in Chinatown but then he hasn't any imagination. One needs one's imagination or else all one sees are the slums.

There are Chinese, Eurasian and black children playing on the footpath, chalking, hopscotch and other things not quite so childish. Do they never go to bed? They have little old wise faces—but here and there, under the dirt, a cherubic face, and from the cherubic mouth comes a stream of language that causes Aussie to talk loudly and hurry me on. Women hang from upper windows and deliver open invitations. But it is no different from any other slum. Then a young Chinese man comes running rapidly down the path and disappears into a dark alley—a second later another follows, and does a knife flash from those wide blue cotton sleeves? Perhaps into the dark Thames that tells no tales, a body will be dropped... There is a blood-curdling squeal and I nearly jump out of my skin. 'Cats' murmured Aussie laconically—he would think of that. Only Charlie Brown's pub[6] is different and it is a showplace now. In the old days when Charlie was alive it had a personality. But there are treasures here. A piece of carved ivory with at each corner a pillar supporting the figure of a saint. There is a German pipe almost six feet long and underneath it an inscription 'If every man is as true to his country as he is to his wife— God help England'. A crocodile hangs from the ceiling and a carved incense burner six foot high is in the corner. In the old days when these treasures were brought one by one, it would have been a rare place—now a parcel of tourists come in and gabble an excited way round (note: must remember I'm a tourist and not be always decrying this very legitimate prey of anyone with anything at all to show or to sell). Got home and then couldn't sleep. The Chamber of Horrors and Limehouse were too much in one day.

4 June 1939

Sunday, and having been to Petticoat Lane where else would one go but to Hyde Park to listen to the Orators. Walked first around the Marble Arch— there was no necessity to do this, but I've wanted to walk around it ever since the song came out. Listened so long to the Orators that I nearly missed the train to Staines and Mrs Watford. Man with one tooth and two hairs nearly convinced me communism was the thing for the world, then I realised he was against communism! A prim, efficient woman, who looked all the world like an infant mistress, had something to say about the Foreign Policy. I asked a short stubby man with a short stubby pipe what it was she was after saying. He took out his pipe long enough to say 'Blest if I know Missy but I know what my missus'll be saying if I don't get home soon—standing 'ere listening to a lot of people talking about things they don't know nothing abaht and neither do I . . .' But they all had a message, and who is to say they were wrong? The things we have taken to be right, have they always been so? They plead lost causes, causes which do not want to be pleaded. Who thanks the woman who puts up a plea for the prostitutes—neither the people who listen to her nor the prostitutes themselves—and yet it is so all great reforms began. At the Corner a dark, intense man arguing on some dark obscure Eastern religion, threw up his hands in despair. He called the English pigs of the lowest understanding, whose dull wits reflected not one ray of light. He positively leapt in the air in the ecstasy of this conviction and came down again off his box! The 'English

Pigs' picked him up, dusted him down and set him up again on his pedestal to curse them again. Queer folk the English.

A lovely run out to Staines to be met by Mr. Watford with a white rose in his button-hole. Met young David and Joey the tortoise. Joey is dropped on the path but apparently survives. Young David but three and already a budding golfer. Sat outside most of the evening. Does it never get dark in England? Coming home on the train and met Fred (who I had spoken to at McIlroy's) coming home from golf. Called in at a little café behind the station for a huge roast beef sandwich and coffee and a chat—a real Cockney crowd—men with scarves and caps and girls with excessively tight dresses. Home and bed and not before time!

5 June 1939

Up well before the lark, grabbed a nightdress and a toothbrush and took advantage of a lift to Bath offered by friends of Mrs Cooke. England in the early morning in the early summer is entirely delightful. There are little pink dog-roses in the hedges now and hikers along the road. I envy them but I will hike again. We slip through little villages scarcely awake, school bells tinkle and women are gathered together to shop at the funny little stores that sell absolutely everything. We did the 107 miles to Bath in record time. Took me first to Somerdale, Cadbury's factory, and then left with arrangements to pick me up tomorrow night. 'Only ones' not usually taken round at Cadbury's factory but fortunately got fitted in with a party. Such beautiful surroundings, pleasant green meadows and grazing cattle. All England knows 'Carnation Milk from Contented Cows' and although it's not a Cadbury's product I'm sure their cows are contented too. A large harmonious building and everything spotlessly clean. A neat little 'guidess' took us round—pointed out the airiness of the place.   First the laboratory with masses of test tubes which analyse ingredients etc. Then the warehouse where piles and piles of cocoa beans are stored. Tasted a bean and shuddered—it is hopelessly bitter. There are big ovens for roasting the beans and then big rollers for squashing the remains into a brown paste called 'mass'. At this point some of it is made into chocolate and the other into cocoa. Began to feel that peculiar longing that always comes over me when chocolate is near. Unfortunately one can buy a quarter lb. at Woolworth's for 2d and temptation is great. Great masses of chocolate is swished round and round, the sight of it en masse might slightly sicken one with more a delicate make-up but I just gazed at it avidly. It is swished long and thoroughly to bring out richness and add smoothness. Milk is added—strange how mere milk becomes something extremely delectable when described as 'full cream milk from British dairy farms'. Moulds travel along at a regulated speed and as they pass the machine, an ingenious dropper, drops just so much in, no more. The moulds pass over a contraption which shakes them thoroughly to spread the chocolate evenly and then deposits it into coolers to harden. At this point we had a sample and my uncontrollable desire was abated for a bit. There are rows and rows of cream tablets with all sorts of centres. Bits of broken chocolate lying about everywhere and no one even eating them! Even the boxes are made here. Girls as deft as artists make box after box with machines that clip together cardboard which has been cut into neat squares. Other girls tie ribbon bows with the accuracy of machines and others pack quickly and calmly box after box. What do their boys bring them when they come to call on a Saturday night?

We returned then to follow the cocoa making. I've never really believed that fresh eggs were put into some chocolate in spite of the advertisements. But there were girls cracking eggs with great golden yolks for the malted chocolate and no egg pulp is used! Eggs come in every day—presumably from contented hens! More samples, even a complete tin full to send to Mum, who pines for chocolate even as I do. In the grounds the gardens gay with tulips and great beds of flowers and the nearby streets all inhabited by employees of Fry's. Rather dear little houses all with gay gardens. And yet in spite of being 'happy in industry' and having beautiful lunch rooms on wide verandas, organised tennis clubs and sports organised by a benevolent firm, my whole Colonial being revolted against 'settlement life'!

By bus then to Bath. It is hard to switch from chocolate to Roman baths. Why has no one told me Bath is one of the loveliest places in England— perhaps they did and I never listened. It had wide, well-planned streets and an old Abbey. Near here is a funny little shop where the original Sally Lunns were made. Later a public-spirited man at the Pump Room asked 'Have you had a Sally Lunn?' I assured him I had but he shook his head sadly 'Sally Lunns aren't what they used to be, Missy. You're about ten, maybe twenty years too late for Sally Lunns'. At the King's Spring he announced impressively 'It's hot itself, it doesn't have to be heated', I murmured in amazement. 'I'll bet you haven't seen its like in the world'. I just couldn't tell him about Rotorua where the geysers flung their boiling, hissing water 20 feet in the air and more. Back to the boarding house to make the acquaintance of Hilda, Emily and their friend Dot. Suggested we should take a car and 'do' Glastonbury and the Mendips tomorrow. New Zealand licence won't do in England but pray no one will notice. Saw about hiring a car—quite reasonable for the four of us.

6 June 1939

Drove off proudly in a Morris 10 with girls, cameras and lunch with paraphernalia dumped in together. It is warmer now and sun every day! There are such dear little villages, the description of each would be the same—an old bridge, a little stream, a castle and a church. The Morris was apparently short-winded on the hills and protested with weird noises which we just ignored. There is a lovely Market Cross at Glastonbury as well as the Abbey and the almhouses. No one in Glastonbury thinks much of King Arthur. They go to hog sales and talk of fishing, but they are tolerant towards tourists. We climbed the Tor and found it worth our while. It was a case of 'Moments like these' when we pulled out of Glastonbury. We were stopped by a Cop. My whole guilty demeanour shrieked 'Licence' at him but he only wanted to know if we'd drop a note in a letter box further along to tell his missus he wouldn't be off till three! It is only about six miles to Wells. I have thought so many cathedrals are fine and then I saw Wells. It is not cramped as at Bath and it has a great West Front. As in Exeter there is indescribable charm about the Close—a picturesque group of buildings that surely could be found only in England. On then to Wookey Hole and Cheddar Gorge. The formations in the caves at Cheddar are good and a wonderful white colour.

There was no other traffic on the road. Just the little Morris and four girls. Somehow for the first time since being in England I felt a long way from anywhere—after all I wasn't so young as I used to be—age was creeping on— perhaps I should be thinking of more serious things. But it was getting late. We hurried back to Bath, I said goodbye and then hustled into Mr and Mrs C.'s car and back to London.

7 June 1939

Ten when I woke, barely in time for the very necessary preparation to look respectable, when Mr. Beckett's Rolls-Royce pulled up outside. To Acton by way of Earl's Court where ice hockey is played at the Empress Hall. Mr. B. quite different to what I expected—a Yorkshire man with a great sense of humour. Very proud, and justly so, of his Works to which great extensions have been made. All round his office a fascinating frieze showing the evolution of coach-building from the earliest days till now. Discussed the whirl-window and was able to give him the information asked for. To the Millet Arms nearby for lunch. It was beautifully served, turtle soup, a perfect steak and strawberries and cream, sherry, coffee and liqueurs. Mr.B. would like to move back to Yorkshire, but this London life draws him too much—the things like the Millet Arms and the theatres—and well just being in the centre of things. Shown round and find it a surprising little factory. So much done by hand, which accounts for the high class goods, and sometimes the high price. Thanked my lucky stars I knew more about B.L.W.s products than any other and had stared at their blue-prints until I knew them backwards.

What a huge car the Rolls is. The chauffeur seems half way to London before we start and all conversation must be carried on per medium of a speaking tube. Decide on return to investigate Chelsea. In the Chelsea Royal Hospital the old pensioners wander and sit puffing speculative and dreamy pipes. It must be the most human place in London. The old soldier who showed us round had seen many battles, his left sleeve was empty and his face scarred, but his carriage was still erect. He walked with us all through the courtyards greeting first one crony and then another. He explained carefully the tattered flags in the Great Hall. Later we visited the Chelsea Physic Garden and had a look at Cheyne Walk. Did a bit of very necessary washing and so to bed.

8 June 1939

And the Parade Ground is the scene of Trooping the Colour. Auntie managed to get me a ticket, miraculously. It was pageantry at its best. The guardsmen are trained with clock and drum. The officers take up their posts in slow time. It seems interminable but no one but me looks nervous lest they should fall or sneeze or break up their immobile tableau. (The old Guardsman next to me whispers that this slow march was instituted in old times to test sobriety—confound them!) The Band plays—it is stirring there in the Parade Ground, something I shall never feel again. I feel that I belong to the great British Empire. Never again will I smile at the sentry at Buckingham Palace. The whole square was filled with God Save The King and every man meant it. If they didn't before or after they did then. I watched one guardsman on the outskirts as if fascinated—surely he was swaying? I longed to do something— yes he was! And then he fell, quietly and neatly, and just as quietly and neatly he was removed. Then the four companies formed order again and marched round the square. As they passed the Duke of Gloucester, who took the place of the King, (for the knowledge of those who read this in years to come our King is just now in Canada) they dip the colour, officers salute with swords and troops are given 'eyes' right. The old Guardsman was leaning forward now, his hands making little involuntary movements, his lips forming voiceless commands. He said the Guardsmen were not what they used to be, never had been since the last war—the cream of the country went then. He is 65 with 28/- a week pension. Soon he will go to Chelsea, and he will not be sorry. He gets up stiffly—they are not bad these youngsters but the training is not severe enough now.

Lunch in a little English restaurant in Soho and in a suitable frame of mind for the Tate Gallery. A great number of Turner's here, did try hard to understand them. A huge big picture by someone whose name I have scribbled too much to read. It is the Resurrection. Figures rise from their graves behind the church, but they rise as they were in life, the bricklayer with his hod over his shoulder, one or two in shrouds trailing lugubriously behind. Somehow it fascinated me. What if it really were thus? Personally I'd rather stay where I was than rise again to type! ... Remembered it's one of Stanley Spencer[7]'s. Passed on to a Reynolds and then a Millais. Realised for the first time that Turner renders so beautiful the luminosity of nature—it is strange how I am determined to 'find' Turner, almost against my will. Hogarth at his best in 'Marriage a la Mode'. Can always chuckle over Hogarth after knowing Dickens.

At night to see Emile Williams in the 'Dancing Years'—a pretty thing, but it was Drury Lane that I loved. Watched the queues for the pit and the galleries. A woman in a long black skirt sang mournfully in a cracked voice and held out a hopeful hand, but no pennies passed. A juggler tossed the balls dexterously but he looked as if a good feed would have done him good. Someone threw a coin and he skipped in a few old-fashioned tap steps to retrieve it, smiling determinedly and brightly. Frankly I couldn't stand any more. They didn't entertain me, they horrified me, and anyone who can stand there and be even remotely 'entertained' by such poverty, be it real or assumed, should be thoroughly ashamed. They are quaint but they belong to the times of Dickens, when messengers ran errands for pitiful sums in inadequate clothes and children slaved as soon as their little fingers could hold a tool. If their poverty is real it should be seen to.

9 June 1939

Decided to wander round the City. Rather unwisely got there about nine, or perhaps wisely. It is at these times, when the workers pour to and from their work, that one realises the vastness of London. There is a sea of Trilby hats, pausing to a man at the Belisha Beacons, those islands marked by orange coloured globes without which one's life wouldn't be worth a tin of fish, and then surging across. For those who are in a hurry even in normal times it is better to use the subway. One dives underground, and it is strange to emerge in quite another place. Advised by the bus driver that to see this part of the city I had better alight at the Bank and, to my eternal shame and disgrace, I asked 'What bank?' When I got off I understood better. The whole district is dominated by this Old Lady of Threadneedle Street. Had a look at Billingsgate but realised the time to see the fish was early morning (note—all language was strictly conventional if broad Cockney). Chatted for a while to a little man who seemed to specialise in plaice and asked the way to Pudding Lane, where the Great Fire broke out. An entertaining man in a cap and scarf who had a philosophy about life. 'It's funny' he said 'there are people like me who 'ave to get up and don't want to, and people like you who don't 'ave to and want to.

Now I cusses every time I blooming well come down the apples and pears in the mornin' and unlocks the Rory O'More. But it doesn't matter how I feels mind yer my old missus she always gets her cup of Mike McGhee'. A woman in her apron and her big marketing basket strolled up inquisitively. 'Look here Ma, this young lady's a tourist. She's walking all abaht 'ere looking at things'. The woman had a friendly face. 'We're alright round 'ere dearie. What was he saying to yer about Mike McGhee?' Had to confess I guessed what 'Mike McGhee' was but why 'apples and pears' and 'Rory O'More?' 'That's the way we talk, dearie', she said, and the little man eased his scarf and took off his cap. 'Aven't you never 'eard of Cockney rhyming slang?' 'Get Missus here to tell yer' he said, 'I've gotta go but she'll put you wise'. So I asked 'Missus' in to a cup of tea. 'I don't mind if I do dearie' she said. A sudden thought struck me. Would she like a glass of beer. 'Yes I would' she confessed, 'but I won't. A young lady like you doesn't go into pubs like there are round 'ere. I'd just love a cup of tea'. So over a cup of tea she initiated me into the mysteries of Cockney rhyming slang. Why and wherefore she knew not but she used it richly and broadly. "Nah then" she says "If I say 'my old pot and pan came home from the pub, threw his titfer on the Romeo Law, took off his daisy roots and went off to bo-peep' yer'd know what I meant wouldn't yer?" Went on my way to the Monument full of new and intriguing thought. Climbed the 311 steps for a superb view from the top. On to St. Paul's Cathedral and then home to Anderson Street to positively avoid everyone to type my diary and to wash.

11 June 1939

After yesterday's visit to the Tower of London a trip on a big Green Line coach, which is luxury itself—and I had the temerity to call it a bus! It was a soft summer's day such as one reads about as happening in England but of which I have as yet had little experience. What a great heavy pile of grey stone is Windsor Castle, blobs of it as firm and immovable as the British Empire. There is something satisfying about a complete castle. I have seen so many ruins. And it is infinitely more satisfying than a Palace. Unfortunately the State Apartments were closed so we took ourselves to the Doll's House. Then into Windsor Great Park which extends for five miles and it seemed we walked every bit of it.

Back as far as Chertsey by boat. There are fine houses sloping down to the river and pretty bungalows. And everywhere boats. It is the house-boats I liked—like floating caravans. Feel tonight as if I have walked all over England—this London life is making me soft.

12 June 1939

And today we continued on the river, a different Thames but, shall I confess it, a vastly interesting one. The Thames of the famous 'smells', barges and commerce. Here I can look at and admire Gas Works and the OXO works unmixed with cathedrals. I can revel in commercialism. Coal barges pass— or I should say we pass coal barges drifting—chug-chugging along so slowly one wonders if they ever get anywhere. Women are on board, weather-beaten women, and even a baby in a pram. One has a traditional 'Hearts and Flowers' painted over the cabin door. The left bank is most interesting, there is St. Paul's to be seen and the Monument. Then it gets more sinister—the Wapping old stairs and the execution dock, where they say Captain Kidd was hanged, and Limehouse! It is strange how I should get more satisfaction from Limehouse viewed from the water than from its streets. The old mouldy buildings rotted into the water. I could see it at night with only the river lights and the eerie hoot of boats—a body being dropped with a dull splash into the water…! The guide stressed the fact that on the right was the house that had once been occupied by Anna Lee,[8] actress. I'll record it because some day I'll find out who Anna Lee was.

The smell of coffee drifted to us from a dirty old brown hulk of a boat. There was a barge full of white stuff which, the guide assured us, was fibre for making silk stockings. They all brought something these dirty boats, something to feed, clothe or beautify England, and to dirty it too. Looking in a mirror at an astonished face with a big smut on its nose, and wondered why I'd come in a light frock. There was a smoky haze over all—gradually it widened until it would seem that instead of a river it were a great sea. Boats, always boats— cargo boats… 'Dirty British coaster with a salt-caked smoke stack'…. While I was still dreaming we were in Greenwich. Greenwich is of great interest to colonials for under the old constitutional theory all the colonies were reckoned as part of the Royal Manor of Greenwich. It also had an eel and pie house! To Greenwich Park and actually stood on the Greenwich Meridian! The O on the maps that I have gazed at so many times. It was an important moment. Back to Fleet Street, to a fascinating place with its sanded floor and old benches, to partake of the famous beef steak pudding. A huge pudding that tasted all the richer for being so huge. It had mushrooms in it to.

14 June 1939

At night to see the Aldershot Tattoo, mercifully fine and the air quite soft and not cold. It started at twenty to ten. Brigade drill, Pipe Bands playing, a mock battle showing the co-operation between land and air forces and then brilliant tableaux—Queen Elizabeth visiting Tilbury in 1588 and the Grand Finale, the Legend of Drake's Drum. There is strength and confident power in the Rule Britannia that follows—but something stuck in my mind 'England Expects'. . . I pray that our men will not be called for that duty for a long time.

Back to town in a peculiarly excited frame of mind. Far too excited to go home just to sleep. It's two when we get back to London. Made up my mind to finish the night in my own way. Walked first across Waterloo Bridge and along the Embankment. Peered in all the likely spots but not a sign did I see of 'down-and-outs' who, according to tradition, sleep there. Enquired of a policeman, who looked at me from a definitely superior height and said 'They all sleep down in the crypt of St. Martin's-in-the-Fields now, missy, we keep them well-lighted'. Let it be clearly understood that I didn't want to violate the privacy of the down and outs, after all why should they get rooted out and looked at, but after all I wouldn't be in London again and ever afterwards, when I read of this peculiar fraternity 'underneath the arches', I wanted to be able to see them. So I walked up Lancaster Place—do a certain type of people never go to bed?—and into the Strand to Lyon's. Then onto St. Martin's. Sure enough they were there in the crypt 'underneath the arches' as surely as if they were under the bridge. The crypt was mercifully heated but no pretence of furniture or bedding, nothing but a pillow, perhaps rubber or something like it. Just, as the warden put it, a place to go. The warden, a kindly man, who let me peep in and as I sat down rather wearily offered to keep an eye on me if I wanted to sleep for a while. I did. Even on the benches it was easy to drop off. There are no ghosts in the crypt, just a loud and prolonged snore and a curse that effectively silenced it.

A cat's nap and then to Covent Garden—an entirely delightful place at 3.30 to 4 in the morning. There were boxes of tiny apricot rosebuds and masses of sweet peas. Their scent mingled with the more pungent but cloyingly sweet scent of the strawberries. There were bunches of fat asparagus and luscious peaches. There were baskets piled upon baskets and men carrying them on their heads with uncanny precision. I drifted out of Covent Garden with a box of strawberries, a bunch of asparagus and a bunch of red roses, wondering vaguely how I got them and decided to see Billingsgate. Billingsgate in the morning is as much a revelation as Covent Garden. Huge plaice and Dover sole, which would grace many an aristocratic breakfast table, lay piled in big barrels and baskets. A little man hurried by with baskets swaying dangerously on his head, but they always righted themselves. I hurried on—perhaps I was rather in the way but the guide book did say that Billingsgate should be seen in the early morning. Suddenly I slipped and heard the only bit of Billingsgate talk since I arrived. I said it myself. I picked myself up and a little Cockney with a bright red muffler picked up my roses and strawberries and retrieved the object I had slipped on—a huge Dover sole. 'Gor blimey' he said 'yer slipped'. I agreed. He patted me into place with friendly little clucks. 'You're looking abaht a bit aren't yer? They often do that, these folks what come to see London. If yer lived 'ere you wouldn't, yer'd just go to work and come home and have your dinner and your pint and go to bed, same as we do. Nah then 'ow abaht tyking this 'ere 'ome for yer supper? I'll wrap it up in a bit of pyper'. It was tomorrow when I got wearily on the Chelsea bus, so much tomorrow that people were going to work. Home to Anderson Street and cooked the Dover sole for us all.

16 June 1939

Ran out at ten to see Changing of the Guard. I stood like Christopher Robin and took it all in. I wanted others to see it as well as myself, those friends of mine in New Zealand who are saving up so hard. It is such a long way to come. And yet when one really comes to think of it, it's silly! It's childishly spectacular, but after all it's 1939 we're in. Looked at frocks in the guinea shops. One must tread warily here. If one hovers but for a moment outside the door out comes a pretty little Jewish girl and you are in trying on before you know where you are. The frocks have delightful swing skirts and nipped-in waists, which is an effective trick of displaying. But clothing is cheap in London compared to New Zealand. Found, hidden away off Curzon Street, Shepherd's Market. It is like a quaint little town all on its own in the heart of London, full of antique shops—queer little overcrowded places where there never seems to be any attendant. You just browse and the time passes. The little streets and lanes are narrow. There are old, old book shops selling older prints. The time did pass. It was late when I fled down Bond St. There are fascinating antique and art shops in Bond St. and jewellers, and also motor car dealers!

In the evening to the Palace with Auntie Mollie to see Cicely Courtneidge and Jack Hulbert rollicking their way through 'Under Your Hat'. Felt just in the mood for the Jack Hulbert type of comedy—songs with a good swing—or at least Cicely swings them so. Later to the Ritz with Aussie and Mrs.C. The restaurant overlooks Green Park—surely this is not London? The Ritz is sumptuous, but no, that is the wrong word. It is grand and the service just perfect.

17 June 1939

Took myself full of sober and intent interest to the Houses of Parliament. Dwelt first on Big Ben that I might never forget him. The hours alone are struck on the famous Big Ben Bell, the quarters are struck on four smaller bells. Then The House of Lords and down the famous lobby, where is the statue of Rt. Hon. Joseph Chamberlain, and into the House of Commons. Where is the pageantry and glory of England? It is so small and gloomy. Surely some better politics could be conceived in a place as wide, sunny and open as the Palace of Geneva? There are two lobbies, the 'aye' lobby and the 'no' into which members go to be counted as they return to their seats. Now I shall always know just where they do all the business of the country—where Britain muddles through. Walked too in that dark sombre place that is Westminster Hall, here Charles 1 was tried and condemned and here Cromwell's head was impaled for nearly 25 years on one of the gables until it was blown down in a heavy storm. Took myself on impulse to Piccadilly to look at the little statue of Eros. Realised with rather a nasty shock that I won't be seeing him much longer. It is strange how one gets dug in in London.

Took young Bernard Ness tonight to Hiawatha at the Albert Hall. What is wrong with the Victoria and Albert Memorial and the Albert Hall? Why should they be permanently objects of derisive sniffs amongst all Englishmen at home and abroad? They are no worse than any other monument and hall of their day. I flatly refuse to uphold popular prejudice. Hiawatha is not played upon the stage but on the floor of the great hall. It is like a fairy tale told when one is very young and Bernard sat with his arms on the rail taking it all in. Not a muscle did he move unless it was his lips as he followed the songs. Somehow it was so much more effective than a stage. One was looking at something real—the hills, the waterfalls, the wigwams... One of the best things I have ever seen.

19 June 1939

Met Auntie Mollie and her aunt and to Derry and Toms in Kensington High Street. On top of this 13 storey building is a garden paradise. The lovely sun pavilion has massive white columns and shining glass. The tea was exquisite and delicious little cakes to toy with. Then out into the old English garden with rockeries and bridges over a little stream. Fruit trees are heavily laden with pears and apples. They are all <u>real</u> and full-sized—not miniatures in tubs. In the Japanese garden there are hundreds of little bridges and pagodas and in the Tudor garden are roses and masses of stocks. It was a delight. Wandered down the High Street and suddenly realised we'd not been to a fortune teller in London. Now these ladies in London are legion. There seems to be no law against them whatsoever. They don't hide away in back streets so that one must spin a yarn about going somewhere else every time one visits them, take a round-about route and jump at the sight of every policeman. They advertise openly and their fees are high. Saw a moderate one and arranged to go in first. If she was good then I'd blow my nose well and heartedly and Aunt Mollie could spend her three shillings. If she wasn't 'any good' I was not to blow my nose when I came out. The fortune-teller spun me a tale about two husbands, an equal number of children and a marvellous future if I'd come for a crystal reading tomorrow to the tune of £1.1.0. Said I was quite satisfied with the two husbands and coming out kept my handkerchief firmly in my pocket.

Have learned since coming to London the absolutely correct wines to serve with different dishes. It seems so important that I tremble to think how little I know. Afraid there is something definitely lacking in my finer senses. Personally I could enjoy a claret with my cheese instead of port. I could positively relish a rich madeira with my poultry. But still to others it may be anathema, so I'll record here the absolutely correct English wine conventions—Soup and old dry sherry or light dry wines, Fish and Rhine wine or white Burgundy, Game and vintage Champagne or red wine, Entrée and light Bordeaux or Claret....

20 June 1939

A teeming day (what have I done to deserve this?) and walked down Oxford Street in search of a frock. Guinea frocks charming in the window but look like half a crown on me. Almost marooned without shelter when the storm came and had to dive into Lyons. Had six cups of tea I didn't want and after the last time in desperation took the Underground to the Strand and back until it stopped! The shops have no kindly verandas as they have in N.Z. Bought a navy frock with silly white flowers that looked like Janet Gaynor but see possibilities of turning it into Marlene Dietrich. Bought a navy bag too for the absurd price of five shillings and navy gloves for 3/11*d* which cheered me up a bit. Went into a little jeweller's in the Strand and the man there cheerfully told me I looked as if I were getting pneumonia, so fled home. Mrs Curzon, a dear, and unpicked the absurd white flowers. Packed and got into a—of a mess. Still teeming. To bed amidst the mess.

21 June 1939

Put on my cream coat in case it should be fine and then put on mac. and umbrella in case it should be wet (it was). Met C.T. and Mrs. C. for morning coffee at Swan and Edgars. Dear old London looked rather fine from the big windows, her chimney pots misty in the soft drizzle—oh so traditional. I have a fine appreciation of these things as viewed over morning coffee in a pleasant warm room full of pleasant leisured people. I'm losing my dash and losing it willingly. To meet Miss W. and the four of us to lunch at the new Indian place. Fascinating smell of curry pervading the street (please note—English ale and Indian curry is not too good a combination), came out with a face like a full moon. Saw Miss.W. back to work (where does she buy those long skirts? Mrs. C. and I come to the conclusion she wants to be individual—too big a price to pay in my opinion). Still teeming. Tossed for another look at the British Museum or the vaudeville at the Prince of Wales and the theatre won. To Aussie's for dinner and then home to bed. Looked wearily at the mess, made a bit more before turning in.

22 June 1939

And Rotherham! The greatest adventure of the trip, and am I nervous! Everything into cases by sheer miracle. Goodbyes to Mrs Davies and the Curzons—taxi to St. Pancras. Aussie already there and Mrs.C. too. Another goodbye—so many now since those of Auckland and Sydney. More roses and books—it's always goodbye and a promise of return. Of course I am coming back to London—for the hop picking in Kent in September. Finally away with the chimney pots and tall grey shapes of stacks in the murky distance. London weeps her sooty tears. Get off in Leicester and ring to meet Mr. Burton. Mr. Burton is not at home—half day in Leicester—so for a wander around. It is an interesting old place. Roamed round the tombstones at the church of St. Mary de Castro. The wind was Arctic. Frozen so in to tea and toast and then to get the train. Would they be there to meet me? Auntie Lizzie, Bessie. Perhaps they wouldn't even like me. The crooked spire of Chesterfield is whizzing past— not just a lean but a real twist. I must come up to expectations for Mother's sake—should I have got a new hat? Then Rotherham. I opened the door and there they were, right in front of the carriage door. "It's Bessie. Eh here's Gwennie. Welcome lass".

Little Auntie Lizzie looking so like mother I could have cried—Aunt Bella, Uncle John, Bessie, Ruth, Malcolm—and I am just one of them. London faded, France, Switzerland, Italy. Life went backwards to Auckland and little Mum. It was as if this was what I had come for. Everything else seemed just something on the way. A real North Country welcome. Talking till far into the morning. Round to Auntie Bella's for a minute to talk there and to kiss Uncle Dick in his 'pit muck' and have a good laugh at my black face. Welcome—welcome everywhere. To bed at last to be tucked in by Auntie Lizzie, to want my little Mum to be there beside me more than anything else in the world—to sleep for the first time since I left Auckland AT HOME.

P.S. The excitement so great the dog had a fit!

23 June 1939

Unpacked and found the chaperone. Hadn't seen him for months. He wouldn't have liked London anyway, and wouldn't have seen anything anyway with his eyes closed. Put him on my dressing table for a fresh start. A run round to 'the girls', Annie and Ruth, to see their homes—little modern homes and beautifully kept or at least the furniture's modern. All the houses are the same plain square upstairs, brick affairs right, or nearly so, on the street. At night with cousin Walter to the dogs! Watched the parade seriously and picked my dog on form. Looked up his pedigree, compared his past performances, picked an honest looking bookie and lost! Only one win and that was not my fault. Teddy Atkins took my three shillings to put on No. 5 and put it on No. 3 by mistake. No. 3 won! They are gorgeous animals these whippets. Lean and lithe slipping like a streak out of their little kennels immediately the door is pulled up. The hare 'click-clicks' ahead—it seems it is just a flash of bodies as they passed and it is all over. They are so eager to get away—you can hear them whine in their boxes, waiting for release. All the posts are tied round with straw. Popped into the Crown before coming home. It's the usual thing here, and women go too. Supper when we got home—a huge one of fish and chips and home-made bread and butter. Everyone popping in to see how got on.

24 June 1939

I'm so bewildered. I don't for the life of me know who's who and who belongs to which family. Have definitely established cousins Jack and George at Auntie Bella's. James, who they sometimes call James Willy, belongs to Uncle John, and today was his wedding. Went round to Uncle John's to meet all the family and then in the cars to the church at Greasbrough (this is the little village where Mother used to go when she was a girl, to sing at their Sunday School). Walked up the path arm in arm with Uncle John to be greeted by the minister with "So this is the bride! This way my dear, this way".

There'd be a lot of 'settling down' to do if I married an Englishman. The way the women run round after their men here is wonderful. A pretty wedding with the bride (Bertha Sanderson) in white and the bridesmaids in gold. Then to have the photographs taken, the cousin from New Zealand is included unfortunately. A wonderful wedding breakfast in a tiny house with a huge fire, then the bride and bridegroom off to Blackpool. Must remember Uncle John's family: Auntie Polly, Uncle John, Irene (married to Walter James with a little girl called Barbara), Don, Maurice, little John aged 8 and of course the smiling James Willy, just married. It was such a jolly little English kitchen—red linoleum polished to a mirror finish, hand-made rag mats and a bright stove with an open fire and an oven at the side high up—never seen any arrangement quite like it before, but it seems quite usual here. The dog in her box in the corner. There's a parlour too with an aspidistra growing in solitary state. From everyone hearty handshakes (they do this much, very much more, than we do) and a "Pleased to meet you lass". I'm getting quite proud of being "You're Susannah's girl from New Zealand". Poor little Mum, she might have always been Susie in New Zealand, maybe Sue, but 40 years ago when she left England she was definitely Susannah. Home to Uncle John's to tea and then back to 42, Park St. One just runs through the 'snicket' to Auntie Bella's. A 'snicket' is a sort of little alleyway from one street to another. Saw the boys' fishing prizes. Did try to appreciate a roach one and a half pounds in weight when I realised that they very very seldom get anything bigger. Had a vision of a few of our hapuka[9] and old Grandfather Schnapper;[10] the boys would go mad with excitement if they had those to deal with. Supper—fish and chips and stout! They have them every night! And so to bed. Aunties, uncles, cousins, friends—and I forgot a visit to the Star where they laugh, sing and bet on everything under the sun, even on the number on a cigarette card every time anyone opens a new packet. It's still FUN ALL THE WAY.

25 June 1939

Sunday and to the cemetery with Auntie Bella to see Charlie's grave, Grandma's and Grandpa's and Auntie Alice's. They visit cemeteries such a lot here, even the children are familiar with them. They run about the grave and describe Charlie's illness and death to the last degree. Perhaps it's just as well in this country where sudden deaths seem usual among the young. And I don't wonder! Frozen stiff in the cemetery. Back to watch 'our' Betty and 'our' Jim do their ballroom dancing. In Yorkshire everyone belonging to the immediate family is 'our'—found that this is really necessary apart from being the custom as there are so many of the same name in different branches of the family.

Dear Uncle Dick, he wouldn't change Auntie Bella for any woman on earth. Auntie Bella is so wholesome looking, with pretty fluffy hair and sleeves rolled up over white arms. Had a Yorkshire pudding with our dinner, eaten first with loads of gravy before the meat and vegetable course, and then a walk through Rosehill Park and Farmer Shaw's fields. All the passers-by nod and say good afternoon. Everyone in their Sunday best with girls and boys standing around in little groups. This it would seem is how they 'get together' here. A lovely idea in the Park, boards tucked away amongst the flowers with little appropriate verses. Looked for and found my little 'Garden is a lovesome thing'.

Malcolm dried the dishes while I washed. Such a thing has never been known before. One doesn't dry dishes here by the way, one 'weshes pots'. Poor little Dusky still having a fit or two but getting less. Vet says it was excitement. We'll never forget the day I arrived and the dog had a fit when he saw me. At night to the Club, Irene there too and Annie and Herbert. The clink of glasses—the chatter of voices—a shriek of laughter. A singer with a strident voice and an ample bosom and next a little soul of the old school in tails standing in approved attitude sings Ave Maria. There is dead silence. Little Auntie Lizzie gazes far away into the distance, I put my hand on hers and we think of Mum. Uncle Albert in the back room, his bald head shining, one hand on his knee and the other on his glass. He has a toast " If tha does owt for nowt allus do it for thissen'. Cousin Walter on one side, young, intense and carrying all the workers' troubles. He comes often to whisper them in my ear. My glass gets filled up before it is empty. It's North Country hospitality. If they like you they do, but if they don't—

Fish and chips a golden brown for supper and a wee talk with little Auntie before bed.

26 June 1939

Morning and nine o'clock. Frantically typed letters and diary and then to golf with cousin Malcolm. Met George who rolls the greens. How the pit-lads tease him for being a sissy. "'Tis said he uses powder". His only crime I think is that he was once a waiter in a 'big house'. Went for a long walk to see the house shaped like a bottle. Beautiful country—soft green fields hiding the sweat and grime of the hollowed interior. Pitmen in their caps and mufflers, their 'snap'[11] on a plate and handkerchief walking along the paths through the fields, even as Grandpa Turner must have walked. Work is life, it dominates everything. "Our Jack is on nights." "Our Malcolm's on afternoons". Always someone coming and going. Always meals at odd hours. The 'pit muck' off, the lads are as clean as a new pin. Children warmly clad, everyone seems to manage marvellously on very little. Things very cheap and wages very low! Took Auntie Lizzie and Ruth to the pictures at Rawmarsh, and home to a family supper. Found that 'days' at the mine is from about six to two, 'afternoons' two till ten and 'nights' ten till six.

27 June 1939

Sun shining and thought the heat wave had come but still as cold as ever. Uncle Albert off to work in the allotment (under protest). The houses have only a scrappy little bit of damp back garden between brick walls, so everyone hires a piece of ground nearby in a section cut up for that purpose and grows vegetables or flowers. Typed letter in t'morning and afternoon out with Uncle John's Donald to walk to Wentworth. It is actually Wentworth that Mother has always told me about where the Earl Fitzwilliam lives when he is here, which isn't often. A lovely walk through Haugh fields, the hedges pink with wild English roses, the larks in the full glory of their song as they rose higher and higher to come down to perch on the nose of the scarecrow in Farmer Shaw's field. Down the bridle track to Greasbrough dam, through barley waving in the wind, and far ahead the shadowy shapes of church spires, chimneys and shafts, all beautiful in the kindly distance, the smoke curtain softening it all, making a mystery of stark reality. There are frogs in the dam. As we gazed at the water coming over the little weir it seemed that we rose and floated on the water. Nothing to do but gaze—a good companion for such a walk is Donald. He should have been a country boy instead of working at the Forge. He has big capable country hands that animals understand.

Onto the next dam to find tiny water hens fussing in and out of the trees. A water lily pond with delicate pink and blue flowers and a rhododendron bush still flowering. A fallen log in the stream and a Jenny Wren's nest in the tree. A little nest with a tiny hole at the top. There is a thin streak of sunlight—just a promise and then gone, but the English countryside shows its true softness under dull skies. Not for it the brilliant blues to scorch that vivid green—soft green leaves trailing in soft still water. Through the Lodge gates where the little pony stood harnessed to a little 'konaki'[12] full of newly cut grass (they don't know what a konaki is here), and then the wide spaces of Wentworth Park. In amongst the huge trees shy deer dart suddenly. A nibble of grass, a rustle in the trees, a quick look up and they are gone—the grass full of shy wild things.

It is breeding time for the pheasants and there are little boxes everywhere containing the broody hens. A keeper comes on his bicycle with a bag of food and the chicks come to his call. It is said that six years after he used to feed them a keeper came again and his call brought them to feed from his hand. When they are grown they are liberated and the Earl Fitzwilliam comes up from London to shoot them!

To the third dam and the swans. We lean on the little bridge and I am thankful for such a companion as Donald. In the centre of the Park is the big house with its 365 windows. The Earl Fitzwilliam is not in residence and it stands looking so lonely. It seems that there should be people on those broad steps and walking over the smooth stretch of green sward. At the side the stables. A little girl comes riding by on a tricycle from one of the Lodges and three miners walk past from work but they never look, it is an everyday walk for them. It seems strange that one can walk through these private parks. With all our freedom in the Colonies a man's estate is his own be it small or large and there are more 'Trespassers Will Be Prosecuted' signs. Certainly we are not allowed to walk up to the doors of the houses. Above the trees rise the shapes of Hoober Stand and the Mausoleum. The dam winds its lovely way round the Park and beyond the trees meet the sky. It is all so English.

Back then to the road past the Needle's Eye—a quaint structure built with a hole through the centre. It is said that a man once boasted he could drive a coach and horses through a needle's eye and built that accordingly. To Auntie Polly's for tea, and so tired. Played darts with the boys and then home. Supper and we talked till so late.

28 June 1939

Morning and wrote letters again. I'm all behind as usual. Visiting with Bessie in the afternoon. We consult the little black address book, knock at the front door, no one comes, it hasn't been used for years. We go round to the back and are made welcome. But first we find a door at the side and knock diligently only to find it's the 'coil oil' (coal hole). See first poor Mrs Downing who shakes all the time since the death of her husband. Then Mrs Broughton. Such a dear old soul—thought I'd discovered another dialect but Bessie says she's tongue-tied. A huge Dalmatian dog occupies the only space in the little kitchen. When it turns its wagging tail either goes in the fire, tickles my nose or sweeps the cake off the table. Some Xmas cake cut for our benefit and as Bessie says "We had us tea". Ran for a few minutes up to her son's place just up the road. Mr and Mrs Clarke next and their son with the cups for bicycle riding. He and his father load canal boats. We've talked so much we stagger home only to be whisked out by Cousins George and Jack.

Walked down Rawmarsh Hill into Parkgate and into Netherfield Lane. This is actually where little Mum lived—the same house No 57 looking, so they say, exactly the same as when as a little girl she ran over the footworn step to school. People stare at me rather curiously and I realise that they don't know Mother used to live there, and hurry on. The school is just a few doors away. Somehow I had imagined it so much bigger. I can see her in a pinafore going to Schonhut's Pork Shop, I can see Granddad setting off across the fields to Silverwood Mine. There too is the remains of the bluebell wood where Auntie Bella and Uncle Dick got lost when they were little boy and girl. There are fields here side by side with iron and steel works. The great wheels of the mines slowly turn, winding men up to the light of day again, the buckets passing in an endless chain. Past Roundwood Mine in the rain, past the cricket field, to scuttle into Cousin Arthur's (Uncle Jim's eldest son). His wife Winnie is a dear, placid woman. Then to the Crown to meet Auntie Bella. A good laugh in the pretty, modern little saloon and then home to 'us fish and chips' and so to bed.

29 June 1939

Typed letters in the morning. Feel very righteous. Auntie made Parkin, instead of doing it by instinct as she usually does used a recipe and it 'flopped'. There's a fascination about 'flopped' Parkin. We all dived into the tin just as it was and ate bits—treacle sticky bits—until it was gone.

Visited again and talked until we knew our little piece off by heart. Routine—stood outside looked in little black book, knocked at front door , went round to the back and started off "I'm Gwynne Peacock from New Zealand. Mrs Broughton…" But we never got any further. "Eh lass come in…" and in we went. Mrs Carr first, invalid poor soul and very weak. Next Mrs Fletcher definitely not weak, full of pep and go. Had a real rest here, just had to sit and listen. She's on every council and committee ever heard of and loves to know everyone's family history. She was waiting for the vicar to call so we took an early departure. Invitation to her daughter's wedding on 12th August. Daughter speaks French, learned it at school. (That's one thing we shall never forget).

Then Mrs Beaumont and a lovely tea. Strawberries and cream, good Yorkshire bread and tea cake. Everyone makes her own bread here. The men just wouldn't eat the bought. A wee budgie here who hops on one's head surprisingly and makes a convenience of one's nose rather embarrassingly. Finally he perches on the cake, puts his head on one side and says absurdly "Kiss Jimmy". The son's wife is Danish and her Mother, visiting for a holiday, not able to speak a word of English. Did I sit and look so remote while on the Continent? I think of my gestures, grimaces and weird efforts to talk Italian and feel that I didn't uphold British dignity sufficiently. Took to the son immediately and then find he has a 'reputation'—a skeleton in the cupboard, or rather a baby to another girl somewhere in Parkgate. It is all so very strange to me here, what must it seem like to the Danish girl? Called then on Mrs Horne in an absolutely airless room with Bessie going paler and paler and myself panting for breath. Would like to have stayed longer but voice is giving out rapidly. Mrs Humphries out (thankfully). Home to supper and to bed.

Here is the recipe for Parkin as the Yorkshire folk make it. There is no other so good—½ lb flour, ½ lb oatmeal, ½ lb treacle, ¼ lb sugar, 1 egg, pinch salt, ¼ lb of butter or dripping, 1 teaspoon of ground ginger, 2 teaspoons of bicarbonate of soda, 1 gill of milk.
Rub the butter into the flour then add the rest of the dry ingredients, the treacle, the milk and beaten egg. Mix well together put into a cool oven in a flat tin and when cool cut into squares.

30 June 1939

My two dears,

I've found that I simply can't keep up with the diary and letters and I'm perpetually as we say 'all behind' so I am going to revert to my old way of combining diary and letters while I am travelling about. Life flows on easily at Aunt Lizzie's. The dear little soul never goes out except to the little shops nearby. Annie and Ruth pop in frequently and there are always meals on the go. "Our Malcolm is on nights" or Walter (Bessie's husband) is "on afternoons". It sounds so funny in the mornings when Walter goes to work. Bessie goes to the door with him and instead of saying "Goodbye" as we do, she says "Good morning". I never know if he is coming or going!

Uncle Albert toddles down to do a bit in the allotment and then to the Club (Workingmen's Club—called the Titanic—more usually 'the 'tanic'). He has a fat face and red cheeks and looks the picture of health but he isn't really, he has the miner's complaint through working in stone dust—it has got on his lungs and he can't hurry at all. We always tease him saying the allotment is only an excuse "to go t' pub".

There are two dear dogs, Bess (whom we call Bessie Horner) and Bessie's Dusky. They are mother and daughter and have really adopted me into the family. I came downstairs at five in the morning and they didn't even bark. They are Bedlingtons—Bess a silver grey just like a curly lamb. They're both put to bed at night on the sofas with a cushion at their head and a cover over them!

To Rotherham with Bessie today—we walked through Parkgate. Raining of course, the promised heat wave not here yet. My transparent umbrella seemed to provoke great amusement amongst the men coming off day shift. Saw where Bessie used to work at Woolworths and heard the story of how, when they were 'courting' Bessie had to work till ten o'clock carrying piles of towels upstairs while Walter waited outside. At length he got so furious he marched in, took the pile of towels from her, kicked them downstairs and marched her off! They're so young the pair of them and have had such bad luck. Walter just started work again after being in hospital. He has the same trouble as Kathleen with his eyes, the retina pulling away from the rest of the eye. They've stitched it back and he's much better. Into the Regal café to give Bessie a Devonshire tea. Devonshire cream in Yorkshire as bad as Yorkshire pudding in Devon and I made the girl take it back and give it another beatup. Bought Auntie a bottle of stout and Uncle some mushrooms for his breakfast.

Cousin Walter in at night with his wife Olga and the two kiddies, Bobby and Betty. Everyone 'bookies' here, in fact it makes me wonder who is left to bet! Today I heard two men lay down a serious and proper bet on whether the town hall or the post office clock struck first! Walter presumably off work for a rest cure but is doing so well 'bookieing' that I don't think he wants to go back.

July 1939

1 July 1939

How the days slide by. Diary, letters and a 'wee bit of crack'. No work being done while I'm here but washing must be done and mighty and intricate are the preparations. Big wooden tubs brought up from the cellar, a day's job in itself. Things are rubbed and scrubbed on the rubbing board, dried as much outside as possible, finished off in the living kitchen by a huge fire and all ironed and aired the same day. We think it's a performance but then we've never had to wash pit clothes.

In the afternoon to Blackpool with Auntie Polly, Uncle John, Eric Watson, Mr and Mrs Watson, their daughter and her husband in two cars. One can begin the day in the afternoon in England for it won't be dark till 10.30 p.m. A beautiful run out through Greasbrough through leafy lanes to Thorpe Hesley and into more open countryside by Smithy Wood mine. Soft green country and big homes with grey stone walls and larkspur and delphinium gardens. Past Chapeltown with a poor little fair spoilt by the rain. Bedraggled fairies flapping home—a clown, his long pantaloons billowing ludicrously below an old raincoat—a Red Indian with his feathers drooping like a defeated cock. "It's a demonstration or summat" says Mrs Watson, and as we whizz past the Red Indian takes himself into the local pub. Through Wortley Woods with soft fern undergrowth and patchwork quilt country, the paddocks, or fields as they're always called here, separated by little stone walls. At Wortley an old fashioned gateway to a church—a big stone in the middle and a gate with chains on both sides. A glorious view on the left—a V of hills in rolling country soft in the light of a brave sun struggling through the fine mist. We pass the

'Black Bull', the 'Stag's Head' and the 'Three Owls' and gardens like pictures. Then the widespread suburbs of Huddersfield, the soft green of the country turning into black houses and poor dirty trees, women in clogs outside the public houses, their arms folded on bosom over their shawls and chimneys, always chimneys.

Up Salterhebble Hill to Halifax and past a strange monument—'tis said two brothers quarrelled, one built a high wall so that the other couldn't look into the garden and the other built the tower so that he could see over the wall. Towards Todmorden with its narrow streets and past the 'Dusty Miller' and the 'Fox and Goose'. Had one at the latter. Past the 'Bobbins and Shuttles' too only to find it's merely an advertisement for a maker of those commodities so necessary to the cotton spinning trade, for we are nearly in Lancashire now. There is moorland country just here, rocky land rising on the left abruptly. A war memorial in the far distance stark against the sky. A miracle—the sun! and the clean clear smell of cut grass. Then Bacup and the trees of the Forest of Rossendale so green and fresh. Through Burnley to Read with its grey houses and chimney pots symmetrically in fours, Mellor and the new aerodrome, then Preston starting well with the Cemetery Hotel! (We thought we would but decided not to). Preston has long streets controlled by wireless, the police broadcasting to the next little box any excess of speed. The Tower comes in sight. It's Blackpool! Sign boards flash by one after the other, 'Christ died for you' runs into 'Slow down excavations ahead'. Right across the road is a red and green archway with 'Welcome' written across. Then the red brick houses start all along the wide road—apartments—apartments.

There is always a bustle at Blackpool. We collected the honeymoon couple at one of the red brick houses and then to dinner. Poor Mr Watson, he ordered bacon and eggs and was still waiting for his second egg at the end of the meal. A bitterly cold wind but at least fine. There were donkeys on the sands, quite philosophical beasts in spite of popular tradition, trotting along obediently enough. A coffee stall in the shape of a huge teapot, miles of sands and promenades. We all piled into a pleasure car for a run to the Fun Fair. These little open electric cars run down the promenades. There is always a lot of laughing and joking on board and waving to those walking along the paths. The young boys and girls in 'gob' hats giggling and pushing each other. The smallest action on anyone's part becomes a commotion. The chief attraction at the Fun Fair is the Big Dipper. It is the biggest Dipper I have ever seen. Saw all the 'up' parts and none of the 'downs'. Held tight to Eric and shut my eyes and hoped for the best. Everyone munched Blackpool Rock—a long stick of candy with Blackpool printed right through it in red so that however much or however little one bit off, there was always the word Blackpool left. Fat girls in excessively tight slacks that looked as if they might give way under the strain any minute. Then girls in baggy ones. Mother, Father and the children singing up and down the street. The 'pie and peas' vie with the 'fish and chips'. The Laughing Cow—a big clockwork figure, whose shoulders shake and whose head rolls in agonies of mirth, sets us all off too.

The honeymoon couple wander arm in arm oblivious to all the din. It would seem that every girl in Yorkshire and Lancashire goes to Blackpool for their honeymoon. The trick photograph man gathers his group together in a smart professional manner. He sits them on chairs behind a red cardboard motor car and lo, when we get back home, there they are waving wildly from out of a nifty little roadster with Johnny at the wheel and Betty sitting self-consciously beside him. He can take one on board a ship complete with lifebelt or behind the bar in the very act of swallowing a bottle of Bass or lifting down a bottle of the best Scotch from the shelf. There is nothing he cannot produce in the way of props.

We're going strong with the rest. Surely there is nothing in the world quite like Blackpool. All year they save for one week at Blackpool, booking at the same red brick house year after year. They buy their own food taking it back to their accommodation to be cooked. The tradition is that if you have any of your holiday money left at the end of the week you just 'bust it oop'. One must come home broke. But it's half past ten with a puncture to mend and then to get back to Rotherham. Back under the red and green arch with its message on the reverse side reading 'You are always welcome'. Back over the moors, eerie under a full moon, everything strangely still, to sleep a little and then to wake for a while to the purr of the engine. We stagger out stiffly at an unknown inn at about 2 a.m. On again in the low coldness of the early morning to Greasbrough. Supper then at James Willy's future home and back to Park Street at four o'clock. Uncle Albert waiting with a cup of tea and a piece of pie. Somehow to bed. "Eh lads it were a reight grand do".

2 July 1939

After all that up early to go fishing with Auntie Bella, Uncle Dick and George. Still raining but we have hopes. Out through Swinton and Mexborough where poppies grow on the roadside. Poor, proud and pretty Doncaster with its famous racecourse. Uncle and George lay a bet as to whether Ted Atkin's car is green or blue. Past the big Bemberg factory (where those artificial silk stockings with no stretch or shape are made) and Auckland Road! Dunscroft with its queer water tower like a pork-pie on legs and then Stainforth and Hatfield pit that is 900 yards deep. There must be men working below us all along here, toiling, black and covered in perspiration. The blackberries are in flower and around a gypsy caravan the tinkers mend their chains. Black slaves under the ground, swearing, grubbing in the very bowels of the earth and above the gypsies lounging on the soft green grass laughing, joking, their gold ear-rings tinkling and the old women smoking their pipes.

We get out at the back of the Crowle Inn where the fishermen gather. Mighty and intricate are the preparations. Big fishing baskets full of gear and betting slips. White maggots, pink maggots and fat yellow maggots, a secret preparation for ground bait. A solemn drawing for places, a donning of wellington boots and oilskins and a fixing of umbrellas. And there they sit all along the sides of the canal, a few yards apart, fishing with concentrated effort. They stare at the water as if the very intensity of their gaze would attract a fish. One wonders how they can stare so long and then one realises they are asleep! A catch! A fish leaps into the air, struggles and is mastered. The spoil is placed pridefully in the basket. It is fully 2 lbs in weight.

Auntie Bella, Betty and I walk round the tow path to watch and having gone about a mile squelch back in the teeming rain. A barge with a huge still sail floats slowly up the canal, on it a baby's pram, or as they say here a carriage, stands at the end covered with a tarpaulin and a dripping man poles stolidly in the rain. We pause by one of the hunched figures on the bank and speak. It turns and scowls. These fishermen have no truck with women. He was just getting a bite and now it is gone; they are always just getting a bite. The long grass entwines itself damply round our legs. So we sit in the car and drink tea until the men arise from their coma in the long grass and gather at the Hotel to check up. Our two men were out of the running so I lost my 'bob'. Home again past Conisbrough Castle ruins to sit and thaw out over a huge fire. Listen to fish tales and eat fish and chips from the shop.

Cousin Albert comes round (Uncle Jim's second son), a genius on the piano but a queer stick. "I'm always alone" he announces pathetically to a roomful of people and the carpet. Find out there is no real reason for his mournfulness, just constitutional. At one stage in his life he was ill and he has clung to it. Feel sorry for him but with that hardness for self-pity loudly voiced, long to tell him to 'Snap out of it'. Find out later that he's met a girl he was interested in twenty five years ago. She's been engaged twice but evidently they were destined for one another. Do wish he'd hurry up and marry her. He seems to be the family 'problem'. Auntie Lizzie nearly had a fit when he turned up with me, he hadn't been there for nine years!

3 July 1939

Up and packing frantically for Aunt Eliza's in Bradford. Bacon and eggs, for who in England ever tackled a journey without bacon and eggs; letter writing and farewells in rapid succession. Bessie to the 'Rawmish' station with me at a spanking pace and then to wait a quarter of an hour for the train. She's a dear is Bessie, never too busy to help. Saw Mr B. on the bus—said 'Good morning' but all I could think of was the infant he gave to the Parkgate girl and then disappeared to Denmark. People really shouldn't tell me these things.

More rain and the man with the flowing moustache in the carriage has catarrh. Realise we change at Leeds just in time. A woman with a huge Dalmatian dog got in. She had paid his fare and can have a seat (providing no one really objects). I certainly don't. He sits next to me stock still and dignified. Every now and then he turns his head to regard me with an unwinking stare and a look of condescension as much as to say 'What are you doing here?' A cross-eyed man kindly points out places of interest but I never find them because I don't know which way he's looking. Then Bradford and little Aunt Eliza away at the other end of the platform. My arm in hers we talk all the way to Lidget Green. She is like Little Mum in looks but not so strongly built as Auntie Lizzie but so like her in ways. A big house of three storeys and a cellar. To Hilda's for tea with her two kiddies, Shirley and Celia, pretty fair children. Later Clem arrived to fill the house. Who would have a cousin, even by marriage, who is a Sergeant of Police, six feet four inches tall and Hilda smaller than I am? Home to meet Uncle Herbert—a dear quiet soul who invents all sorts of gadgets for domestic use and for use in the mill, but somehow someone always grabs them from him before he takes the patent out. As soon as he comes home he disappears into his old shed across the road. Talk until far into the night about Little Mum. Saw with horror the Peacock family photographs which we'd given a decent burial years ago. We say 'Good morning', too late for goodnight and so to bed in a huge room.

4 July 1939

A cup of tea and up at 9.30. Laughed at a Yorkshire expression in connection with Americans and their food. 'Tis said "they eat what they can and can what they can't". The Yorkshire folk, indeed all English people, don't use long vowels like we do. They talk about dance to rhyme with manse not with the 'A' sounded as 'Ah'. Hear Auntie Eliza's side of all the family history. She knows so well all the stories that Mother has told me. Does Mother remember going to the shop for ————? for the dogs, forgetting the name and asking for 'hypocrite'? For lunch a luscious bilberry pie made for my benefit. The bilberries are little tiny black berries that one picks on the moors. With a tongue dyed a deep purple we proceed to Harry's for tea.

Harry, the driver of a trolley-bus, is a thin-featured nervous man but I like him. His wife Edith with a milk and roses complexion. Somehow I always feel like a gypsy in spite of my fair hair amongst these English girls. The little girl Audrey, a dark hollow-eyed pixie, and young Harry, as Aunt Eliza puts it, 'a little devil'. Home again to Uncle Herbert. Dear Uncle Herbert, he comes in regularly from his shed at half past nine, puts on his coat, turns to Auntie and says "Dusta want 'owt?" A wee bottle of stout maybe or some fish and chips for supper. He brings them but never for himself. He always sits down to a big plateful of bread and butter and a cup of tea.

5 July 1939

Jim and Elizabeth to visit today after we'd done the shopping at the little local shop. Elizabeth is Edith's sister and just such another English fair skin and dark hair. The two wee boys are such quaint little souls, solemn-faced and dark-eyed. They've nothing to say except a gruff "no" and a howl when things go wrong. They stand stolidly in front of their grandmother and say with a scowl "I don't like you".

English children do have such expensive toys. Hilda's two girls have prams costing £3 each. Harry's and Jim's boys bikes and trikes to burn. Went next door to see Mr and Mrs Wilcox, Edith's Mother and Father—real Yorkshire. Mr Wilcox is a dear and a humourist too when I can understand what he says. Was a bit 'flummoxed' when he said to Edith "Yo know whoam ah mean. They'm used to live down by way".

The women do all the papering of the houses here, nearly every year a room must be done and the curtains are washed every fortnight. All pay into numerous Clubs—a shilling a week for the Doctor—a shilling for clothes. One called the 'Diddle-um Club' just caused a lot of consternation. It was true to its name. The woman who ran it spent the money!

Perhaps I'm recording a lot of queer things, but they are so strange to me. I've never met anything like them before. It is forty years since Mother left home and there are many ways and customs she has forgotten. The folk here just laugh when I write them down—to them they are everyday things, generations old.

6 July 1939

Into town with Hilda, but first to Mrs Smith's to have our fortunes told. Hilda leaves with the threat of a baby boy that won't live. For myself a husband to be picked up in England—a dark man with a dog. She sees a white boat with red on it—a short journey soon. But first, indeed very soon, I'm going Harrogate way where I'll see lots of dogs. There's no doubt about it, dogs predominate but it was good fun. We left with Mrs Smith's blessing and a tantalising smell of fried onions coming from the kitchen. Into Bradford to look at marvellous bargains in summer frocks. By the feel of the weather they should give them away. I've certainly got a summer frock on but wouldn't relinquish my fur coat summer or no summer.

Clem can beat me at talking. He used to be one of those romantic individuals mounted outside Whitehall in the shiny breastplates—a Life Guard! So he has something worth telling.

7 July 1939

Still raining. Arranged to go on Ilkley Moor but would have to paddle. Auntie says in shop "This is my niece from New Zealand. She's going on Ilkley Moor this afternoon". The butcher gloomily hacks at a steak and adds "Not baht 'at she won't" and we didn't. Clem, Hilda and I went to the New Victoria instead to see 'Honolulu'. Can hardly realise that I'll be there some day. It seems more remote now than it did in New Zealand. The New Victoria is a huge theatre seating over 3,000.

8 July 1939

A day with Auntie writing letters and reminiscing. Cold getting better but a bit hoarse in the mornings, still with the amount of talking I do it's a wonder I have any voice left at all. Aunt Eliza removed twenty six times in her married life, practically all in the same district. A big photograph of Grandma and Grandpa Turner in the dining room. Neither of the dears look as if they really wanted it taken. Auntie says according to family tradition Grandpa was one over the eight and Grandma furious with him when it was taken. Found out too that there's gypsy on Grandma's side; that accounts for a lot of things— Grandma's cousin so much so that he used to go round in a caravan. Edith and Harry in in the evening. Bed at 12.45.

9 July 1939

Teeming but went with Clem to look over the fire station. Here there was a marvellously equipped ambulance with a good type of half drop window. Just push it up or pull it down and fix it in position with the lever at the bottom. The big engine is a revelation when properly explained; the ladder 101 feet with a telephone to speak to the man at the top. A mechanism controls the length of the ladder according to the angle at which it is raised. When they dash out they always have to avoid an old gas lamp on the other side of the road. Asked why they didn't remove it as it's not used now but just met with the vague reply "Oh it's always been there". It's like that in England—once a thing's there it's always there. The place is full of new air raid fire-fighting apparatus—all grey and streamlined. Stroked the big police horses—Angus, Peter, Diamond, Sportsman, Hussar and Tom. They polka, waltz and nuzzle into your pocket for sugar. Strode back trying desperately to keep pace with Clem's 6 feet 4 inches.

In the afternoon a visit from Uncle Herbert's brothers; all the image of each other. The plumpest, Harry, is a magistrate and tells long and involved stories of cases. He's an Oddfellow and has a decoration medal with inset diamond— the family's pride and joy. He has been to Paris on a 'convention' but doesn't take his wife. She is a dear soul who hangs on his every word, nodding her head in confirmation. I was reminded of the Most Prominent Citizen and giggled helplessly and alone. Saw too today the inner workings of a police box which appear at intervals along the road. A log book, a list of beats and duties, a telephone, a gas ring and kettle! There is a gadget attached to the telephone whereby the public can open a door outside speak into a grill and the police at Headquarters answer immediately. If police are wanted a light flashes intermittently and the first policeman passing has to pop in to see what to do.

Well my dears I've written screeds but I want to record it all. Some of the customs are so new and strange. I'm having such a happy time here. I've got to go to Auntie Bella's on the 14th as Elsie will be home. Then I must go up to Scotland and Ireland before the summer goes. It's a marvellous life, my only worries are letters and my diary. I just can't get them written. Hope to meet Auntie Mollie at York about the 24th for a little farewell celebration as she leaves about the end of August. This is being written in bed and Auntie is just bringing me a cup of tea. I help as much as I possibly can. My love to you two dears and love from all here too. All the children know of Auntie Susie. I'm posting a knitting book with a nice jumper for future reference. Hilda and Auntie both knit beautifully. Your work has been so much admired. I'm always thinking about you and a big kiss goes right to New Zealand every night. Isn't it wonderful to think I am actually here?

10 July 1939

To reminisce again with Aunt Eliza and to recall the feud between the Rawmarsh and Parkgate children. They'd all line up on the border, Mother among them, and yell "Rawmarsh bulldogs fastened in a pen. Can't get out for Parkgate men". Old Heskith who used to wish fire and brimstone on the children who played in his field and Paddy Mahon who had the fields beyond (the children all called him Paddy <u>Mion</u>). And then the little story of the three saucers which Susie and Eliza bought. Susie broke two going home. Later when 'fettling' the dishes Eliza jumped at her and shouted 'Boo'. Bang went the third saucer and Susie's reproachful voice wailed "For shame our Eliza and me trying to wesh pots and sing and sound my aitches!" Now Little Mum will smile at those far-off days. Forty years is a long time. And what happened to all those Parkgate boys and girls like Florrie Capril—a reight grand old woman now like her Mother. And what about <u>the</u> family of the district—the Bergens. Fatty dead and the youngest and oldest unfortunately sunk rather low. Only the middle one an ordinary respectable person but definitely uninteresting and slow of wit. And this the family that all the Turner children envied so. Miss Hague, the schoolteacher, dead now. She married a Mr Wannop, a grocer, and her daughter is definitely a little queer. Gazed again at the photograph of Grandma and Granddad—so many years together and only two short years apart at the end. I shall never think of Grandma as a little old lady; instead always as a slender-waisted, dark-haired, dark-eyed, gypsy-looking woman and Granddad, the strong, short, square Staffordshire man sitting stiffly on the chair. I have a clearer perception of their lives now that I have seen Netherfield Lane, the entries, the smoke and the bluebell fields. The South and the West of England were beautiful but Yorkshire lives, it has a past, a present and a future for me.

Uncle Herbert is at teatime and does not go over to the shed with his beloved inventions. Dear Uncle Herbert, he sits for interminable hours and just 'studies'. But he emits a rare chuckle. Does Susie remember that she once said he was going into consumption. He hasn't gone yet. He eats great piles of bread and butter and gets not one scrap fatter; but then it's Auntie's home-made bread. Auntie wanted to give me the recipe for Yorkshire pudding. Surprised her by making one of my own just as good as hers. Explained that I'd been brought up on them since childhood. This afternoon to the Park to see the rehearsal for the police parade. It's a fine day. What have we done to deserve this? Took rather an unusual photograph today of an old mounting stone in one of the main streets—used in the old days to mount one's horse with dignity. Six police constables pass and salute. I bow graciously a la Queen Mary and trip over the dog leash. Harry and Edith in at night; Harry hates to say Goodbye to anyone. At last to bed at 1.30.

11 July 1939

And so to Derbyshire. Said Goodbye to Aunt Eliza for a little while. Viewed the interminable chimney pots of Bradford through half-shut eyes and dozed to Chesterfield. Fell out in a hurry and finding no one knew anything about the bus to Bakewell fell in again as far as Ambergate. It is such a pretty ride to Bakewell, through little villages, the scent of new mown hay in the air and the fields full of waving poppies. A woman washes in a tub outside a grey stone cottage, swishing the clothes with a peggy. Another draws water from a well with a bucket and a windlass. There is a grassy bank running down to a river and behind rising to the skyline a leafy mass of green trees. At Derwent an old woman gets on with a basket of eggs covered with a spotless white napkin. Pink roses climb up grey walls to grey slate roofs and blue delphiniums and lupins bloom down a crazy pavement. Cromford and an old man rests on a seat, a young man, a typical young farmer, passes. "How are you goin' on old 'un?" The old man nods, "Oh just tidy tha knaws". His head sinks lower into his knotted scarf, a red spotted one. It is knotted in front with the ends tied to his braces.

We pass Willersley Castle, the old home of Sir Richard Arkwright. All round Cromford is his country. We have just passed the Sir Richard Arkwright Co. Ltd. mills. It is strange how every little bit of England has some association, maybe with beauty and a lovely lady as at Camelot, maybe with vice and dark days of terror as the hall in Exeter where Judge Jeffries held his court or sometimes with industry as here at Cromford. And then Matlock. There are four distinct Matlocks—Matlock Bank where one goes to 'take the waters', Matlock Town which is the little village nestling quietly in the hills, Matlock Bridge where one listens to the band on summer evenings, where coloured lights are hung on gala days and immaculate youths in white flannels boat on the lake and Matlock Bath where there are lovers' walks and caves. The High Tor rises protestingly above, the Derwent below drops in little rapids in silvery dashes. There is a swing bridge over a gorge and on the skyline, old Riber Castle. It is like a castle in a fairy tale, as if when the clock strikes twelve it may vanish away into the clouds. Learned later, rather disappointingly, that it is not old. It was built by no knight of old for his lady fair but by one Mr Smedley for use as a hydropathic institute. Something went wrong, no one seems to be able to tell me what, but is now just a castle on the hill. We pass the Grouse Inn where John Manners fought the duel. We pass from the history of industry to romance. This is Dorothy Vernon country, she of Haddon Hall. She rested at the Peacock Inn which we are passing now, an old and venerable hostelry with a stone peacock over its door.

Grace to meet me at Bakewell and then to Lathkill Lodge, the case left at the grocers to be sent on afterwards. There'll be a little bit of my heart left at the Lodge with Billie and Dolly. A little grey house 200 years old, little latticed windows, arched doorways and a motto in stone letters on the chimney. And the setting! Broad fields of waving grass gently rising to the slopes of oak-clad hills, a lighter grass carpet patterned by grey stone walls dividing the fields. The private road to the Stanton Estate edged with hawthorn. There is a big iron gate to be opened as the car from the Hall goes or comes. Across the road one gets just a peep of Haddon Hall but the Duke of Rutland lets no one through and has planted hundreds of trees by the road which when grown will stop the view. There is always that shadowy look of great still trees and distant hills.

Inside the Lodge, a corner fireplace with a bright fire, blue Dresden mirrors over the mantelpiece, a paved floor and arched doors made of a single piece of timber fitting solidly into the wall. Two bay latticed windows and budgies on the little window seat. An exquisite Venetian Louis cabinet of walnut. It is a lovely work this, the grained wood being ornamented with metal inlaid with enamels. I believe it was originated by one Charles Andre Buhl, an Italian cabinet maker. There is also a French gilt clock with a tinkling chime of sugary sweetness.

Billie is a retired war ministry man. He is a courtly gentleman indeed, punctilious about speech and manners but full of fun and delightful mannerisms. Dolly is a genuine Lancashire woman and a wonderful cook. There is also Little Jenny, a half wire-haired terrier and half Sydney Silky, warming her tummy by the fire. There is an adventure about sounding new personalities and making new friends. It was late when Grace and I crept upstairs to bed. The little lattice window was a frame for a harvest moon.

12 July 1939

Raining of course but who cares. My case turns up after being sent to the wrong Lodge. Billie is the best entertainer in the world, subtle repartee is the order of the day. Heard a delightful little verse, so appropriate to the English climate:

> First it rained ant then it blew
> Then it friz and then it snew
> Then we had a little rain
> And then it friz and snew again.

Ghost stories at night with the lamp low (there is no electric light here, away in the Derbyshire Dales) and the firelight flickered. Lurid ghost stories. Grace and I fly upstairs with our candles, scared out of our wits. We jump into the little bed and pull the clothes over our heads. There is a tapping at the window! Summoning all our courage we jump out and grab the broom Dolly is waving against the glass! Gradually the house settles, the lights of Haddon Hall go out. There is no sound except—I wonder if there is a ghost after all?

13 July 1939

How the days slip by. Had a delightful day of reminiscences of the old War Ministry days and further back to Billie's school days. Somehow one likes the schoolmaster who looked over the top of his glasses across the table and said "When eating soup let it be a personal affair. I am not interested and I don't want to be".

A fine day and so we visited the Matlocks. It is like going calling on a family to visit these three old world towns, especially with Billie, for we are all dressed in our best. Billie's hat is at just the right angle and his cane taps in placid rhythm. It is like returning to the days when one 'Took the air'. We visited Matlock Town first and went into St Giles Church to see the Woolley monuments. On a slab of black marble is an inscription to Adam Woolley who died at the age of 100 in 1657 and his wife Grace who died in 1669 at 110. The inscription reads: 'For the purpose of recording so extraordinary but well authenticated an instance of longevity and long continuance in the state of wedlock, their great-great-great-great-grandson Adam Woolley of this parish, gentleman, caused this monument to be erected in the year 1824'. Behind the door is a glass case containing a number of wreaths. These were carried at the funerals of maidens in olden times. In the churchyard a really queer epitaph in memory of one Phoebe Bown in 1854 died at the age of 82.

Here lies romantic Phoebe
Half Ganymede, half Hebe
A maid of mutable condition
A jockey, a cowherd and musician.

We sauntered down to the side of the lovely Derwent always leisurely in Beau Brummel style, stopping to admire the thickly wooded slopes of the hills on either side, the Heights of Abraham and the tors, these great faces of rock rising sheer up from a bed of soft green trees that seemed to float in the still cool waters of the river below. The grey stone houses back right on to the cliffs. They are all the same colour and it is as if the houses were just a piece of the cliff hollowed out.

Matlock Bath has many attractions and its residents know them all. No one there we were told proudly has ever been known to have phthisis[13] on account of its health-giving waters and pure air. I marvelled and privately made a note to look up and see what phthisis was. Evidently the Matlockers think the outside world is full of it. The baths are a pleasant place, the water naturally warm. In the new Bath Hotel the roof of the bath-house is a perfectly rounded arch but frankly they are not half as good as ours at Rotorua. After all one must be fair. In front of the Pavilion is the fish pond. It is such a shallow pool and yet carp, chub and roach swim round in perfect peace and harmony. For 2*d* we enter the Petrifying Wells. Here bowler hats, eggs, nests and even a rabbit are petrified by the waters which are strongly charged with carbonic acid. This dissolves the limestone through which it passes. When the lime-laden water emerges into the open some of the carbonic acid gas escapes and as a consequence the water cannot hold the whole of the lime and throws it off on anything it touches. The shops are full of Blue John souvenirs—a lovely stone like a transparent marble streaked with bluey-purple lines. This comes from Castleton. It is called fluorspar, a crystalized combination of lime and fluoric acid. It is said that it is found in Castleton only and nowhere else in the world. Somehow I'm glad I put on my Paris frock.

Home to tea, an English tea, leisurely, witty and pleasant. There's nothing quite like an English tea. Draughts in the evening and I am given an opportunity of showing just how dull I really am. Rolled a great quantity of cigarettes with a fascinating patent roller. I feel as if I'd been at the Lodge for years. I must record a notice in one of the Matlock shops—'Harlequin jelly good for the belly, 4 oz. a penny as long as there's any'. More ghost stories by the firelight, impromptu ones told by Billie and me, each trying to surpass the other. Ribs for supper. Getting still fatter but why worry.

14 July 1939

Drifted into Bakewell with Grace for a little shopping. Everything proceeds slowly with long conservations before change is given. The girl at the chemist wraps up our film, holds our £1 note in her hand while she tells us of her Grandmother's marriage and her niece's holiday or the other way round. Our bus is going and we champ at the bit but nothing stops the flow. We bought a Bakewell pudding. A Bakewell pudding is a sort of flan with a custard therein but one does not get the recipe. It is a long cherished secret of Bakewell. It is good and rich, so rich that a little goes a very long way. There is 'something' about Bakewell. The guide book describes it as an 'air' that can be directly traced to ducal ownership. There is a sort of quiet dignity. One naturally drifts to the Parish Church—at least travellers do. In this church in the Vernon Chapel are buried all the families of the Vernons and Manners of Haddon Hall. Here is the monument to Sir John Manners and his lady, Dorothy Vernon, the same Dorothy that eloped with him so romantically and rested at the Peacock Inn. There is at least one quaint epitaph in the churchyard to one John Dale. It just says—'The good man's quiet—still are both his wives'.

Tonight Dolly has given me THE bracelet—200 years old; I croon over it all night. It has a history. The story goes that in the little village of Morten-cum-Hardy in Lancashire a great lady once stayed at a little country inn.

She seemed in great trouble and sent the 'boy' with a note and the bracelet up to a neighbouring house to give to the young Lord. But the boy was a lively lad; he called at another inn with a few pals, lost the note and presented the bracelet to the barmaid—a comely wench. Frightened he returned with a story of having delivered the note and bracelet to the young Lord. So the lady waited and waited—watching the road and starting at the sound of each horse that drew up by the door. She ate not enough to feed a bird and grew paler and more wan. Then one day she was found in the little village stream— no one knew who she was or from whence she came but all they knew was that she was a lady. And now it's mine. I wear it every day. It may attract romance or repel it. I know not or care not and yet what if it did carry a curse?

Another clever little bit to be recorded:

A CLERK is a man who knows a great deal about a very little and who goes on knowing more and more about less and less until finally he knows everything about practically nothing: WHEREAS
A MANAGER is a man who knows very little about a great deal and goes on knowing less and less about more and more until he finally knows practically nothing about everything.

15 July 1939

Teeming, thundering, lightning. The echoes in this part of the country are wonderful, a clap of the hands and the whole district echoes again and again. It is a different Derbyshire today. Salisbury Plain in such weather is a dreary windswept affair but these hills and tors are grand. We pull the curtains and light the lamp early. The wind whistles round the Lodge. It is a night for ghost stories and ghosts. 'The door slowly opened' said Billie 'it was opening of its own accord. A dark shadow waited outside and the spirit left one of those who were seated round the fire....' I shifted my eyes from the flickering flames to the door, it seemed that I went all cold and Billie's voice was far away. It was opening of its own accord. Grace's eyes had followed mine and a little moan escaped her lips. Dolly's eyes looked as if they were set in two black caverns—a dark shape appeared. With astonishing clarity I wondered which of the four of us seated round the fire that shadow would draw. My hands clung involuntarily to the chair. It wasn't going to be me. Then the shadow came in, its voice boomed heartily. 'What's the matter with you all? I nearly knocked my hand off'. We all talked loudly, quickly and at once and not one of us admitted to Farmer B. that we had taken him for the shadow of death! We decided unanimously to play draughts for the rest of the evening.

16 July 1939

'And then we had a little rain' but nevertheless to Rowsley Church with Billie, past quaint old cottages with picture gardens. There is a private chapel here for the Haddon Hall folks. The vicar, young and apologetic, read his sermon carefully and without imagination. It appears that having once got his 'living' he stays here for ever! Suddenly I felt sorry for him—he must always remember that Lady —— came socially before Mrs ——, that Billie, socially if not financially, came above Farmer B. He looked so young to be buried, to be always remembering little pettifogging conventions. I was introduced to Mrs M. She bridles! Often have I read of people bridling but never actually seen it. She is incredibly sweet—married for seven years to the stodgy M. and still adores him. Past the cottage of the oldest inhabitant on our return, with its lupins and roses round the door, and took shelter in the Peacock Inn. The Peacock Inn is terribly expensive, so shelter was all we took, besides we were straight from church!

Home to a marvellous dinner of roast and Yorkshire. None of us could say 'Goodbye' just 'Au revoir' and made up a little story about my going away on a holiday and I'd soon be back. Dear little Lodge in the Derbyshire Dales. Surely these dales are the most English part of England. English and yet right in the heart of it. Along a beautiful ravine opening out of the road between Cromford and Bonsall, is the Via Gellia![14] Somehow I'm right back to Rome walking down the Via Sistina and up the Via Dell Impero. How come that drive has such a Latin name? I can find no explanation but just as a sharp reminder that we are in England the Via Gellia runs past the Pig of Lead Inn!

It was a lovely ride to Sheffield in spite of the rain. There is a coral pink glow in the sky over Curbar village, a quaint place with narrow streets. Past leafy woods with dense undergrowth, and the Fox House Inn. There are little bits of history all along this route. Got off to investigate Eyam, just a picturesque little village out from Calver. Here in 1665 when the Great Plague was raging, its people earned the title 'The Brave Folk of Eyam'. It is said that a box of clothes was sent by a tailor from London and the person who opened it immediately contracted the dread plague and died. The plague spread and nearly three quarters of the people died in a few months. The people naturally made to flee from the infected area but their minister, one Mr Mompesson, realising that they would take the plague with them into other parts of England persuaded them to stay. It succeeded and the plague was kept within the limits of the village. But it was a sad village. Food was brought to the village from neighbouring towns and placed on rocks. So many died that there was hardly a village at all when the plague had run its course. There is a quaint sundial on one of the doors of the church and at least one epitaph worth mentioning:

In seven years' time there comes a change
Observe and here you'll see
On that same day come seven years
My husband's laid by me'.
Anne Sellars Jan. 15th 1731.
Isaac Sellars Jan 15th 1738.

Sheffield, definitely late and a long walk from bus stop to Exchange Street to get the Rotherham tram. A cheerful looking man offers to carry my case. "A bit o' help from one traveller to another" is his explanation. The conductor straps it up on the driving apparatus and it falls with a thud on the head of a 'real tough guy'. (Note—Sheffield cussing excels anything I've previously heard.) Home to Aunt Bella's and a reight royal welcome. The ride from Sheffield to Rotherham is a long straight road through manufacturing towns that run into each other without a stop. Attercliffe and Tinsley—just a long line of iron and steel works spitting showers of sparks, glowing like fireworks in the black night and always the dull rumble of machinery. Went to the 'Star' to meet old friends again and to join in the singing of old songs. Elsie's a dear girl and I like Frank very much. Ran round to Auntie Lizzie's to collect the mail. Mrs Rogers in France has returned my Tiki[15] with snaps and a nice letter. To bed at an unearthly hour.

17 July 1939

Today just slipped by. Tried to write a few letters but not a hope. I'm entertained every single minute. Learning to play snooker, not brilliant, but not so bad for me—I do not throw a pretty dart but a decidedly dangerous one. For a walk with Jack and Frank, Hooton Roberts way—a quaint little village on the way to Doncaster. It's strange how soon one gets out of the towns. There were grey stone farmhouses here with all the stables, dipping sheds and milking sheds crowded rather near the road and the whole lot near the house! Realised of course the cattle are bedded in for the winter so they won't want to go traipsing into paddocks miles away like we do to milk. Took shelter in an empty house, iron hooks hang from the ceiling and there's a jar of pickled onions on the shelf. The wind whistles and the rain keeps up a steady tattoo on the roof. Investigate the cellar but find nothing but a musty smell. Called at the Cemetery on the way home and froze. Read still more tombstones of people who died of pneumonia. Have not the slightest desire to lie amongst my ancestors.
Tonight to the Regent at Rotherham with George—a good variety of tumblers, comedians and others who didn't really intend to be funny at all. It is so long

since I saw anything like it in New Zealand. English humour is so boisterous, people generally don't appreciate subtlety, they like it straight from the shoulder. Know now why English comedians aren't so popular in N.Z. Uncle John's youngest boy, little John, taken to hospital with fever. No wonder! Still raining.

18 July 1939

Washing day and nearly fine. Wrote letters solidly. At night to Rodeo Riders performing in a field. Gorgeous horses jumping through burning hoops to the accompaniment of wild and woolly Cossack yells. Rather enjoyed the gathering of blocks of wood as they dashed past. In fact 'rather enjoyed' it all. How the kiddies cheered! And so did I. Even selected my own particular hero—a real South American Joe on a small wiry coal-black mare. Jack, like a little gentleman, carried Elsie's umbrella for her and then when it rained insisted on using it himself! George and I to the Crown at 9.30. Greeted specially by Uncle Sam's friend, Matt Rogers. Said to tell Uncle Sam he was just the same as he used to be.

19 July 1939

George decided not to go to work. So off to walk, the four of us—George and I, Elsie and Frank, to Worksop. First the bus as far as Maltby, through Wickersley and Bramley. They build dear little bungalows for pensioners here. They are called bungalows because they have just the one floor but have very little resemblance to our bungalows, being just square brick houses. No one other than a pensioner or a widow would think of living in one. All houses are upstairs and sometimes all joined together in a row of six, then an entry leading to a path running at the 'backs', then another six houses all joined. The newer council houses are only three joined together. Folk here can't understand why I prefer the bungalows to the houses! Extracted a midge from George's eye—he seems to attract everything like a magnet.

Rested for a while at Maltby Crags—a glorious view with the delicate spire of Laughton church always visible. It is high but not phenomenally so but it must be the contour of the surrounding country that makes it stand out. 'Tis said that in the last war it was visible from the North Sea. It is strange how these little bits of Latin names keep springing up all over England. Laughton is really Laughton-en-le-Morthen. A real English walk to Roche Abbey with woods on either side. This green loveliness is something never to be forgotten, and well it might be green! It is raining, thundering and lightning and we shelter under trees, behind hedges or just around, laugh and get wet. These ruins of England are such well-educated ruins. Roche Abbey, or what is left of it, stands in a shaven lawn, its loose stones piled neatly up and not a blade of grass to hide its nakedness. The entrance is through a lovely archway with fowls picking at the base and chickens—a little yellow fluffy balls under one's feet. Pigeons coo in the old grey stone walls and the rain drips down. So into the house for lunch—a long lunch! The wishing well next. One takes the water into one's mouth, walks backwards up the hill, swallow and wish. I'm so busy keeping my balance and wondering if the water is contaminated that I forget to wish.

Into the woods then—a lake with a perfect reflection, white swans and grey cygnets mirrored in the still, still water. The gentle drip of rain and a clean earthy smell. On the road again and a different smell, a typical English farmyard. Old grey stone buildings and fat pigs. More thunder and lightning so took shelter in a garage and nearly got run over by someone who looked like one of Britain's traditional aristocracy. On again past Sandbeck Park (Earl of Scarborough) and the finest hunting horses I've ever seen in a field. Signs everywhere to Firbeck Park but all point in different directions. We never found Firbeck, maybe the income tax collector has silently carried it away! At Oldcotes Elsie and I go into the King William the 4th Inn but came out quicker than we went in—dog. The tower of old Blyth church in the distance and we are at the crossroads. Tossed which way to go and Worksop won. So George and I tramped and Elsie and Frank followed on behind—far behind. The squat solid tower of Blyth fades away, Langold, North Carlton, South Carlton—I feel like the three jolly farmers as the villages flash by. Here we find a holly bush with red berries and it's only July! Surely such early holly means a long hard winter? Wouldn't it be wonderful if I could stay for Xmas, but that's a whole five months off. There are glorious chestnut trees in Carlton Woods. Now I always associate English woods with the steady drip-drip of rain. Waited for Elsie and Frank to catch up specially to boast of our endurance and speed. We weren't tired. Oh no, but no one flew into the Victoria Hotel quicker than we did. Rather an intriguing dart-board with doors which when closed made it look just like a cupboard. When open the doors form a protection for the wall when people like me play.

Walk for a little way through Worksop into the Dukeries. This is Robin Hood country. There are lovely homes and gardens. Walking back past the Greyhound Hotel a real Mother Gamp sidles up to George. "Hello luv 'ow about taking me in for a drink?" We tease him about her all the way home. Back by bus through Gateford, Woodsetts, Lindrick Common, South Anston, North Anston and Dinnington—old grey stone villages. Colliers going to work on the night shift—weary-looking, their clogs clanging along the streets. But under their caps their faces smile always, their mufflers are neatly tied.

They all carry the round water tin called a Dudley moon and an oblong tin of 'snap'. 'Snap'—that's what we all want, so off to the fish and chip shop and home to supper.

20 July 1939

George decided not to go to work again. Morning spent taking photographs— the Congregational Sunday School and Day School where Mother went, No. 57, Netherfield Lane and the old 'Travellers Inn' where Granddad used to 'reckon'. In the old days a man would sometimes get coal by contract. He himself would employ his 'trammie' and other men to help him, paying them himself at the end of the week and for that purpose they all gathered at the Travellers Inn, to smoke and talk and discuss the merits of the latest whippet. They still have whippets—thin lithe miniature greyhounds in little red coats.

Home to dinner and then to walk again, and walk we did. Saw first the old pit shaft of Knapton's Pit where the men used to go down in the cage controlled by a pony walking to and fro. Across the fields to the Haugh where Cousin Walter lives in a little row of cottages standing all by themselves. They are called Greenpiece Cottages—just about half a dozen in a row with all round fields of waving corn. Past Monkwood reservoir to the Mausoleum. One gets the key at a sweet little Lodge surrounded by a garden of old English roses. There are deep red ones hanging over the path with an almost unearthly scent. It is true that English roses smell sweeter than ours in N.Z. They are richer coloured. The vegetables have a stronger flavour too and the meat.... The little old lady who answered the door asked if we'd wait while she finished "weshing pots". The Mausoleum is a peculiar place, a sort of large monument built for Chas. Watson Wentworth, Marquis of Rockingham, who died in July 1782. Inside is an exquisite marble statue by Nollekens—surely it is Italian marble? The ermine collar is delicately done, the lace ruffles soft and the face true. There is a little tale about the statue, 'tis said that the sculptor accepted a bet from a friend that he would make a perfect statue and if any fault could be found with it he would take his own life. He finished a masterpiece but there was a mistake, the stitching on one side down the trousers was missing, just above the garter and he lived to carve no more stone. Busts of members of the Marquis's Cabinet stare at us all round the wall, Sir Geo. Savile, Sir Chas Montague, the Duke of Portland and the old lady looks at them reverently. She locks the door carefully on the Marquis and we paddle back to the road.

We crossed stiles all the way to Wentworth Park. Cannot quite get over the way one can walk through farmer's property here and what is more they put little paths for you to walk on and stiles for you to get across. I'd like to see us creeping under the 'post and rail' fences of the N.Z. farm. Pheasants call from the grass and moorhens paddle amongst the lilies on the second dam. Over many stiles to Thorpe and I learn to climb them a little more gracefully. There is thunder, lightning and a queer yellow light. Stone stiles now three steps projecting out of stone walls. Miles and miles of Scholes Coppice and Keppel's Column. Say it over and over again, it fascinates me somehow—'Keppel's Column in Scholes Coppice'. Just like one of those things one says quickly and gets hopelessly tangled up. If you can say it quickly and correctly you're quite sober! Greeted at the Lodge by a dear dog with muddy paws. Keppel's Column is a queer narrow round tower build possibly in the old days as a look-out. We went up the steps, all 217 of them, dark winding stairs. The more we toiled the more we giggled; it seemed so ridiculous somehow but we just had to get to the top. A marvellous view, but as the guide books say 'visibility poor'. Back, as George puts it, 'through t'sludge' and on the road again.

They are such funny little villages—these Yorkshire ones—sometimes just twelve little grey stone houses huddled together. It's still raining—throwing it down as they say here. Stride along like a couple of athletes and meet George's particular friend who enquires re his health. It appears that George hadn't gone to work because his rheumatism is too bad and his friend has just been along to Auntie Bella's to sympathise with him. Auntie did some quick thinking and said he'd gone out for a wee walk to try to get his strength up to go to work tomorrow. We pause in our manly stride to explain that he has rheumatism very badly. Leave the said friend grinning broadly. Looked at maps till about half past eight and then remembered Deanna Durbin at the Regal and fled for our lives.

21 July 1939

George thought perhaps he better go to work—pay day. In the afternoon to Auntie Miriam's at Canklow. Somehow Auntie Miriam is different to all the rest. She has jet-black hair in spite of all the trouble she has had and such a lot of ornaments on the dresser. There are birds in cages, canaries and love birds, two little mysteries that sit solemnly side by side, never moving, never blinking. Sat in Grandma's rocking chair and Granddad's Windsor chair with the high back. There was a stuffed parrot in a cage too that Mother gave to Grandma when she was a very little girl. In Auntie's bedroom on the wall facing her bed is a photograph of Mother and Mr and Mrs Foster taken in the bush among the ferns.

At night to Parkgate Feast! How often have I heard of Parkgate Feast where Mother went when she was a small girl with her sixpence to spend just how she liked. Rode on the Noah's Ark (like a miniature switchback railway) and tumbled about in absurd little motor bikes until well after midnight. Teddy

Perkins, his round honest face shining with pleasure, wins a pair of china dogs. He looks so soft and yet when he picks up the balls and throws back his arm lazily and carelessly all goes before him. But they're not china dogs here they're 'pot dogs' and all the fashion. The black sludge is ankle deep at the end of the evening. We've thrown three-penny pieces on little square boards and gambled on everything under the sun until we've no money left. And then Teddy slipped. He drew his arm back, swung his bulk round and let fly at the coconut. His feet seemed to shoot from under him and he fell flat in the black mud. Never have I seen a man so muddy. We fished him out wiped him down but he'd hit the nut! Back down Chapel Street the four of us to buy our supper on the way home. Sat till two chatting and George decided not to go to work.

22 July 1939

Up late, very late and into Rotherham for a spot of shopping. There's a glorious peal of bells from the Rotherham church. Somehow this church dominates the whole town. The streets must needs to go round it. They even cut through it and we walk on old flat gravestones the inscriptions on which are long since disappeared. In the afternoon walked again, past the Chemical where George got more bits in his eye. Past the Fitzwilliam Arms where Auntie Bella used to work. Up Potter Hill to Bryn-Cot to see Mrs Senior, a pretty little woman about Mother's age. I can hardly believe that she is Leah Causer. Always in Mother's stories came the phrase 'Then Leah and I went to Greasbrough'—or 'Leah and I used to sing'. This was Leah; how I wished Mother had been there. Mr and Mrs Brown were there too. Mrs Brown was Lucy Machon, another of the trio—Lucy, Leah and our Susannah. They still go to the Congregational Sunday School where Mr Senior had taught for 50 years! In England it is like that. Then I think of the changes and the moving about our life has brought. Mrs Senior has one child too—George, who plays a Wurlitzer professionally. He is married and living Morecambe way. Poor Mrs Brown is very deaf and also Mr Senior.

Back to Auntie Bella's and shouted my way through tea. The Feast again at night and I ate the famous whelks. Never have I attached so much importance to things to eat. One sprinkles vinegar and pepper with studied discretion on a little plate of these delicacies, and I liked them. Plates of peas are very popular too. Can't get over the eating of things like this in between meals; an ice cream or a milk shake maybe but to settle down to peas and chips and whelks! Still I can take it and enjoy it. Paddled around in the black mud. Shoes hardly visible and the bottom of the men's trousers just caked with it. Stayed on the Noah's Ark for three quarters of an hour! The four of us home, mashed a cup of tea and sat talking till twenty past two.

23 July 1939

It's Sunday and on Sunday in England one has mushrooms for breakfast. Walked out to Conisbrough Castle through Ryecroft and Kilnhurst. It is strange how Sunday in an industrial town looks Sunday. Everything is at rest. The fires in the brickworks are low and the smoke from the mines lazy but underneath the soft green countryside men still toil for they take Sunday shifts too. Past the tiny cottages at Hooton Roberts to the Holy Well. There are a lot of these wells in England, carefully fenced off. They seem to bubble up perpetually, no doubt an outlet from some underground river. Gazed right down into its mysterious depths, clear bright and cold and at the bottom there lay a bully beef tin still labelled 'Best New Zealand'. And then Conisbrough Castle high on the hill. Gaunt grey stones softened by the green dripping trees. Enquired for admission at the Lodge. A tall gaunt woman appears. 'It's time you went back' she rasped 'eating me out of house and home'. We backed off involuntarily. 'It's my son' she explained 'he is valet to Lord—'. We gazed inside and a hungry looking youth was wolfing pie rapidly. There is not much of Conisbrough left. In the guide books it is Conisbrough , on the buses Conisbro. There is just the keep tower of fine grained limestone. Even in the time of Henry VIII this old castle was a ruin. But I have learned to reconstruct ruins. There are holes on either side of the entrance where the chains would be that operated the drawbridge across the moat. The walls are full 15 feet thick. It is even possible to reconstruct the domestic life of the castle. There are little recesses hollowed out in the walls placed so as to allow the water to run off outside. These were the 'bathrooms' of the Castle. And the fireplaces! They have been noble structures in their day and must have taken gigantic logs. The mantelpiece is 12 feet long and the stones sort of dove-tailed into one another. Stone ledges run all round the rooms evidently used as seats. One hopes that tapestries and cushions were plentiful. There is a little recess too that is the 'small oratory' mentioned in 'Ivanhoe' where the noble Edith, mother of Athelstan, prayed during the burial of her son. For it is Ivanhoe which has kept the castle alive. Its history is so obscure that it is almost legendary. There is a large hole in the ceiling of the first floor and it is said that in the old days food and water would be passed from floor to floor through these holes by means of a pulley. Right in one of the buttresses is a room of hexagonal shape, not a large room perhaps 13 feet by 8 feet. Long narrow slits in the stone admit light and air. It would seem that this is the very chapel where lay the bier of Athelstan. Now when I re-read my Ivanhoe I'll know just where the noble Richard with his faithful Ivanhoe disguised as the Black Knight of the Fetterlock .....

We climbed to the very top. Down below the wind clanged the big door and whistled round the broken stones. In the distance is Cadeby mine, the trucks all filled ready for Monday. Below the river wends a pretty way. The viaducts with their twenty one arches are shadowy in a misty haze. Somehow I like Conisbrough better than all the ruins for it is not a 'tidy' ruin. The grass grows wild around it and creepers wind riotous over great piles of stones. It is strange how these old places came by their names. It is stated that in writings of the 12th century that 'Conan began a berg, in all the world there was not a berg so fair. When the berg was made with much strength he set on it a name after himself, often he rode it through and through and named it Conan's berg'.

Home in time for dinner. Had a sleep by the fire in the afternoon and sat writing my diary. Another walk round and about, sometimes sheer beauty can come from such prosaic things. There could be nothing more lovely than Rawmarsh church dark in sharp relief against the red glow of the chemical works.

24 July 1939

Never again, a bottle of stout and a piece of Schonhut's pork pie for supper. Thoroughly bilious but packed for stay at Honley. Slept solidly on the bus past dear little villages from Barnsley to Huddersfield. Much better by that time, and by the time I reached Honley everything was O.K.

Gwennie spends the next few weeks visiting acquaintances and other parts of Yorkshire, the Lake District and then some of the sights of Scotland. We catch up with her again near Glasgow staying with Mrs. Mcq.

August 1939

7 August 1939

A gorgeous day and actually hot, with SUN. Mrs. Mcq. lends me a kilt and a tammy. Must say I like the kilt it is so warm and has such a free feeling. In the afternoon into Glasgow. Things are so cheap! and the temptation to buy so great especially at the Irish Linen shop. Coal is 1/10 per cwt, good hard stuff, against N.Z. 6/3 for a one and a half cwt bag. Potatoes 2*d* for three and a half pounds. Here too, as in England, ale and stout is sold in grocers' shops. But very few drink beer in Scotland unless it's to follow a whisky, which strangely enough is no cheaper than it is in England. All the little girls are in kilts and nearly all the very small boys—diminutive ones with huge safety pins at the side and the lads with leather sporrans. Why do all the Stuart lassies with the flaming red tartan of their clan have flaming red hair?

At night queues waiting to get into the continuous pictures and still waiting at 9.30 p.m. A few look as if 'Glasgow belongs to me' but the Glasgow people will tell you that they're the Irish. Ill-feeling between the two—the Irish they say come over and take the jobs at cheap wages. Glasgow is a big city where the buses stop and start in the same breath and you watch the traffic lights then run across for dear life. Woe betide the lagger. It is still a city of slums but its slum clearances areas are cities in themselves. It seems that there are acres and acres of square blocks of houses in the suburbs.

8 August 1939

Another summer's day. Somehow I can still imagine it raining in England. But it wasn't raining up Loch Lomond. Got a real early start by bus to Ballock—20 miles each way for 2/- Out through the suburbs of Glasgow seemingly never-ending. The vast building schemes are certainly more for utility than beauty but they are at least new.

There's a jolly crowd of hikers on the boat up the loch. 'Och man' says one old man to another 'But our laddies are grand wi' their packs on their backs and their kilts swinging' and grand they were indeed. All down the sunny lengths of Loch Lomond we sang 'I'll tak the high road and you'll tak the low road'. A clear blue sky that made the dear old loch as blue as an Italian lake. Wooded sides ran up into barer hills. It is the Trossachs—the magic country of the Lady of the Lake. It was not for nothing that I wearily learned the Lady of the Lake at school. Little camps are everywhere. I got off at Rowardennan to walk with the hikers towards Ben Lomond. How I longed for a kilt to waggle behind. Picked handfuls of purple heather. Then we boiled the billy and drank innumerable cups of tea. Had haggis for dinner—one can buy them in all shapes and sizes. I like it—yes I definitely like it, but a little goes a long way. To put it colloquially it is 'filling'. Haggi (after all what is the plural of haggis?) are made of chopped lungs, heart and liver of sheep mixed with suet and oatmeal and seasoned with onions, pepper, salt etc. The mixture is packed into a sheep's stomach bag and boiled. And as sheep have varying sizes of stomachs so there are consequently varying sizes of haggis.

Played rummy but not brilliantly. I was still thinking of Rob Roy and the squirrel in the park at Ballock who peered down on me from the trees.

9 August 1939

Another big day seeing Glasgow with Mrs S. We did 40 miles of 'tramming' for 1/0. A good lining of porridge in the morning with just a wee bittie salt—no sugar, and some good haddock. Firstly King's Park, and the flowers! Everywhere there is colour. Scotland gets all its flowers at once. Whoever heard in N.Z. of stocks and chrysanthemums blooming together. In the more mild climates the show of flowers is spread out over the year but here they come all at once. There were flowers in the East flamboyant and startlingly bright, but they were foreigners, these are our own flowers, and growing just like they do on the seed packets!

I had to be dragged away from a flaming garden of orange and red antirr—(hang it all, snapdragons) to ride through Paisley, where the thread comes from, and Renfrew to the banks of the old Clyde. The Clyde—the Mother of ships. Those same ships, that bring home their strange cargoes up old Father Thames, are cradled in their babyhood on the bosom of old mother Clyde. Her youngest—the pride of her eye—is just about ready to leave the family nest. She is the Queen Elizabeth[16]. Is it that I have seen so much that she doesn't look so huge, and yet she is a great bulk. She is like nothing so much as a huge block of buildings afloat. Everywhere there are ships, some being built, some being repaired, and others it would seem just come home to die. Saw too those sturdy if not beautiful things called hoppers that carry away the mud from the dredges. There is a strong smell of the sea. Across the ferry for a ha'penny and tram to Glasgow.

Then to the slums. There are still slums in Glasgow in spite of the vigorous slum clearance schemes. Why didn't people wake up 50 years ago to the vital necessity of this work and maybe now we would have people housed as human beings. The women are in shawls with always a baby on their hip. Almost children themselves, many of these women, and always sitting on the kerbing and, fighting on the pavement, are babies and more babies. Up through an entry, dusty and dirty with bits of greasy paper floating about, into a little yard, the biggest part of which is taken up by the ash-hole. Tall black walls transform the place into a dungeon. From the windows above blowsy, frowsy women hang unkempt, but all with their lipstick on! There is an occasional window box where some poor soul tries to look up instead of down on the mess below. One puts up a silent prayer for the hastening of the building schemes. There seem to be more slums than in London, but then England rules. Scotland still hungers comparatively silently for Home Rule. A big notice is chalked on the church 'No money no religion'. One wonders how John Knox would have reacted to that! But Glasgow does not pander to tourists—when it is shutting up time they shut. The statue of John Knox stands formidable and grim—I don't like John Knox.

Back past a man entertaining queues at theatres, tap dancing and fooling for a few coppers. He is thin and red about the nose. I am 'not amused'. I feel vaguely uneasy. These things should not be.

Home to a good dinner.

10 August 1939

Into town early complete with lunch. Finnan haddocks for breakfast to fortify me for the Ayr country. It is strange how Scotland is segregated into various 'countries'. 'The Scott country', 'The Burns country', 'The Rob Roy country' but I was a stranger in the Burns country. I know him not as I know my Scott. It is a lovely country that one passes through, friendly with so many whitewashed biggins and little shy girls and aggressive small boys.   We stopped at Kilmarnock first. An elderly woman, who I feel sure would belong to a Mothers' Union, mournfully shook her head in its indefinable black straw hat and murmured 'poor wee laddie'. I nodded assent though I don't know why. It is the spirit of Burns and his writing I get here. I am no Scot to find the rhythm in 'Is there, for honest poverty/ that hings his head, and a' that/ The coward slave we pass him by/ We dare be poor for a' that'. And besides I don't agree with Burns. I'd hate to be poor. I hate even the small degree of poorness into which my lot has been cast. Not because I want wealth and position or power but poverty means daily drudgery (not hard work, that is different), drudgery that keeps one in the same place year after year, tied by necessity to a thousand pettifogging miserable money-saving devices so that one may in a brief flash enjoy some of the most minor of the good things of the world. But wealth properly controlled can bring freedom to roam the world. A man may do it in poverty if he has a tremendous courage or a desperation but the world is against a woman for things like that. A man is a slave if he is poor in spite of what Burns says—a slave to small mean things—and we all know it otherwise why do any of us with any 'guts' at all fight so desperately against poverty?

Burns cottage stands beside the road at Alloway. There is a special building, incongruously modern, that houses many of his relics—part of the original manuscript of 'Tam o' Shanter', the big family Bible and a bit of glass on which he has written with a diamond. I found myself wondering if in the event of my own unlikely sudden rise to fame all my little bits and pieces would be suddenly gathered together and exhibited. Made a mental note to destroy most of them when I got home. Sighted a big spreading building near the cottage and enquired diligently what it was. A morose Scot turned bushy eyebrows on me. 'It's where all Englishmen ought to be Missie' was all he said. I learned it was an asylum.

At night to the pictures to see 'So This Is London', a good laugh. Haggis for supper and dreamt vividly that I went to John O' Groats when I should have been at Land's End.

11 August 1939

Washed my hair and just lazed in the sun—wrote letters and prepared for my Scottish tour by taking things vaguely out of my case and putting them back in again. Finally selected the minimum of things needed for a nomadic, carefree life I was about to begin and stuffed them into a haversack. Went for a walk with Mr. S. round the braes. Yellow stooks of hay and a cropping machine cutting its mathematical way amongst the corn. A peaceful, rustic scene, and rising straight behind, blocks of tenement houses. Glasgow is like that. In the distance Glasgow chimneys and her slums and behind us the bonnie banks and braes.

12 August 1939

All bustle today, the initiation has ended and I'm Scottish. Goodbye to Mr and Mrs. S. Off to Stirling Castle and the spirit of Mary, Queen of Scots. I dreamed of the murdered Douglas then heard a raucous voice of a Sergeant Major at raw recruits in tartan trousers! This was no sixteenth century! I came to earth suddenly to find myself in a narrow stone passage at the head of an impatient company of braw young Scottish soldiers. I had perforce to march at their head until I escaped thankfully into a side passage only to pull up suddenly at a door marked 'Soldiers' latrines'. Fled from there and gave up dreaming of the past with the present so vital. A crowd of tourists taking photographs of the troops in the courtyard drilling. One particularly, right in the front, looked like a German. He can take that photograph home if he likes. Is Scotland preparing for war? I'll say she is.

It is a strange thing that all Scottish castles are whole and in good preservation and all English ones in ruins. Felt I could safely slip back into the past again and found the room where Douglas was murdered by James the Second. Just imagined it beautifully and gazing at the famous stained glass window when a voice says behind 'This is where they done it Gladys, the dirty dogs!'

To Dunblane and a local inhabitant shows me the Cathedral. It is rather a lovely 13th century cathedral with two beautiful wooden tombs. I wonder how John Knox tolerated this beauty without doing something about it. But there it is still. I look longingly at the path by the river again but the Youth Hostel is a mile up the road. It is such a jolly Youth Hostel, full of Scotch lads and lassies who definitely don't want to go to bed. We sit with mouth organs, toast and tea till twelve singing 'Roaming in the Gloaming'. There are dances too, Highland Flings and sword dances with a couple of pokers for swords. They're singing even as I write this 'Should a body greet a body coming through the rye'—Do I like Scotland? Och aye!

13 August 1939

The hostel at Dunblane is a model hostel of green corrugated iron. The roof of the dormitory is all glass. No meals are served cooked in the Scotch hostels as in the English, everyone must cook one's own. So breakfast—a huge plate of porridge with two Scots girls and then awa' to walk to Doune. Going well when I'm offered lift (my conscience lodged no objection so I took it). There is mystery in the early morning mist in Scotland and the sun when it shines seems brighter after it. I watched it lift over Doune Castle. The world was moist, tender and expectant. It was still only 7 a.m. The old caretaker at the cottage blinked uncertainly. It was early, could I go over the Castle by myself?

I know my heart missed a beat, several beats as I followed the long path up to the massive door. The Castle was mine, all mine. The caretaker had given me the key. It took all my strength to turn it. The door groans open and then clangs behind me. Decide to explore the dungeons first. It is pitch dark and there is a peculiar cooing, shuffling noise. Summoned up courage to carry on and discovered nothing more fearsome than an old bicycle! I opened a little door leading to the castle proper. I sit in the little wall alcoves and gaze down through the narrow slits in the massive walls. It is one of the loveliest sights in the world. Returned the key and on the road again. Caught up with Hector, Jock, Flora and Mary from the youth hostel. It is a pretty road from Doune to Callander. The boys sometimes sleep out and carry all their pots and pans. They clink and clang like tinkers as we walk.

Callander is a bright little town, obviously an entrance to the Trossachs, that loveliest of all Scotland, the softest and greenest. Sometimes we are silent, especially Flora and I. She enjoyed things silently like I did. The trees—surely they are not already turning colour for Autumn when it is but August, but they are. Perhaps it is rather the ripeness of summer—a maturity rather than a decay. It was late when we got back to the hostel. I crept out again while the others slept to listen to the stillness of the Trossachs. There was a noise behind me and Flora stood there shivering slightly in a raincoat over an absurd nightdress of celanese and lace. 'What are you doing?' she whispered. 'Just looking' I said, and with our arms round each other's waists we just continued to look.

14 August 1939

We have roamed again this morning. We swam in the Loch, and the Loch is not warm. It's a nine mile walk to Strathayre along the side of the lovely Loch Lubnaig. Hector and Jock turn apologetically into the pub and Flora and I find a teashop. Announce my intention of taking the train to Crainlarich. I'd better be getting on a bit. Just about to board the train when Hector races up the platform. The train goes sailing out while we learn that the boys have got a lift and got their benefactor to take us all. The benefactor hovers in the background then comes forward and introduces himself as Ed. B. He's a solicitor from the South of England and touring alone. He is not only 'alone' but lonely. Would we join him—all of us? I repeated doubtfully 'All of us— we'll fill the car you know' but he only laughed. The Gods having sent Ed, we piled our haversacks into the car and ourselves on top of them and away. We little knew how much we were to see of that little maroon Morris. The four of us did rather seem to take possession of it. We had dinner by the side of the road. The boys have a spot of difficulty with the fire, over which we will draw a kindly veil, but we bless Ed and it was lots of fun.

It was sunset when we came to Glencoe—came to high cragged peaks and the yellow glow of a vanquished sun on scalloped hills. The spirit of the McDonalds and the Campbells were there and Jock was a McDonald. His eyes never left those wild hills 'This is the land of my forefathers' he exclaimed digging Ed in the back. 'I know old chap, but for heaven's sake sit down'. But sit down was more than Jock could do. His red hair stood on end. His nose sniffed the air. Heaven help a Campbell who might come along at that minute. 'Hector listen this is where the skunks did them in, right here'. We stopped the car and Jock got out. He planted his feet firmly on the soil of his forefathers and announced his intention of camping there for the night. And so we left them, Hector, who was not a McDonald, grumbling mightily and Jock staring at those giant crags. Ed to a hotel and Flora and I to the Glencoe hostel, a fine one, to laugh over the memory of Jock. We crept into our bunks, one above the other. I was just dozing off when a head was lowered over the side of the top bunk. It was Flora. 'I hate the Campbells, don't you' she said. I nodded and muttered 'Uh, uh'—and what is more at that moment I really did!

15 August 1939

Met Ed as arranged and explored the actual scene of the massacre. Jock definitely subdued and slightly apologetic. He didn't know what had come over him last night but I assured him that he was no true McDonald if he could view Glencoe without emotion. We drive slowly to Ballachulish and then along the loch side to Fort William. We were just in time at Fort William to get into the little West Highland Museum. It was here we saw the 'secret' portrait of Prince Charlie. And then Flora got the giggles. It was all over Prince Charlie's breeches. They were of Stuart tartan and must assuredly have fitted very very tightly. They looked so absurd she said standing there. She had never thought of Prince Charlie's breeches apart from Prince Charlie before!

I've seen some Highland cattle, great shaggy ones like you always see on Scotch postcards. Soon there won't be much that I've heard about that I haven't seen. That'll be the day! Of course there's still the Loch Ness monster.

16 August 1939

Have made several tentative suggestions to Ed that we might be a bit of a bally nuisance cluttering up his car with our haversacks and heather but he always wants us to go on another day, and we always say 'Yes'. We'll be reluctant to break up our five-some now. We've grown comfortably familiar—we can relapse into silence, wander off on our own and have ceased to be just polite. This morning we ventured up Ben Nevis. It is the hardest path on earth. It is cold too. The path zig-zags so we must go three times, nay four times, the distance of the proverbial flying crow. Down in the valley the road becomes a ribbon. All around there are hills menacing. It is hard going, rocky country through which streams abound. We are silent long since—even the little lake near the half way hut fails to bring forth a sound. In the little stone hut we find our breath. It is as well we did so that we might have some to lose, for the view from here is superb. These mountains take so much out of one—not only physically but mentally. It would be easier if one were a genius, for having expressed audibly a thing it is no longer one's master. But I can't express the Highlands and I am forever subdued.

And so to Fort Augustus. The boys plant their little hiking tents and Ed, Flora and I find a little 'bed and breakfast' close by. A quaint little house with an attic room.

17 August 1939

Bacon and egg, toast and marmalade. Do we look that English! and a teeming wet day. Somehow I no longer feel a stranger in Scotland now. We drove up the western side of Loch Ness and never a sign of a monster did we see. Inverness comes gradually heralded by islands and houses. It still teems. We prowl round the shops and have a hilarious lunch of sausage and chips. Another look at the deluge outside and then—whisper it very low—into the pictures. It rains still and we paddle to the car park. A big Scottish policeman pulls us up. 'Ye dinna ken this is a one way street?' We assured him we 'dinna kenned' and pulled out towards Nairn. The windscreen wiper wig-wagged cheerfully and the rain stopped as we pulled up at Culloden Moor. So it was here they fought. On a lovely road from Inverness to Nairn and past a little village called Ardersier—a quaint old grey stone place full of soldiers and their girls. We wonder vaguely why the soldiers in such quantity. We sail unconcernedly through an archway. A soldier steps out smartly. We stopped suddenly purely because he is in the way. He gazes at us and we gaze at him. He says 'What is it ye want?' 'We don't want anything' we return and we all gaze again. It seems it is Fort George we've found and now used for the training of troops. A young officer in a dinner suit gazes at us enviously it would seem from an upper window. A wail of energetically played bagpipes comes from the mess quarters. Half past eight or so is a queer time to come visiting a Fort. The young Scottish soldier in his tartan trousers shows us round. He is only about 19 and going to Shanghai next week. And is he rebellious.

It was late when we left Fort George. Left Ardersier where there were girls in khaki uniforms too. Past a Temperance hotel at Ardersier, and hovered, but a look in at the window revealed a stuffed hawk with a kindly but bleary eye, and an aspidistra, so we went on again. We ran into Nairn and into Mrs. M's cottage, a dream of a cottage complete with hollyhocks, a fire, a hot water bottle in one's bed and fish for breakfast.

18 August 1939

Up all of us really early—a perfect morning. Walked into Nairn before breakfast, a good clean town where the shops get an early start. Lazed on the beach all morning and watched the tide. It is good clean white sand with little striped bathing sheds dotted about, seaweed and a washed-up octopus. A fine figure in a kilt passes the time of day. So I'm from New Zealand, and am I no afraid to come so far? I'm only a wee lassie, maybe I'd be about twenty-one now (and me thinking I was in Scotland not Ireland!). He strode off his kilt swinging behind. I wished I'd been staying in Nairn. But travellers like us don't stay anywhere. We all sat quietly thinking one thing—the time had come when our little party must break up. Ed was going South, the others West and myself North.

We travelled back to Inverness through Carrbridge and watched a grouse shooting party at work. They arrive at the scene of action in a brown wooden van. We watched through the glasses the beaters at work then the birds in flight, the sudden pop of the gun and the dogs retrieving. Everywhere dotted about are the stone semi-circular shelters from behind which they shoot. But somehow this slaughtering of things even in sport always makes me slightly sick. I saw rather the craggy mountains with the little streams, the black-faced mountain goats and always the purple heather.

At Inverness we parted. It wasn't an easy parting. I must stay the night in Inverness and it seems the whole of the 'Hielands' had congregated there. Not a single room to be found. An Irish woman, a delightful soul, told me of all the people she had staying, showed me where they slept, gave me a full and complete list of all who had enquired for rooms that day. Told me how long she'd run a boarding house and how it didn't pay her, and when I finally stopped the flow of words admitted reluctantly she hadn't any room. Finally sought help from the policeman at the car park. A kindly Scotswoman with high cheekbones and huge hands admitted that she had a room for 'the poor wee lassie' and she tucked me up in bed with a hot water bottle and a promise to waken me early in the morning.

19 August 1939

Dragged out of bed in the wee small hours and practically propelled to the train half asleep by the Scotswoman's husband. Blinked myself thoroughly awake in the railway carriage. Surely the face of the man who sat opposite with his wife was familiar. 'Did you get fixed up last night, lassie?' he asked. Surely the fame of our wanderings had not spread through Inverness! And then I remembered he was the policeman at the car park. He still looked like a policeman in spite of his tweeds. He was combining a spot of pleasure with a spot of work at the sports at Lairg's Highland Games. Found I'd taken a ticket to Thurso instead of Wick. Argued with every guard who came through, blamed the Railway Company, the Government, the weather and everything else I could think of, and then suddenly realised that it didn't matter much after all. Realised I'd have to 'pull up my socks' and stand on my own feet. I'd been looked after too much since I entered Scotland. I was SOFT.

A six hour journey to John O'Groats. I'm getting excited again—I can feel it rising. The country up here is so flat compared to the rest of Scotland. There is a big naval base at Invergordon on the Cromarty Firth. Battleships and seaplanes swooping about. And then I remembered—the sounds of war were in the air, I'd forgotten that. They were still rumbling—even as they had rumbled when I was in Italy, only perhaps a little louder. We dropped the jolly Bobbie at Lairg. Along this wild coast they say a shoal of whales were stranded not long ago—surely an incident strong enough to pollute the entire British Isles! On the farms women work with their men throwing the hay up into the carts. Their implements seem primitive especially the scythes in use. The corn falls straight and true after each rhythmic sweep. At Helmsdale we run inland again. The moorlands are all dug into trenches where peat has been extracted. On the hills bracken fights for precedence over the heather. Little whitened or grey cottages appear, some with thatches and all with their peat stack.

I forgot that my ticket was for Thurso and no one worried. The great thing about Wick is that this romantic little town, which the guidebooks say is the seat of the Scottish herring fishery, is 'dry' by a 55 majority vote. The men blame it on the preponderance of women in the town and go grumbling to Thurso for a drink, or maybe there is a little hidden somewhere among the heather!

I go straight into the bus for John O'Groats. Somehow this top of Scotland is so satisfactory. It is just what you would expect the top of Scotland to be like. Scattered little homesteads in flat country—waddling geese, fields dotted with stacks of hay and peat stacks. And a bus driver who said 'O.K. Baby'. There are tourist buses in plenty. It is surprising the number that drive 150 odd miles up and 150 back in a day to satisfy their vanity so that they may say they have set foot in John O'Groats. Perhaps I'm like that too. It was sheer vanity brought me up but sheer fascination made me to stay. Wandering vaguely down a rough road to where the fields ran right on to the sea shore. Rather disconcerted at finding myself on a private farm and apologised to the farmer for trespassing. Well now I was a wee lassie to be on my own. Was I camping? If I wanted somewhere to stay maybe his wife could tell me of some place. 'Dinna ye go to the hotel, lassie' he said 'the folk come up from the South and stay there just the one night and they drink'. So I trotted up by the side of six feet of Scottish brawn to the 'wee bit hoose'. Fowls around the door, a stone floor, the guid wife in her mob cap and the daughter just in from milking the cow. 'Wouldna ye stay here wi' us lassie' she says 'we've a wee bit room upstairs and we'd like to have ye'. So she made me a cup of tea with cream and scones and pikelets and at six appeared six fresh herrings, potatoes and milk. I looked at Father's medals and his war time kilt. He was a Seaforth Highlander. I fed the fire with peat and made the toast for supper. But first down to the beach with Nellie in her kilt and a white silk blouse to count the seven lighthouses, to clamber over rocks and watch the men bringing in the lobster baskets. I did some washing in an enamel basin on an iron stand and filled a stone water bottle with hot water to put in bed. These stone hot water bottles are called 'pigs' here and truly it only needed four little feet and a curly tail to make it revoltingly like one of those little round pink things one sees in dozens round an old sow! The bed was filled with chaff! but very comfortable indeed. I'm tucked up in it now and writing this wretched diary.

19 August 1939

Last night I saw the Aurora Borealis! Now that it is daylight I wonder if I did actually see it or have I dreamt it. For it is just like something one would dream. The whole sky was lighted up with bright luminous beams. There were colours but they were indefinite cold colours, more just flashes of light. They are vaguely disturbing. I don't know how long I stood in my nightdress at the window but I know that I suddenly felt alone—a realisation came that I was here at John O'Groats as far from my home as it was possible to be, looking out on the desolate Pentland Firth with these weird lights dancing in the sky.

But the morning came and Mrs. B. with tea. Mrs. B. was still in her mob-cap. I am not at all sure that she doesn't sleep in it. We take our porridge by the spoonful and dip it in the milk. Every person has two basins—a basin of porridge and a basin of milk. I didn't realise as I took my porridge that I'd be called upon to face bacon and two eggs beside! A perfect day and away with Mr. B. and Nellie to the lighthouse. The fields full of a small heather and a bigger bell heather. The sheep have the funniest faces—long inane ones. I believe they are of the Cheviot breed. At the fences we don't climb, Mr. B.

lifts us over with the greatest of ease and roars a mighty boom as he holds us suspended in the air. Up to the lighthouse—everything so white and clean and shining. Advised to put my notebook away in case they think I'm a German spy. The war's not far away they say.

A belated dinner on return—half a chicken at least, vegetables, scones, cream in my tea and pancakes. And the bill was 5/6. Buy a few souvenirs at the little store. Is there anything that little store doesn't sell? A wee woman comes in—another in a mob-cap and big boots. She buys of all things a tin of Heinz Steak and Kidney pudding! We see the bus coming—I take a hurried departure across a field my haversack bob-bobbing on my back and a bunch of heather and a tin of shells grasped in my hand.

Walked two miles to the hostel in Lairg arriving at an unearthly hour and met Mr Garr from Auckland. We seem to know all the same people, belong to all the same clubs and yet have never met. Swapped experiences till 11.30. Left him the address of my John O'Groats friends and so to bed.

20 August 1939

Up at six and feeling fit. Drank innumerable cups of tea and walked three miles to the station. Inverness again. Did I ever comment on the camping coaches? They are everywhere—railway carriages made into furnished caravans, £3 a week to hold six. The Railway will trail you to a siding wherever you want to go charging ordinary individual rail fares. A crowded train to Aberdeen and the very first thing I see is Woodside and Tinkertown where the gypsies live. They are a queer collection of caravans with lines of washing, puffs of smoke from the tin chimneys on the caravans and the most delightful collections of little urchins in the oddest collection of clothes I have ever seen. Ask a swarthy woman with great gold ear-rings if I can take their photographs. She is a pleasant soul and promptly rakes in all the mothers. They grab their respective, wildly protesting offspring and scrub them clean, dumping them in a prim unhappy looking row by one of the vans. I took the photograph but the charm of the picture had gone.

But I had made some friends. Would I like to see inside a caravan? Sure I did. It was clean but definitely muddly. There were bunks in such odd places and even then there seemed a lot more people than beds. There was a bright little dresser and gay covers. I had a cup of tea with these women. We sat on the grass and waited for the kettle to boil over an oil stove. Strangely enough I didn't tell them who I was. They knew I was travelling Scotland and no doubt thought I came from the south of England. And then the men started coming home. Their chief occupation seemed to be mending chairs. They shook hands heartily. Wouldn't I like to stop for dinner? The pot was already boiling. And sure enough it was—a big black pot swung on a tripod over a fire. We had a kind of stew—once or twice I thought that black eyes twinkled more than usual under bushy brows as I praised it. And then they asked me if I knew what it was? It was rabbit maybe or poultry and yet not quite like either. It was hedgehog! A real gypsy dish. I gave a weak little 'Oh!' I have expected to regret eating it but I didn't and I confess to having a second helping. It was definitely nice.

We sat on the grass for a long time. Out of one of the caravans came Grandmother Gypsy. Maybe she was Great Grandmother, she was so brown and wrinkled. Her long ear-rings dangled against her withered skin. She looked at me with piercing black eyes and my presence was explained. 'Sit down' she commanded. I sat fascinated at her feet. 'I will tell your fortune' she said. The women gathered round 'You're lucky' they whispered, 'it isn't often...' One woman went into a caravan and returned with an object wrapped in black velvet. The old woman took it in her hands, unwrapped it and revealed a crystal. She sat with it in her lap gazing at me and then into its unfathomable depths. Even the children were quiet then. 'Lassie' she said 'you have some of the tan in you too'. I felt my heart miss a beat. How did she know? I had only just found out myself. 'You've more in you than you think. And you're not always very happy because of it. You're what we call a blue-eyed gypsy. You're only really happy when you're moving on. When you stay in one place you're restless. I can feel it here. . .' She put her hand to her throat. I could only gaze fascinated. How well I knew that feeling. She nodded 'I know—I know it's the strain that will not die. You'll know no rest all your life because of it, but it can't be helped you must just go on'. 'You don't belong here', she looked at me suddenly and there was a stir through the company. 'You belong . . .', she paused and her hand waved hesitantly in the air, 'As far away from here as it is possible to get. Away to the other end of the earth'. And most assuredly I did. She paused and we waited. Then with a sudden almost impatient gesture she wrapped up her crystal. 'That is all, I can tell you no more. There are clouds gathering... It's not you, lassie' she said. 'It's not your fortune it's something else crowding in..' I thanked her. I would have crossed her palm with the biggest piece of silver in British currency but she shook her head. So I dug up my threepences and pennies and gave them to the kiddies. I thanked them and left them waving by their caravans.

A sudden impulse made me get on the bus for Ballater. I felt more like a Youth Hostel than a hotel. I met Jim. W. with his haversack and both of us bound for the hostel. And henceforward we saw things together and it was little we missed between us. We had a good night at the hostel. Shot off to bed about twelve with the warden in the middle of an argument on Scottish Home Rule. Strange how this keeps cropping up. I really believe they're serious.

21 August 1939

Up bright but not early. Jim just as bright but later still. Made our tea jointly left it to draw and someone else drank it in mistake for theirs. I had no bread and Jim no butter so we pooled our resources. Westwards then further along the Dee Valley. We watched fishermen up to their thighs in the stream wielding great salmon rods. We met the village postman toiling up the hill to Balmoral Castle. The flag is flying, the Royal Family is in residence. The king they say is out grouse shooting. I do not envy him. I envy no man just now. We walk on to Crathie. It is a dear little church and simple. Even Jim in his shorts and myself in my waterproof hat (the only thing I have to cover my 'crowning glory') seem welcome. Call for a cup of tea but the local store doesn't cater for 'hikers', in fact they look slightly disapproving—perhaps we better pretend to be cousins. In Braemar we took bed and breakfast at an old English cottage. We had two little rooms with rosebuds curtains and two little Scottish ladies to fuss round us. Braemar was their world, the Queen and the King their Gods. The clans are collecting already for the Highland Games. At night the pipes rang over the hills. There were kilts in the streets and magnificent sporrans. There were preliminary practices of dancing and tossing the caber. Found to my amazement that the caber is as huge as a telegraph pole—there are few Scots today who can toss it as it should be tossed.

22 August 1939

We parted reluctantly at the crossroads, Jim to Aviemore and myself back to Aberdeen. The local paper shows disturbing headlines but we just don't look. There are funny little streets in Aberdeen such as Nether Kirkgate. It is narrow and cobbled and on one corner is found the Wallace Tower. Went out to the fish market—not quite such a bustle as early morning but still fascinating with small weather-scarred trawlers in and boxes and boxes of fish. The men wear their sack aprons split at the bottom and tied round their legs—their hands are big and red—it is not an enviable job. On a sudden impulse get on a full train to Arbroath. It is a crowded train. Rather wondered when I got into a little compartment and sank gratefully into a seat. Suddenly realised that the compartment contained a newly married couple complete with confetti, so got up wearily. There are audible sighs of relief as I depart. I thought of lots of things on that journey. I thought of all the bags of sand at John O'Groats all ready to be carted away for A.R.P.[17] work in the cities. Everywhere they expect the war and fear it. Even at the furthest point where the tides meet in an agitated ripple. Just like the world today. It was raining hard in Arbroath and sure enough all the hotels were full. Wandered around, poked into a few back streets and spotted the Y.M.C.A. Got a little cubicle room for 3/-.

23 August 1939

Breakfast starts with long prayers, very long prayers. Almost I could have wished to eat my egg and say my prayers afterwards, for prayers do not go cold with waiting. Peggy (who I met at the Y.M.C.A.) and I walked as far as Auchmithie—a quaint fishing village on the edge of the cliffs. An old 'salt' (what the Yorkshire folk would call a 'real 'un') smokes his pipe and it is a strong one. He has a peaked cap and the smell of his daily toil clings to his jersey which buttons up the side. Seabirds swoop and scream among the rocks and beyond the horizon, faint but clear, is the Inchcape Rock lighthouse. Groups of fishermen sit and talk about fish and about the war. It is coming and soon—but no one knows just when.

Peggy says I can come home with her to Kirriemuir. Our route lay through farmlands, hay in stooks, busy men and busy women. All the talk of harvest— Germany had a bad harvest, they say there will be no war. Peggy's father it appears has a brother in Wellington or thereabouts. We talked and talked until at nine o'clock they announced I'd just have to stay and sleep with Peggy. We slept in a big double bed with a fire in the room.

24 August 1939

It's morning at White Gates and Mr. P. makes the porridge—Scotch porridge with lots of milk. Had it all ready for me and just dying for me to get up. It was on the table and I just had to eat it before even a drink of tea or water. And what's more I ate it and enjoyed it. Learnt what 'Gulls' were—thick porridge, so thick that when it is cold it can be cut into slabs. Mr. P. keeps bees. Looked at and admired these with a net over my head. Swarms of them it seemed came and buzzed round us making a sizzling sound and looking extremely vicious at being disturbed. Peggy's 'boyfriend', Don, comes round and we go fishing. But oh! the beauty of Kirriemuir sheltering in the foothills of the Grampians. Its old name is Thrums. Few people now know the meaning of Thrums. They were the loose threads used to catch up broken threads in hand loom weaving. For in the days about which J. M. Barrie wrote, the hand looms clacked in every house. The houses are so quaint, many with their backs to the street as if they would rebuke curious sight-seers before the start. There are lovely views around Kirriemuir. Climbed the Hill—I saw it on a rare day when it is not obscured by smoke, for the hand looms have given way to power looms and factories with their smoke and muffled roar. From the top Glen Clova lies broad, deep and bare.

Don goes fishing and Peggy and I walk on to the moors—on to purple hills to lie in the heather and scramble down to a little stream. It is so fragrant and clean. We talk, dream, sleep and munch toffees, and take photographs and gaze at the sky. It would be so easy to get lost, so easy to slip over one of those rocks—we realise suddenly that clouds are coming up. The hills are suddenly lowering, hiding their heads in a thick cloud of mist. It seems to follow us as we race down into the Glen. We take a bit more time to eat wild raspberries and tease Don because the fish just wouldn't bite. At home Mr. P. has let the fire out. There's water to pump and we all turn to. That's one of the joys of living in a romantic-looking cottage. Sit round the bright fire at last having eggs and bacon and a wee drappie[18] of something Scotch in our tea. We talk and laugh and look at snaps. Outside the trains thunder past—inside it grows hotter. Later the two of us creep into bed at last and whisper far into the morning.

25 August 1939

I'd have given the world to stay in Kirriemuir or perhaps being a traveller that's the only thing I wouldn't give. Being a traveller I must travel. So with peas in my haversack from the garden, some honey and potatoes for my next meal I set out for Glamis. There are grand old trees and herds of cattle here. I had to struggle to be interested in Dundee after Glamis and Kirriemuir but Dundee has to be 'found', the veil of smoke has to be lifted first. It is Dundee's people that I remember. Little old women, such a lot of little old women, sitting round the church. Hair scraped back and huddled into their shawls. One old woman (but was she so old after all?), her face furrowed and grimed, her hair wispy, answered my query as to the whereabouts of the caretaker to show me up the church steeple. 'Wait here, lassie' she said 'I'll fetch him' and she ran—not walked—round the church looking for him, returning with him in tow. 'There you are' she said triumphantly and trotted off before I could say a word. I felt horribly guilty. Somehow if I lived in Dundee I'd always feel guilty about something. Had a good look round the shops. Things quite expensive and all Autumn goods on show now. Good Scotch tweeds, I liked them but my increasingly sturdy figure would not look too well in Scotch tweeds.

I looked across at St Andrews—the famous golf course by the sea. It isn't by any means a spectacular course. It gives one the appearance of being almost casual. It looks so easy but I am assured it isn't. Those queer little sand dunes give a lot of trouble. An interesting little booklet says 'It is very seldom that the Old Course can be played on two successive days in the same direction'. It would appear that by Act of Parliament ratepayers and members of their family resident in St Andrews enjoy the privilege of free golf over the Course. I wouldn't have dared to desecrate its sacred turf. I was content with the Eden course, and so excited I could hardly hit a ball. The golf house looks just like the pictures we always see and everywhere plus fours, golf clubs and golf talk. Chummed up with a little Austrian girl who thinks she'd better get home because the war is coming. Always this threat of war.

26 August 1939

Dead tired—think I did too much yesterday but Perth is a restful place. It must be pretty in Spring when the lilac trees are blooming. Walked round the river and saw a notice. It is a bright spot in Perth's matter of fact life. 'It is near here' it reads 'that Charles 1 watched the Morris Dance by thirteen members of the Glovers' Corporation from a floating stage of timber'. Somehow I had a ludicrous vision of Aldermen in knee breeches in varying stages of obesity prancing and footing it lightly—and broke into an uncontrollable grin. A young woman with a baby looks at me enquiringly. 'You're a stranger to Perth' she said. Only she pronounced it Pairth. I admitted I was and pointed out the humour of the memorial plate. But she saw no humour in it and merely shook her head. 'I come here nearly every day' she said 'and I've never noticed that before'.

I took the train to Edinburgh and crossed the Forth Bridge. I always want to do bridges again and again. It is a bonny bridge—one end of it almost disappearing into the misty distance. Our train seemed to be suspended in mid-air the water was so far below.

27 August 1939

The Youth Hostel at Edinburgh is well out of town but I had no trouble in finding it last night. I've shaken off the fatal complacency of Kirriemuir, it seems today not that I am 'finishing Scotland' but that I am beginning Edinburgh. I walked along Princes Street in the very early morning when the mist still hung in the air. Is there anything more beautiful than the fairy mistiness of the Castle seen across the Princes Street Gardens? One would think it was a mirage seen across the valley. The noise of trams, the glitter of shops in a great city and rising in its very midst a rugged memory of Scotland's dark brave days. I made my way up to the Castle as early as I could. There were others already there. A child waited with her father at the ticket office. 'Daddy who built the Castle?' 'Daddy why did he build it?' Daddy what's it built of?' ' Daddy will it ever fall down?' I took my tickets with a prayer of thankfulness that I didn't have to do sightseeing complete with offspring. All over the Castle and lastly the dear little St Margaret's Chapel. It is here that the Scottish soldiers can be married. A tiny exquisite little place holding about sixteen people. It makes me remember that little church of Maria Della Spina in Pisa—it is a long, long time ago now.

It is a long way down the Royal Mile—every speck of it redolent with history and a peculiar smell that has nothing whatever to do with history. The Royal Mile knows its tourist. One is surrounded immediately by little urchins with a monotonous tale of 'This is Lady Stair's house and it's got writing above the doors. I'll show it to you—give me sixpence lady', all in one breath. The littlest ones are learning but they learn the most important part first. They hold out hot sticky little hands and lisp 'sixpence lady sixpence'. The smell one can cope with but the rapidly increasing urchins drive one out reluctantly but hastily. It is said that St Giles Cathedral, with its many memorials, is the Scottish Westminster Abbey. It is strange how Edinburgh and London are akin. They are the elder sisters of a noble family that include Exeter, York and maybe some others that I have not seen. It is as full of history as London, and as lovable.

Called to see Mrs McSwain at St Peter's Place. Rather nice suburban homes out that way. Her daughter in the Royal Infirmary with appendicitis. Had a good talk about Auntie Leslie near whom she used to live in Dunedin. Her boy is at sea. More war talk—rather disturbing. Somehow one feels that it is near. Picked up letters at the Post Office—about two dozen. No wonder the man asked me who I was to have such a big fan-mail. Home to the Youth Hostel to read them until far into the night.

28 August 1939

Up very early with a mind full of things to do. Past the Castle again to smell the smells of yesterday morning slightly intensified. Bought more 6*d* admission tickets at the Palace of Holyroodhouse (have spent more money for admission tickets in Edinburgh than anywhere else). History starts immediately. In a way it is a shame that the most violent pieces of history should be laid before us first. There is an old doorway between the Chapel and the Quadrangle. It is through this doorway that the murderers were supposed to have gained admittance to the apartments above where Rizzio dallied with the Queen. The passage itself covers the last resting place of poor Rizzio.

I left Edinburgh reluctantly but feel rather as if I had done a great work. I had collected and duly classified so many memories. I caught a train presumably for Carlisle, for the Roman Wall that I hadn't seen still haunted me, and then got off in a hurry at Galashiels. To get to Abbotsford, Scott's home, I need to take the Ferry. It is a goodish walk to the Ferry and there, at a little cottage, I enquired about crossing. A dour man with bushy brows came out. Without the ghost of a smile or a change of expression he said 'It's 2*d* per person per

1 James and Elizabeth Turner were Gwennie's maternal grandparents and she was fascinated by them. James was a coal miner all his working life and Gwennie believed that Elizabeth had gypsy blood. Gwennie caught herself staring at their old home in Netherfield Lane, Parkgate when she came to England.

2 George and Susanna Peacock (née Turner) were Gwennie's parents and they lived in Auckland, New Zealand. Gwennie often referred to Susanna as 'little mother' and she was still living at home at the time she began her round-the-world trip.

3 SS *Orcades*, the ship that carried Gwennie and her Auntie Molly from Australia to Villefranche in Southern France in 1939. *Orcades* was a Royal Mail Ship and was sunk by a German submarine off the Cape of Good Hope in 1942. Gwennie took very readily to life on 'the ocean waves'.

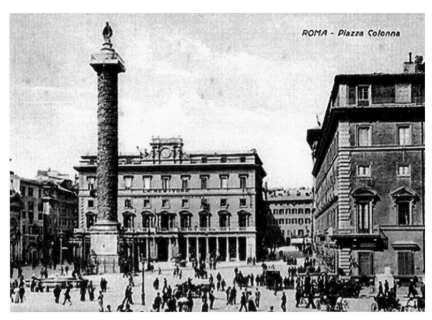

4 The Piazza Colonnia in Rome. Gwennie visited Rome soon after setting off on her own having left the Orcades. She loved Rome but was less impressed by Benito Mussolini whom she heard haranguing a crowd not far from here. She was also present at a Holy Week service led by the Pope in St Peter's Basilica.

5 A view of gondolas on one of the canals in Venice. She was so excited about being in Venice that she typed, 'I give little squeals of delight every time I look out the window at the Grand Canal'.

6 Gwennie with Auntie Bella, Uncle Dick Roe and a neighbour at their home in Rawmarsh, South Yorkshire. Gwennie stayed with Bella and Dick for some of her time in Rawmarsh. (Isa)Bella was a sister of Gwennie's mother, Susanna. Gwennie met Bella when she arrived initially at Rotherham railway station and then Dick at home when he arrived from work in his 'pit muck'.

7 Gwennie with her Auntie Lizzie outside her home in Park Street, Rawmarsh. She could not get over how similar Lizzie looked to her mother in New Zealand. The dog is presumably the one who had a fit on her arrival such was the excitement of Gwennie's first night 'at home'.

8 Malcolm Brown, Gwennie's cousin and one of her constant companions while staying in Rawmarsh. Gwennie was with Malcolm when the unfortunate incident with the Air Raid Warden in the black-out occurred.

9 Gwennie with her cousin Annie. This must be soon after the 15 January 1940 as the snow is thick on the ground. Gwennie is wearing her beloved fur coat and suddenly seems a much more confident and extrovert person. She had never seen it snow in New Zealand and was ecstatic when it fell in Rawmarsh. All the neighbours seem to have been excited for her as well.

10 Uncle Albert Brown with his grand-daughter Marion at his allotment in Rawmarsh. Albert was teased by Gwennie and the rest of the family that going to the allotment was just an excuse 'to go t'pub'!

11 Schonhut's butcher's shop on the main road through Parkgate. Gwennie knew this shop well before she ever left New Zealand. Her mother, Susanna, had obviously told her many times of the famous Schonhut's pork pies and sausages. Susanna often spoke of her visits as a child to the shop from her home in Netherfield Lane. The window display is like a 'meaty' work of art!

12 Mr Leonard Schonhut, proprietor of the famous shop was described by Gwennie rather irreverently as 'clean and pink like one of his own sausages'. He had recently visited the Continent and was keen to talk about this with Gwennie. She was less keen as the conversation was held in a refrigerator!

13 Broad Street, Parkgate, the main shopping area close to where Gwennie stayed in Rawmarsh. Schonhut's butcher's shop was on the right hand side of the road here and further down on the left was the Traveller's Inn where Gwennie was delighted to see the place where her grandfather James 'reckoned' the wages of his team from Aldwarke pit.

14 The Rockingham Pottery kiln at Swinton that Gwennie visited on one of her numerous perambulations around the countryside near Rawmarsh. She was surprised how often people went out for a walk in England with no particular destination or purpose in mind.

Left: 15 Gwennie in her 'pit muck' on the 25 January 1940. She begins that day's diary entry with, 'This is the greatest day since I left home . . . for today I followed in the footsteps of Granddad Turner and went down the mine'. She was smuggled down Aldwarke pit and spent a whole shift below ground, going right up to the coalface. Her description of the working conditions makes for an engrossing read.

Bottom: 16 Aldwarke Mine pit-top close to the twin settlements of Parkgate and Rawmarsh. Many of Gwennie's relatives in the area worked either in the local coal mines or the huge steelworks in Parkgate.

17 The Congregational Chapel in Greasbrough which Gwennie visited on her trip. Greasbrough is a neighbouring village to Rawmarsh and Susanna, Gwennie's mother, used to attend services here when she was young and sing in the choir. Gwennie met up with several people from this Chapel who knew her mother well before she emigrated to New Zealand.

18 The Chemical Works at Mangham near Parkgate. With her positive outlook Gwennie found beauty in the most unlikely places. She even enthuses about the night sky over Parkgate lit up red by the glow from the 'chemics'.

19 Auntie Lizzie with her dogs. Gwennie was struck by how closely Auntie Lizzie resembled her mother. Before Gwennie arrived Lizzie did not travel very far from her home at all but this was to change with Gwennie's prompting.

20 The parish church of St Mary's at the top of Rawmarsh Hill. On Boxing Day 1939 Gwennie was bridesmaid at the wedding of her cousin Elsie to Frank. At the crucial moment of the ceremony she wondered if her stocking seams were straight.

21 The two volumes of Gwennie's diary as delivered to Malcolm and Noreen Brown's bungalow in 2003. The open page shows a tracing of the key Gwennie used to open Doune Castle near Dunblane in Scotland.

How it rains, but to be perfectly fair

e train with haversack and golf coat
g on a great Adventure. Away through
that I've ever read about - green luscious
ttercups, roadsides blue with bluebells,
s and lazy streams winding round trailing
.

ss, and almost right across an ever winden-
duck. I saw that before on a quiet Lake

There are Surrey homes set in large gard
et. There are laburnums like a shower of
o. Sticking out of my haversack is a
from Fontainbleau - it is so real still.
o]

Off the train spontar   a dear little town
half way to Southsea. A b;   can see, but still
lovely, with old English   an emigrant at the
station, a poor little gi   f and a group of
not very understanding Ha   make her understand
that Mrs. Patterson could   tation but she was
to take the bus and they'

Told her all about i   ome than I have done
since I left Europe. S   hree days having
come from Budepest, and n   did she know.
Thought hard things of Mr   dn't get herself or
anyone else to the statio   l waved pathetically to me as I went up i   re of the town.

Found a little place
garden. Such a pretty pla
a shelf, a hot water bott
terryfied of it falling o

13/5/39: I'm the luckiest girl in the wor
thanks to the Maharajah of Baroda!   This dist
who owns Tennyson's home has allowed it to be o
for one day only, and this is the day! Aldwort
Tennyson composed so many of this poems. Where
Idylls of the King.   The ground it is said was
in 1867 because of its quietness, and the house
by one John Knowles. .

So I walked through the quaint little town
homes set amongst English trees, gardens bright
and forgetmenots, and harbouring placid content
about. Walked up Tennyson's Lane where he wand

22 Drawings of the three different versions of the 'Chaperone'. These drawings appear in
the diary occasionally to represent the extent to which Gwennie was embarrassed by her
behaviour on a particular day. They seem to relate to the nature of her relationships with
some of the men she met on her travels.

23 The impressive east front of Wentworth Woodhouse near Rotherham. This 'big house of 365 windows' struck Gwennie as looking rather lonely and she was amazed that anyone could walk right past the front door without passing a 'Trepassers Will Be Prosecuted' sign.

24 The keep of Conisbrough Castle only a few miles from Rawmarsh. Gwennie liked this castle more than any other because it was not a 'tidy' ruin. She knew of its literary links with Sir Walter Scott and the story of Ivanhoe.

Left: 25 The chapel set into the walls of Conisbrough's keep. Gwennie was thrilled to be at the exact spot where the 'noble Edith, mother of Athelstan, prayed during the burial of her son' in the Ivanhoe story. She also investigated the keep's 'bathrooms' i.e. toilets!

Bottom: 26 A view of Whitby Abbey on the Yorkshire coast, high above the town. She knew this view so well for she had grown up with a picture of it hanging in her New Zealand home. She looked at it from every angle to imprint it on her mind.

27 The skyscrapers of central New York. Gwennie paid her dollar to ascend 'almost to heaven' to the top of the Empire State Building. She thought, 'perhaps the Tower of Babel was not a myth after all'.

28 Coney Island close to New York City. Mitzi whisked Gwennie here almost before she had arrived at the Y.W. It was here Gwennie first suspiciously sampled sausage and syrup together and decided it was really 'quite good'.

29 Gwennie with her friend Anne Anstead in New Zealand about 1990. As far as is known Gwennie never left New Zealand after returning from her world tour. She married Tom Vivian in 1947 but was a widow for over thirty years of her life.

30 Gwennie with her cousin John Turner in Auckland in 2002. John and his wife, Betty, travelled out to New Zealand from Rawmarsh in 2002 to meet Gwennie. John was a young boy when Gwennie visited Rawmarsh and can remember the excitement of her arrival at Rotherham station.

trip'. Always ready to help along a joke I returned 'Or per part of per trip' but to him 'our Albert[19]' was evidently unknown. He frowned slightly and only repeated irritably '2d per person per trip'. So I stifled a rising giggle and paid 2d. True to the tale the river was so shallow I could have walked across.

Met a woman taking tea to her farmer husband so we sat on the grass. They shared my buns while I drank their tea. The farmer said I was a reight bonny lassie and wasn't New Zealand somewhere in India or was it Africa? We had blacks didn't we? I explained that in Africa there were Zulus and our Maoris weren't 'blacks' they were merely 'browns'. He nodded easily. 'Well they're much the same aren't they? It doesn't matter a great deal away down there'. It is only a mile or two to Abbotsford from the Ferry through farm country clean with the good smell of hay. The first introduction the visitor has to Abbotsford is the wail of the pipes. As one approaches one finds the piper in full regalia strutting up and down outside the gates, and charabancs! And inside are the people out of the charabancs. I have found that people in charabancs are a people unto themselves. Whatever they may be in private life the charabanc moulds them into a certain pattern. They are as far removed from 'hikers' as the Zulus from the cheerful farmer on the road from the Ferry. Of course there are differences in charabancs. There are the Mothers' Union charabancs and the escorted charabancs. It was a woman from one of the latter who was taking a photograph of the house. She had done much manoeuvring climbing on garden seats and trampling on flower beds. Finally I opened my camera and asked her which was the best place to get a photograph from, surely she must know. She lowered her camera, gazed at my haversack as if it was something contaminated, edged away and muttered distantly that she didn't know she was sure.

The Scott family it appears still lives at Abbotsford and they certainly encourage charabancs. They have installed quick, efficient guides to deal with the crowds. Several of these guides work at once with difference parties starting at different points, their main object being to keep moving. More than occasionally they meet and shout each other down. Ours being old lost badly. I got a lift on the road to Melrose—a quiet woman who seemed absorbed in her own thoughts so that I left her to them. She drove calmly and steadily. I had a lazy walk round the river. Melrose, it would seem, is a prosperous little place but the news is ominous. One cannot ignore it entirely. Children are to be evacuated from London and other dangerous centres. In the ruined Abbey pigeons coo—surely the old Abbey will not know another war? We drove on through the Scott country to Dryburgh and Jedburgh. I thanked the silent little lady and she replies with the cryptic utterance 'There is so little I can do for anyone' and she is gone, slipping the gears in noiselessly.

Arrived in Carlisle at a disgraceful hour. The shy warden welcomes me like an old friend. Fell into bed. Feel like I have been whisked through the century.

29 August 1939

I'm back in England again and it is still raining, 'chucking it down' as they say in Yorkshire. Has it ever stopped since I left? A real early start to see the Roman Wall. We sit four in a carriage—the man next to me catches my eye, smiles and nods towards those sitting opposite, and no wonder. The two opposite are both reading their respective newspapers. One is the Methodist Chronicle and its headlines blazon forth 'The Joyous News'. The other, a local daily paper, warns in huge type 'Situation Ominous'. The 'Joyful News' man looks like an escapee from Dartmoor, while the 'Situation Ominous' has a face like an angel.

Bardon Mill and a walk of 5 miles to Housesteads Camp. There's not a car in sight to rescue me from the rain, but it is rather fun. A woman explained the way to me. She has a peculiar ring—just a circle of gold and on the top are about 8 sixpences stuck together. The Camp and the Wall are away up on as hill past a farmhouse, through long grass but it really didn't matter by that time. I got the ticket for admission at the farmhouse and was told to present it at the little house by the entrance. The little house seemed deserted, so I wandered in.

The stones are easy to follow on the plan—the kitchen and then the Murder House. (Was this a domestic or a military necessity?) Murder is a strange thing to think of in that wild lonely place with the wind shrieking around the old stones. A hawk swooped down and squawked in my ear and a voice boomed suddenly from behind a pillar "Tickets!" I did more than jump—I leapt. A vision in oilskins and no teeth suddenly appeared and I handed to it the piece of sodden cardboard that was the ticket. As a guide he was superb. He clothed every odd stone until I could almost see the place complete with Roman soldiers. It is at Housesteads he said that the remains of the only gate in the Wall is found except of course the gates in the forts and milecastles. The wall here in some places is six feet high. I have always wanted to walk on the Roman Wall. There is a wonderful view across flat country and peculiar cloud effects. The Wall was slippery and overgrown and I walked right off the edge. I picked myself out of a little stream. The guide still walked ahead, I could vaguely hear his voice explaining......

It is said that when the excavations of the camp took place a bunker of coal was found in one of the courtyards and in one room a store of arrowheads. It is possible to pick out the barracks, long narrow buildings just like barracks today. Outside the fort are the remains of the baths. There were strange gods worshipped at Housesteads in those days or, as it was called, Vorcovicium. There is a relic of a temple to the Persian sun-god Mithras—I wonder little at their efforts to invoke his presence in this England of ours but I doubt if he ever came.

The 5 miles to Bardon Mill was much shorter when you know the way. There is a quaint little sign post to a village called 'Twice Brewed'. It seems there is also a 'Once Brewed'. I took the train to Newcastle and then to Durham. There is a funny little station just before Bardon Mill, we passed a sign, Haltwhistle. I began telling a companion the story of my mistake on the Isle of Wight where I had thought Long Whistle the name of the station. This time it appears the train did not halt and whistle. It really was the name of the station! One never quite knows in England. I had a little time in Newcastle—time enough to find some quaint old streets and to see the swing bridge. Alongside is another bridge built by the same firm that constructed the Sydney Harbour Bridge. It looks like a miniature so much that I wanted to laugh. I spent the rest of the day and the evening in Durham Cathedral, in the loveliest of lovely churches by the river. I was sitting and looking at the great wheel window and the bells pealed. A service for peace is starting. Peace with a world waiting and ready for war? Took myself to the Youth Hostel—the coming war is casting its shadow before. I'm the only girl—and besides are only two boys. It is a queer fusty place with a grumpy old warden. Next week he says they are closing down and the Hostel will be elsewhere. I would think it would gladly be elsewhere.

30 August 1939

Train to Darlington and picked up my case which I hadn't seen since Glasgow. It looked slightly dusty and forlorn. Bus to Richmond to Mr and Mrs W. Dear old Mr W. looks just the same, his wife a kindly energetic little woman. Don't I look well and haven't I got plump. So I was just skin and bone on the boat was I? And me thinking I looked so nice!

Both Mr and Mrs W. are air-raid wardens. Realise for the first time just how organised England is. Everyone preparing for war with one hand and hoping for the best with the other. Mrs W. is expecting her nieces coming to get out of London. All streets being whitened at the corners and along kerbings for when the blackout starts. There is a big camp near Richmond and the streets were full of soldiers (and girls).

Richmond is one of the loveliest little towns in England. The castle on the edge of the River Swale looking down on verdant pasture, old English trees and the market-place all rough cobbled with the Trinity church in the centre. It seems one goes upstairs to church. The ground floor of the sacred building is devoted to shops! It is a town that still delights in old traditions. Mr W. says that once a year the councillors still walk the boundaries and at 11 a.m. on Shrove Tuesday one of the smaller bells in the church is rung to 'Bid housewives tend the fire to cook the pancakes well'.

Rushed off for a walk straight away to Easby Abbey. It is as the guide book says 'These ruins are more beautiful in their setting than in themselves'. They are scattered ruins in peaceful, fair 'dale' country. The walk is round the River Swale along well wooded banks. We called first at a farm for a glass of milk and a chat. The farmer—a man of 63 and a wreck from the last war, poor man—has just married a young wife. They have a wee puny baby. Old Mr W. is in his element poking the Wensleydale sheep with his stick. He is a councillor and 'someone' in Richmond. Everyone touches their hat and the men from the 'Old Men's Home' call him Sir. His every word is what they do in New Zealand. In Richmond at any rate New Zealand will not be confused with Africa!

We had tea at Barnard Castle—chocolate biscuits because I said I liked them. Toasted teacakes because we had them on the boat. There was more talk of the good old boat days, of Monte Carlo, of Villefranche—it seems like another life now.

31 August 1939

Last night Mr and Mrs. W. to an air raid meeting, there is a tenseness still in the air and a waiting. Did I report my inability to get my passport visa'ed for Germany? Glasgow refused to do it, and Edinburgh, and now a refusal from London. Sat up in bed and ate a huge breakfast. It is England again we have porridge, bacon and egg and toast and marmalade. Went this morning to walk on the moors where the Yorkshire heather grows. Somehow it is not as purple as the Scottish heather or is it that I am slightly resentful at finding heather in Yorkshire at all? We pass a lonely little house and has rather a funny story attached to it. Mr. W. had instructions from the owner to offer it rent free to anyone who would live in it and keep it habitable. Two people turned up. One a woman complete with furs and jewels who enquired if there was electric light and the other a man who wanted his groceries delivered. On the way home we call to see the Playhouse in Richmond—the oldest almost in England. A small room with a gallery running round. It is a second hand shop now—just pure junk.

To the pictures at night—and half listening for a preliminary raid. Richmond is not complacent, its air raid precautions show that. Never have I seen a town more prepared.

September 1939

1 September 1939

And German planes bomb Warsaw. Hitler calls on the German Army to 'Meet force with force'. What will Britain do? We start early and go up the tower of the Castle. It is a fitting thing to leave for the last for the tower commands a view not only of Richmond but a wide stretch of the surrounding countryside. I leave Mr. and Mrs. W. to their air raid activities. Their nieces come tomorrow from London. It is another goodbye and many thanks.

Away by bus to Whitby over good farming land with never a hint of war. Fat homesteads with signs 'Teas, Real Yorkshire Fare—Ham and Eggs'. Fields and fields of potatoes and little villages –the like of which I know so well now. Fruit is heavy on the trees that are trained up against the sides of houses. A church is open all day for prayer. The bus stops and the driver and conductor get out and disappear in the direction of the church—I look at them with a new respect and then find out that it's a short cut to the pub. The service stations here are called 'Filling stations' (so should pubs be). Past Thornton Le Dale and hills wooded with soft green—past the Fox and Rabbit Hotel—grey stone houses and red roofs. The driver jokes with a girl of the local cricket team. A notice 'out of bounds' at intervals along a farm fence reminds one again of war. I see a pack of hounds and red coats, my first glimpse of hunting, and a hill with a compulsory stop for cars and buses. It is such a little hill compared with our New Zealand ones.

And then Whitby and the Abbey! This was an epoch. Since I was a tiny girl the old picture of the Abbey has hung in our house side by side with Bolton Abbey. And always I have known I was coming—I walked round and round the ruin viewing it from every possible angle. I wanted to imprint it on my mind. It was just like the picture—the famous pond in front but instead of cows a group of ducks and ducklings. There are 199 steps to climb to the Abbey. Somehow that made it more deliciously exciting—this climbing up to a thing one has always coveted. The hostel was right in the shadow of the Abbey in an old building said to be at one time the stables. The old fishing port of Whitby is a delight—narrow streets soft and mellowed by the years. Hiding in every corner memories of Captain Cook who set out from here in the Endeavour to plant the flag of England in new continents. The quaintest and narrowest of streets, Tin Ghaut, leads from Grape Lane to the harbour. Washing hangs at the end and the tide is out. Tall-masted fishing boats lie at their evening rest. Fishy smells emit from sheds containing smokie and haddock. Around the narrow corners the old women at their stalls sell the Whitby jet and the mysterious ammonites—the latter a sort of petrified spiral fish.

I sleep in the shadow of the Abbey I love best of any of them because I have known it the longest. I saw the sun set with a pink glow and loved life as I found it with a deep content. Hitler says 'The hour has come'—for me it had, I cared not for the morrow.

2 September 1939

The parish church is quite near the Abbey. It had a lovely Caedmon Cross in the churchyard. Actually solved the mystery of the smallness of Captain Cook's house in Melbourne. It appears that it is only half its original size being cut in two for the purpose of widening the road at Great Ayton. For heaven's sake why don't they make things like that clear in Melbourne? Located the house where Captain Cook actually lived in Grape Lane overlooking the harbour. It is neatly labelled as such and the most respectable surgery of two doctors. The English air is at its best at Whitby. It is like wine—almost heady. Went across the harbour to the sandy beach where modern Whitby plays. According to the guide book there is a cocktail bar, a high class café and a licensed buffet. Felt a bit guilty—perhaps I had been neglecting the other side of travelling—perhaps I had been concentrating on ruins and cathedrals too much—but I didn't really want a cocktail or a licensed buffet. I couldn't even imagine to myself that I did. And then it rained and rained and rained. Bought little John some games, looked at the rain and set off for Scarborough. Towards Robin Hood's Bay it cleared. Robin Hood's Bay is the quaintest little place. It is built just higgledy-piggledy on the side of a steep cliff. It vies with Mousehole in its thrilling stories of the sea. It is about fifteen miles to Scarborough and I hitch-hiked the final five or six miles. Some Devon ladies in a small car were hurrying home—it would break any minute they said excitedly and the driver put her foot harder on the accelerator as though it was a race against time. Maybe it will come tomorrow.

I left them at Scarborough—a true English watering place. It has a lovely beach but somehow the holiday spirit had left it. It would be strange if a war came just when my homing instincts had brought me home. I got the train for York and changed for Rotherham. At 10.30 I walked into 42, Park Street with my haversack on my back, a tartan ribbon in my hair and a bunch of heather sticking out behind. We talk and talk and talk and then I slip in beside Auntie Lizzie and talk again until the early hours.

3 September 1939

Today history was made. Another war has begun. The Prime Minister's speech comes through. It is a sad speech but determined. My heart aches for the man—he has put up such a fight for peace. Has a man ever humiliated himself or his nation so much in an effort to preserve a peace? And with it all war has come and we must face it as best we can. All the time, while I've been tramping over the heather, they have been preparing. We're blacked out at night with old curtains, pieces of linoleum and black paper over the windows. Soon we will be rationed. But a nation cannot prepare to fight overnight and we must be far behind. This is the hour that I have always dreaded not for myself but for the nation. The hour when the war-lords would strike, encouraged to strike because they have seen us for years grow soft under the talk of peace and comfort and over-civilisation. The world is not yet ready for the kind of civilisation Britain was settling down to. It has been the same all through the ages—when a country shows any sign of being weak there are always those ready to pounce. I thought a lot today of Bob and Jim—they are not fighters but they will fight—of Auntie Molly who sailed for New Zealand on the 1st— of Mrs Broughton who is due to sail and of Mother and Daddy worrying so far across the sea. If only I could shout to them across the sea that I am safe, that I am glad I am here.

Daily life goes on just the same. It is surprising but after all what can else can one do? Round to Ruth's in the morning and Auntie Bella's to report arrival and then to have a good wash up, wash my hair and tidy up my suit cases. It has its funny side already this war. Night comes and I have everything spread out in the bedroom ready to pack into suitcases. There are bits and pieces of clothing and souvenirs on the floor and on the bed. Suddenly word comes to black out. There's no curtains up at the window so out the light must go. Malcolm and I peer round with a torch helplessly, poke a few things away and finally Auntie and I scramble into bed in the midst of it all, giggling all the time. We seem to have expected it so long that it is nothing new. Barrage balloons are up—great silver balloons—about thirteen of them. If an aeroplane touches one it blows up. Sandbags everywhere and little wartime tags springing up already. To the tune of the Chestnut Tree we sing—Under the spreading chestnut tree / Stanley Baldwin said to me / Have you got your gas mask / Don't ask me / Ask the blooming ARP. The ARP by the way are the Air Raid Precautions.

4 September 1939

And the tragedy of the Athenia.[20] The old horrors of war are starting again. It seems such a little while since the Lusitania. I put up a prayer for Auntie Molly on the sea. War is a settled fact now—last night an air raid alarm at 3 a.m. Walter home with a rush from the Forge—we could hear his clogs long before he got here. Some people went to the Park presumably to be in the open. Thought we'd better go down in the cellar but by the time Auntie Lizzie got me awake and fully conscious and we'd groped our way down it wasn't long before the all-clear went. Can't in conscience say I really heard the siren myself. Must practise waking up quicker or else get Auntie Lizzie to go without me. Annie and Herbert sat up in bed with their gas masks on (or so she said!) Typed diary solidly—the diary will be the death of me let alone air raids.

Round to Mrs Senior's (Auntie Annie Turner's mother). A sturdy self-reliant old lady who has twelve children—'all born and christened as she says'. Looked at all the old snaps and photographs and told them as much as I could about Uncle Sam and family. Promised to take home a parcel of odds and ends they're dying to send to Auntie Annie. Mrs Senior has made Yorkshire teacakes—they are fresh and the butter is golden. The little house is just a replica of the one Mother was brought up in and is spotless. Did I ever record the interior of these houses? One enters at the back door into the back kitchen. In it is a cooking stove, a sink (on which is often a gas ring) and a copper. (On washing days big tubs are rolled up from the cellar to be used in conjunction with this copper, all complete with gigantic rubbing boards). A door leads to the 'house-place' a sort of second kitchen with a cooking stove just like the other and a cupboard at the side. This is usually furnished with table, chairs and a sofa and always the dresser with a mirror over it. Another door, still leading towards the front of the house, leads into the parlour—a tiny, entirely unlived-in, room used chiefly as a repository for coats and hats. Found this strange at first until I realised what it meant to toil upstairs every time one wanted a coat or hat. The stairs are narrow, treacherous affairs and appallingly steep. They lead to two bedrooms as a rule—quite big bedrooms and above them again a huge attic. Below the kitchens are the cellars—a mysterious place into which Auntie Lizzie vanishes, bringing up butter, milk, bread etc. One day I explored. It was so cold and clean. Nothing ever seemed to go dry or stale down there. The bread is kept in big earthenware crocks. I am afraid now the war has come that cellar will no longer be a mystery. But as Malcolm says we will at least be where the 'eats' are.

Those of course are the older houses. The newer ones like Auntie Bella's are slightly different. One enters into a kitchenette with a dresser, a sink, a small table and a hand washing machine. Of the stove only the oven shows. It is heated from the next room where there is an open fire. The living room with the fire is a fair sized room and a comfortable place furnished with chesterfield and chairs and always the big family table. Upstairs the bathroom and the toilet and bedrooms, smaller than in the older houses but then even in England families like Mother belonged to, of sixteen, are no longer the fashion. They still have bigger families than we do and share rooms more without any ado. For the older houses the rent is about 8/- a week and for the newer, the colossal sum of 13/-. Everyone is vastly amused at my writing down all about the houses and can hardly realise that New Zealanders have never seen houses quite like them.

5 September 1939

We're still at war but not much more news. No pictures and Youth Hostels closed so my wanderings finish for a while at least. Troops in the South being rushed to the North and those in the North being rushed to the South, can't help thinking it would have been a champion idea to leave them where they were. Typed diary frantically and feverishly. In the afternoon to Mrs Cooke (formerly Lizzie Cottrell), a frail delicate little lady who has been ill all her life. Dear little soul, she cried when she saw me. Still sings in the choir when well enough and still has the organ she used to play on when Mother and she ran to school. Do wish over and over again that Mother was here. Feel a poor substitute but do my best. Mr. Cooke is a pleasant sort—been on mean test for years (sustenance) but they manage and have a nice home. It is said that British planes flew over Berlin and dropped millions of leaflets. That'll do a whale of a lot of good. Many of the boys who go up to enlist in the army are sent back again with instructions to wait until they are called. George and I round to the Club. Everyone remembers me and shakes hands until I feel like a life-long member. No longer do I have to sign to enter and pay the visitor's fee. I just go in with a nod. No fish for supper! All trawlers commandeered they say so Auntie cooks potatoes, beans and bacon for ten o'clock at night. Crept into bed beside Auntie Lizzie and talked—no more air raids.

Bread baking today—revel in the smell of new bread with golden crust even as I revel in a field of new mown hay. Remember an 'aesthetic' woman I met in Glasgow who rhapsodised on a field of hay and then wrinkled up her nose and looked vague when I mentioned my weakness for new bread and its smell. 'She—ah—didn't really know, she never had to bake'. Pointed out that after all the bread was only one step further on and didn't she think a crisp golden loaf was an artistic triumph? She obviously didn't and melted away with a look that said plainly she was vastly disappointed in me.

6 September 1939

Typed diary again. A bit sick of it but if that's my only worry I've nowt to grumble about. Went to Rotherham and took Auntie Bella's Betty. We all have to carry our gas masks in a cardboard box. Left mine in the post office for a start. Bought a grey skirt—white one worn out in a continual fight for existence. Latest gas mask story of Joe at the pit, who is not a beauty.

Jim: Hie oop Jo-a why doan't thy tak off thy gas mask—raid's over?
Joe: What does tha mean lad? Ah haven't got it on.

You'd appreciate that if you saw a gas mask. It is a fearsome thing of rubber that covers one's whole face. One peers through two goggles. The nose and mouth part extends into a huge 'snout' with a perforated end. In this snout of course are the 'doings', filters and so forth I suppose. The breathing is sort of gaspy, like the preliminaries of having a tooth out by gas. The latest is that since the air raid scares started two firms are going out of business—Beechams and Carters![21]

7 September 1939

Not a light in the streets or showing from the houses. If you show so much as a crack or a glow the air raid warden comes knocking. All infringements to be fined about £10. Cars painted all round with white instead of having lights. Corners of all houses all painted. Rather absurd really when all the town is in blackness except the chemical works which emits a great red glow all over the sky! Walked with Jack Roe to see Rotherham Museum—closed when we got there as a 'place of entertainment'! Walked through the Park and saw Uncle George Henry's name on the War Memorial, then up to Silverwood mine and back by way of Aldwarke Lock—a good nine miles and yet I don't take off any weight. Young Jack says 'If they doan't hurry oop and call me ah'm goin' to enlist again me'. Youth hasn't changed a bit since 1914. Going to stay with Uncle John next week.

8 September 1939

This evening with Auntie Bella to the Crown and then to the Star. It seems she goes to pay in her Club money. Must find out more about these clubs. The chief one she runs seems to be a birthday club. You pay in each week and on your birthday receive a cash payment. Frankly I can't see anything in it. You don't get any interest. Why not put it in a bank? The only one who really gets anything out of it is the one who runs it for a slight commission. Of course they club together and get things at wholesale rates from Littlewoods and chocolates for Xmas etc. I think the whole idea is that they haven't a bank account and if they kept it at home they'd spend it.

All the crowd know me now. We sit in the 'little room' and chat. Everyone very, very generous. It is amazing all the same how little they drink all night. One glass lasts through interminable fish stories, items by the artists and discussions about the work at the pit. A second glass and it is time to go home. Go out with one of the boys into the big room. Some of the men had brought their whippets in. Saw one lap up nearly a pint of stout! A crowd gathered round it pridefully. It had won an important race and didn't that animal know it. It stood condescending, quivering as those skinny and hairless dogs always do. Meant to be Doncaster races today. Remember how Mother used to tell me that as a girl they went down to the main road to watch the crowd go by to the Doncaster races. There will be no crowd today because there are no races. Everything like that postponed. It seems a queer war with meagre details over the wireless.

9 September 1939

With Ruth and Bessie to Parkgate to see Schonhut's shop, famous, and justly so, for Pork Pie and Sausage. It is the same Schonhut's shop which Mother used to run to from Netherfield Lane. Leonard, one of the sons, is clean and pink like one of his own sausages. He has just been to the Continent. Showed me round and we stood in the refrigerator talking about Switzerland for a quarter of an hour. Suggested that before we discussed Italy we went into the room with the boilers. Asked me round for tea on Thursday. Met Lily Liversedge coming home. She never speaks to anyone but Auntie Lizzie. Doesn't seem a bit like one of my cousins. She had to stop and I made sure that Ruth and Bessie were included but she looked thoroughly nervous. It would be difficult to hold a family feud—you meet everyone too often!

To the pictures at night with Ruth—open again for the first time and home to supper. Malcolm and I creep home in the dark clinging to each other, falling over things and giggling. See a figure at Auntie Lizzie's gate—a broad portly figure leaning over the gate. Give it a hearty slap on the back and a broad 'Heigh opp lad what's tha doin' art toneeght?' The figure turns with a splutter and it's not Uncle Albert but the Air-Raid Warden! I fly dragging Malcolm after me. We fall over the clothes prop, tread on the dog's tail and land into the house in hysterics. The black-out is going to have its funny side until we get used to it.

10 September 1939

Sunday. Up before Auntie Lizzie, 'weshed pots', set table and snared a bit of Parkin. With Walter and Bessie to see over Aldwarke Pit Top. No idea there were so many 'doings' at the pit top. Coal comes up from the mine in little wagons passing over the weigh-bridge. Young boys sort out stone from the coal and put aside all bits containing copper. The coal is then washed—the resultant water is black with a thick residue that is called 'jubilee'. (In the time of strikes, when the miners' coal supply is cut off, they collect this 'jubilee' and roll it into balls and burn). The coal is then shaken to separate the little bits from the big lumps and then weighed again. Saw also the mechanism working the lifts for lowering and raising the men working down the mine. A man sits at gears with a huge indicator before him—a big black dial with a big black indicator. Huge dynamos provide power for the working. Everything, absolutely everything, filthy with coal dust. All the men very friendly and willing to explain. Windows all blacked-out and some work necessarily stopped at night on account of being unable to black-out. Saw the lamp room and the lockers where the men's 'snap' and coats are kept. All meals taken to work are known as 'snap', mostly sandwiches and tea cake packed in an oblong tin along with a small tin full of tea and sugar mixed. And never ever do they 'make' the tea. They 'mash' a pot of tea. They all look the same going off to work, the round tin water bottle called a 'Dudley' or 'Dudley Moon', the oblong tin snap tin, a cap on their heads and a scarf round their necks. Some mines are equipped with up to date baths but the old miners shake their heads. It 'gies' them cold they say to come out sweating from the mine—to go under a hot shower and then out into the cold early morning air. The coal is all moved on running belts of thick rubber. Not all the pits have these gadgets but cleaned and sorted coal demands a much higher price.

At night as we sat by the big fire a piece of coal exploded like a miniature bomb and shot right across the room. 'Metal' explained Uncle Albert laconically. So that is why the young boys are so busily employed taking out all the pieces of coal with metal in. Played golf with Malcolm on the little local putting green. 'George' in charge remembers me and tells Malcolm he thinks I'm a very nice young woman and he wants to see me again. Poor George, the boys think he's a 'sissy'. His only crime seems to be that he was once a waiter or something in a big house. Anyway as I pointed out to Malcolm he's shrewd enough to get on very nicely without much work. Strangely enough in their half-amused pitying toleration they'd never thought of that.

The soldiers' marching song so they say is to be 'Boomps a Daisy' and I'm knitting socks for soldiers. These socks are the family joke. No one seems to have knitted any here before. Round to Annie's this afternoon. Has a huge radiogram with a constant supply of new records. Played 'South of the Border' until I just about wore it out.

11 September 1939

To the Co-op Stores with Auntie Lizzie and on the way saw through George's brickworks. 'Our' George—not the George of the putting green which goes to show how necessary this 'Our' is in Yorkshire. Lingered a long time in the ovens and felt a new person when I came out warm. Stood on a floor over the ovens down which they feed the coal through little holes and burnt my shoes into a pattern. Piles and piles of bricks in an oven several thousand it would seem. They are put in and left for weeks. Some ovens can't be used on account of the fire showing outside in the blackout. Others were full just ready for the roof to be built over—had never thought of it being done like that, all the bricks piled in and the roof built on afterwards. A machine cuts the bricks into shape with a special machine for odd-shaped bricks.

Auntie Lizzie walks two miles every Friday to Kilnhurst Co-operative Stores because they give 3/- in the £ dividend against the 2/- given by Rawmarsh Co-operative. I thought of the winter and the snow and the raw fogs—she is such a little thing. This afternoon round to Uncle John's to stay and how they teased me about those socks for soldiers. Donald on nights and comes downstairs at about three o'clock dead tired after a patchy sleep. It is no good for the young ones. Uncle John off with his back.

13 September 1939

And little Mum's birthday. Thought about her all day. Uncle John is not strong but on the other hand he can put away a good meal and walk miles so presume he carries on as best he can. The dear is still having bits of shrapnel removed from his leg—a little souvenir of the last war. He's just dreading going back to the mine on nights again. 'Nights' means leaving home at 10.30 p.m. and coming back about 6.30 a.m. 'Days' are 6 till about 2 p.m. 'Afternoons' are about 2 till 10.30. That of course includes travelling time. Little John's a dear.

I'd take him and finish his bringing up any day and that's a whole lot for me to say.

Out today with Mr. and Mrs. Cooper to Newstead Abbey. Next week everyone will be rationed for petrol—six gallons a month. Out through Maltby and Worksop and through Sherwood Forest. Here Robin Hood had his band. I could almost hear the glades ring with their laughter. Stopped at a beautiful grove of silver birches—almost like grey ghosts in the morning mist and then an avenue of beeches. We prayed in the quiet air for the peace of the world— and even while we prayed a lorry full of soldiers thundered by on the road. They were singing 'Keep The Home Fires Burning'—all the old songs over again... Standing alone in glorious old English grounds is Newstead Abbey, the home of Lord Byron. There is a Japanese garden with a little stone bridge over water that flows with crystal clearness from rock to rock. In the Abbey is Byron's helmet which he wore when fighting in Greece and I held his sword out of its scabbard. It was to this lovely house that Livingstone came to write. It is strange there are two such opposite influences at Newstead—the wild turbulent Byron and the patient Livingstone.

Back to Rotherham to Herringthorpe Valley Road for tea with a first-class blow-out of a front tyre on the way. Home in the black-out. The buses are with purpley blue windows and subdued lighting. In the darkness everyone coming home from the Crown and Star seem like conspirators, whispering in corners and peering furtively. It is easy to see how suspicion and superstition reigned in the old days without lights.

14 September 1939

Helped Auntie Polly and went for a walk with Uncle John. Just round and about—they do a lot of that in Yorkshire. We never seem to just walk in New Zealand, we always have a definite object to justify the going. In the afternoon to Schonhut's to tea. Talked ourselves tired about the Continent. (The housekeeper Miss. C. not there. Local gossip says she's wanted him for years and years). Sent me home with a sample of everything in the shop—just what Mother used to buy—a veal and ham pie, 1lb. of sausages (and sausages are not the makeshift dish they are in New Zealand, they are fat luscious things and ½lb!), one black pudding and a duck. I wonder if Mother will remember what a duck is? It seems to me that it is what we call a faggot—a mincemeat ball seasoned with onions and sage. Wash-day dinner at 57, Netherfield Lane used to be mixed vegetables in a saucepan and two or three ducks from Schonhut's put in at the end. Everything at the shop is spotlessly clean. All the meat is killed on the premises and the shop right on the main street! Don't seem to have any municipal slaughter houses. What a horrible thing it must be to hear those pigs squealing! Exchanged reminiscences about the Continent. It will be a long time before anyone goes again I'm thinking.

Round to Arthur Turner's at night (Uncle Jim's eldest son). Arthur works in the pit. His wife, Winnie, a Lincolnshire woman—a pleasant soul who is not too strong. Joan, his daughter, about 18, a pretty, dark girl just beginning to realise life and loving it. Turn up at the fish shop at 10 p.m. for a usual supper. It would seem that each member of a family states definitely and decidedly what they want. The one who goes takes a basin covered with a cloth and the various portions are wrapped separately in paper and deposited in the basin. We had hardly got ourselves settled in the queue when the crowd moved up one. The little woman in the shawl leaned across the counter and taking a deep breath said rapidly 'I want a pennoth and a fish, a pennoth and a pennoth of fish bits, a pennoth and a pennoth of scallops and a pennoth and a fish cake. She paused triumphantly. The fish man duly considered. He took his little pieces of paper and muttered as he filled them—'a pennoth and a fish—a pennoth and a pennoth of fish bits'. Putting the lot in her little basin the woman went out. The queue moved up a few more. We wait patiently—it is bright and warm and always someone one knows. Presently a small child pulled aside the curtain that blacked-out the doorway and a small voice piped up 'Please, Mother says you've left summat art. What she wanted was a pennoth and a fish, a pennoth and a pennoth of fish bits, a pennoth and a pennoth of scallops, a pennoth and a fish cake'. By this time the fish-man's wife, a busty woman in a big white apron, came forward. 'Get out of the way' she says smartly. 'Now what is it you want?' She took the parcels and the child nothing loath started her recital—'a pennoth and a fish, a pennoth and a pennoth of fish bits…' So she shovelled it all back into the hot fat and started again, muttering as she filled the packets. We moved up a bit more—it was our turn and our basin was filled with little parcels. Just as we were going out the woman came in 'Tha's gied me wrong agin' she was saying, 'tha's left out fish-cake. I said I wanted a pennoth and a fish…' We left them to it—there's no object in letting one's own fish get cold.

15 September 1939

Friday and a walk with Uncle John over the fields, meeting old pals of Granddad Turner all the time. All can see the Turner in me, except the strictly truthful ones, and all wring my hand mightily. Then to see Auntie Polly's relations. They all seem to work hard and love it. Tiny houses with bright red fires and lots of sandstoning.[22] Mothers look as young as grown-up daughters, evidently they have married very young. It is so with young Mrs Glossop—she has a round neat figure so seldom seen out of England. It is neither fat nor lean, compact is the word. In the afternoon to see old Mrs Glossop (Auntie Polly's Mother) who lives in one of the little church almshouses on Dale Road. In was in such an almshouse that Mother used to visit the old ladies on the P.S.A.s (Pleasant Sunday Afternoons) to take them tea and a mite of sugar— sing a hymn and say a prayer. It is a dear wee house, comfortably in the middle of about four others exactly the same. Just one room and a kitchen, everything spotless and the fire so bright. Knitted the sock and just about finished it. All the other little old ladies peer out of their doors to see who it is. One a tiny soul in a dress of about fifty years ago with a white starched collar. Mrs Glossop has Grandma Turner's lustres and a pair of big vases.

George and Teddy came round after tea and took me to the Star. Uncle Dick in full swing telling a fish story. I love to listen to Uncle Dick telling a tale. 'And ah said to him as fished by me—'Tha knows our Gud came second for t' last three years. Tha knows...' Shall I ever be able to talk this Yorkshire dialect as it should be 'spoke?' There is a cheerful chatter, George argued on gas masks, Auntie Bella's laugh rang above the lot and Mr. Doughty kept saying ' Av another luv'. Everyone is 'luv' here. Even Malcolm when he goes over to the grocers is greeted by' Nah luv what dusta want?' and being one of the younger generation and only 19 doesn't he hate it!

16 September 1939

For a walk with Uncle John to Piccadilly to see Auntie Polly's George Willy who has tennis courts and a lovely garden. Rather close but I get a bunch of roses as a gift and the family nearly fainted. A long walk round Dalton, Thrybergh and through Hooton Roberts to home. An old whipping stone at Thrybergh and, on the way to Aldwarke, the locks opened to let a boat through—a barge full of wheat. A real old bargee with an historic pipe (redolent with history in fact). His wife worked the puffing billy engine—a weather-tanned face, a print mop cap, apron and good substantial boots. Her Lord and Master threw the lock man a penny on to the bank, swore at him and passed through. A glorious morning—the blackberries promising along the roadside—I feel the fatal call of the open road.

Afternoon—just had a laze and needed it, knitted sock and finished it. Donald says he could do with a pair of socks let alone the war. George says 'Is that the other one?' and Uncle innocently remarks 'Is that all you've done?' Sallied them all up just as James Willy and Bertha came to tea. Cornered James Willy to ask him confidentially what they call him at work. Find out he's Bill—and heave a sigh of relief. If I ever had to say James Willy I'd die. Bertha, Irene and I to the pictures but couldn't get in. George came round with Teddy and took me to the Crown. The boys are spending far too much on me.

Every day seems to be happy in spite of the war and a few warnings. Russia they say is coming in with Germany. Why should the Poles have to suffer so—is it their lot to go on so all through the generations? So many are asking what on earth are we in this war at all for. Dreamt I was in a gas raid and found myself suffocating at the bottom of the bed under the clothes. Auntie Lizzie's Annie is a scream. Poor kid she's suffering from rheumatism in the feet but insists she's joining the army and hobbles along saying 'Pick 'em up Brown—pick 'em up'.

17 September 1939

Sunday and 'reight' busy. For a walk with Uncle John, George and Jack, the latter stalking ahead in true Jack style. Up on top of Greasbrough Hill to see the guns—great sinister things swinging silently. The balloon barrages overhead wave like silver fish. Dreamt of Venice, of Paris and of Scotland and came to life in time to hear George say 'Ah just towd him it was nowt to do wi' me' and realised the tale was finished. Called on George Turner, another of Uncle Jim's sons. He works in the pit and is a fireman in his spare time. He and his wife Doreen are so plump and healthy looking and their kiddies three of the nicest I have met. They were off to Sunday school, Margaret in a white frock and a big pink sash.

Albert to tea and afterwards for a walk with him. Round to Auntie Lizzie's for letters and Uncle Albert beams. Asks Albert how he is and then asks him why he hasn't the guts to get married? Make a hasty farewell and departure— these things will happen in the best families. There are two doors to go through before one emerges from Auntie Polly's kitchen into the garden. The first leads into a little square passage, then the other leads outside from the passage. Take the cloth out to shake it talking all the time, laying down the law vigorously at something, open the first door and shoot out the crumbs into the passage. Still getting teased about it.

18 September 1939

Weather getting definitely colder and fires larger. Helped Auntie Polly with dishes, the house place and all the beds. In the afternoon to Mrs Marriott's for tea. Donald came to fetch us home in the blackout and, not knowing quite which house, listened at the window. Unfortunately it was the wrong window—people came out and exit Donald feeling definitely small. War much the same. Pamphlets issued today on how to deal with a bomb if it should alight in the yard. Personally I'd rather not deal with it at all. Russians fighting now—afraid it's the finish of poor little Poland. Brickmakers head the list of men who are not required for service—that exempts George. Jack says at the pit they've been told they're wanted at home.

19 September 1939

And to the farm with Donald at Wickersley. Old Mr. Lloyd a dear and insisted on giving us tea. A real farm kitchen with a bright fire and on the hearth a thirteen pint copper kettle shining until it reflected every single thing in the room. Put on overalls and had a great time bottling milk by machine and putting on stoppers. Arthur Green offers me a job any day as a farm hand so I'll not be stuck when my money runs out! A most peculiar fowl strutting about. Thought at first I'd had something stronger than tea, then discovered it is a cross between a fowl and a turkey. Small turkey head—a red, rather revolting, featherless neck and a fowl body. Looks for all the world like a fowl with its neck half wrung. All prepared for Xmas at the farm—jars of mincemeat, puddings and cakes. Rationing won't worry them. Home by bus and then a glorious walk from Rotherham—a perfect night the black shape of the Power Board works clear against the sky. A red glow diffuses the sky. (What price the black-out?)

20 September 1939

Uncle John and I to Rotherham to find out the time of trains to Manchester. Train services very much restricted. People here not very used to phones—will go all the way to Rotherham before it dawns on them to ring up. Teeming with rain. In the afternoon to visit James Willy (After all it is more fascinating than just plain Billy) and Bertha at their little house at Greasbrough. Mrs Sanderson (Bertha's Mother), a real Yorkshire woman. Talks with a broad accent in short sharp sentences. I find myself 'beg pardoning' an inexcusable number of times and then smiling vaguely. Oxford Row is a quaint little group of cottages grouped round a central yard. In the centre of the yard are a group of toilets to which one has one's own key. A long walk home in the black-out through woods and over fields. Finished one sock. Donald is sure they'll be both for one foot. Outcry about too much money being spent on A.R.P. wardens. Those on full time getting £3.0.0 a week. Slowly but surely all 'out-of-workers' being absorbed on such work. Latest tragedy of the war—Mr. X of Rawmarsh has been found a job—been on Means Test for 15 years and raising a family on it quite satisfactorily. Poor man nearly died of shock!

21 September 1939

A glorious day but getting cold. Balloon barrage still shining in the sky—occasionally our planes get tangled in them and go up in smoke. Washing Day at Auntie Polly's—all complete with huge tubs and peggies. What a to-do it is. George sends S.O.S. to Uncle John's—would I go round as soon as possible. Thought someone dead at least and fled there at 6.15. The only trouble was that they hadn't seen me since Sunday. Round to the Crown. Lectured George on spending too much money and after a long explanation of the peculiar psychology of the British miner we reach the Travellers Inn. All they ask for is 'a nice going on' and if they spend—well there's plenty more where that comes from. Pointed out that it's darned hard-earned but he just shrugs.

Now the Travellers Inn was Granddad Turner's old haunt. Here he used to 'reckon' on pay-day with the men who worked with him. Sometimes they would take on contract work –particularly when a new face or seam was opened up. The firm would call some of the older men and let them take a contract on their own—picking their own men to work with them. If the new working proved good all to their advantage, if bad then they lost, but the old hands very seldom made a mistake. The head one would be paid according to the amount of coal taken out and he paid his men as previously arranged. This explains a lot of the visiting of pubs in those days. They were the recognised meeting place for paying out. Sat in the same seat that Granddad sat in and met Mabel Doughty there—she married a Rotherham man not too fond of work. She remembers 'our Susanna' well. She says that there had been a woman knocked down in their entry by a man in the black-out. The story is told afresh to everyone who came in—'An 'e knocked 'er darn and tried to strangle 'er—'er who married Bill James' boy and she had her rubber boots on an' all'. Tried in vain to discover what the rubber boots had to do with it.

On the 22 September Gwennie leaves for Manchester and spends well over a week visiting relatives and people with New Zealand connection in Oldham, Rochdale and other places in Lancashire.

October 1939

4 October 1939

An epoch in the Peacock history. This is the day when Gwynne, daughter of George Peacock, son of James, son of William, crossed the Irish Sea. The Traffic Inspector by the bus wishes me the best of luck and no torpedoes. The station at Liverpool was blacked-out. They had made a thorough job of it. I stepped cautiously off the train. I found two policemen—there was little hope of missing them. They stood facing each other—big Irish policeman—and there was no room to pass between them. They looked down enquiringly. 'I'm going to Belfast' I whispered. 'Are you now, missie' said the bigger of the two. 'Let's see your card and we'll see'. But everything was in order. They drew themselves in and I passed between with instructions to walk left. I walked obediently. I could hear water going 'gurgle-gurgle' but not a thing could I see. I know now where Moses was when the light went out. He was in a long tunnel or covered wharf going to the Belfast boat. Then a glimmer of light ahead and a gangway. I was peered at by two officials and ushered into a cabin. Cabins at 2/- for the night seem to be a luxury, most people sit in the lounge. Took one look at the lounge through the haze of smoke and retreated to my cabin. Made the acquaintance of a young girl in the lower bunk, a bride of seven months whose husband has just left for France. We joined a jolly crowd up on deck, many of them RAF men,—appears there is a big camp in Ulster. In the black-out one learns to distinguish voices rather than faces. There was 'bass voice' who sang 'Silent Night' simply and sincerely, nearly reducing us all to tears. There was the Cockney who said amidst sniffles 'Gor blimey mate' and broke the tension that followed.

The boat crept out silently and secretly sometime during the night, we scarcely knew when. Collected the little soldier's wife and down to our bunks—hard as nails but I slept—awoke but once with a weird impression I was standing on my head. I was—we were evidently having a rough passage.

5 October 1939

Came the cold grey dawn. Up rather reluctantly to see the Loch as one enters Belfast. There were no formalities in getting off. I set foot firmly and decisively on Ireland. Jim, who had sat next to me on the deck, was beside me as we queued to get off and he had hours to wait until his transport went to the airport so we had a spot of breakfast together at Mrs. Mcgillycuddy's. 'Ach now and you're from the Airforce' she beamed and because Jim was from the Airforce we had a huge plate of ham and eggs for 9*d* each! And the morning paper thrown in. Got to the bus depot just in time. The conductor was a genial soul—a true Irishman of the Irish books. He recognised me as a stranger within the gates and introduced me to the whole bus. In turn they pointed out to me all the points of interest. There was Lisburn. Lisburn was expounded on by an elderly man in bright green socks. We passed through Portadown and I got off at Stone Bridge. I took the road to Kilmore. Purple damsons lay hidden in the grass. The trees themselves were golden—behind the hedges apples hung thickly upon the tree. A pungent smell comes from each little white-washed cottage on the roadside. And then ahead the church at Kilmore. Even when every day is an adventure and life is very very good, these moments are rare. I was there in Ireland looking at Kilmore Church, the church where Grandma and Granddad went when they were young. Where James Peacock passed his Bible under the pews to Jane Loney and she opened it and found written in big childish letters 'I love Jane Loney'. I have that Bible now.

There is a little store cum Post Office by the church and in it I enquired my way further. Could they direct me to Monie? I was looking for Fred Peacock's at Monie, I said. 'Peacock' they reiterated and shook their heads and then they brightened. 'There were Paycocks at Monie. Would it be the Paycocks now I was looking for maybe?' Paycocks or Peacocks what did it matter, so I nodded but before the road was pointed out the questions repeated 'Who did you say you were?' 'I'm a Paycock too', I said in desperation,' and I come from New Zealand'. There was a sudden flutter in the little shop. Children appeared from nowhere—an old man and another woman—all to look at the Paycock from New Zealand. At length I got away. I passed public pumps on the side of the road and stopped to consume more blackberries. Still couldn't see the cottage and turned in at a cottage on the right hand side. A woman came to the door.

I stated who I was, where I came from and what I wanted in one breath. I had found that one might just as well in Ireland. 'Well now' she said, subsiding into a chair and folding her hands under her apron. 'What do you know! You just sit right here and when Patrick comes home from the goats I'll tak ye round myself'. And so I drank tea and discovered that this very house was where Granddad Peacock had lived before he left Ireland. The only difference was the thatch had been taken off the roof and iron put on. The clay floor, as hard as granite, was still the same and the stove. Here Granddad and Uncle Oliver sat and made boots. In those days there was a big window to let in the necessary light but otherwise the house is just the same—the wee windows, the little front porch and the pump at the side.

Fred Peacock's was just round the corner. We turned in at the gate past stacks of sweet hay crowded together into a dear muddy yard, here an old cart and an old plough rested against a background of trees thick with red cheeked apples. And there stood a long low mud-walled cottage, simply whitewashed. The remains of pink roses straggled up to its thatched roof. I shall always love that yard—the muck heap behind the shed and the fowls scratching in the little wild flower garden where the shamrock grew more plentiful than the flowers. Somehow I didn't want to knock. I didn't want to break the spell. The low-latched door opened and a woman of about sixty appeared with a full skirt and a blouse, her hair scraped back and big farm boots of her feet. I put my arms round her and kissed her and we went inside. There I found Uncle Fred (Daddy's cousin) and his sister Minnie. The woman who came to the door became Auntie Lizzie (Uncle Fred's wife). I sat on the low wooden chair by the fire and suddenly, quite suddenly, I was one of the family. I seemed to know that little room as if I had been there before. The clay floor, the fire of peat built right on the floor and spreading itself into the room, the big iron arm that swung over the fire which dangled a big iron pot. On the dresser six pewter plates were reflecting the fire. There was a willow pattern set, plates with an old fashioned brown pattern, mugs and in front a double row of porridge basins. The fowls came and pecked at our feet as we sat and talked and drank tea, for tea I must have, and a boiled egg. Soda bread too made in a big flat cake on a griddle.

We talked until the canary sang again. They had received my letter to say I'd be coming but as I hadn't been able to say quite when, they had just waited, and they hadn't even known whether I'd be a boy or a girl! 'Gwynne' in Ireland is so often just a surname or a man's name. And then they asked me to stay. I could have cried with sheer delight. It meant much more to me than they knew. Apart from all sentimental reasons too I had a vision of a long long walk to Armagh if they hadn't! Precisely at nine we had supper. A big bowl of porridge and goat's milk rich and creamy. Auntie Minnie takes me to my room with a candle. She leaves me with the candle at the door and goes in first to put up the black-out—an absurd piece of paper about 6 inches square—over the window. I thought of Monie all covered in fruit trees, of the little cottage with the thick walls, the wee window inset to about two feet, of the little flickering light of the candle—surely Hitler's planes would have a better target than that to concentrate on! But the Ulster people are law-abiding—terribly law abiding. They are more conservatively and Victorianly English than the English themselves! It was a little room with a clay floor covered with pegged rugs—a big and incredibly soft feather bed and dear old patchwork quilts. Surely I can say this is the apex of the trip?

6 October 1939

Take down the black-out and find it's a glorious day. Shake up the feather bed and smooth over the patchwork quilts. Feel as if I'm up bright and early and wonder if the household already stirs. A knock on the door. It's Auntie Minnie getting a wee bit worried. Believe she thinks I take sleeping powders or something. It's a quarter to ten! I 'took my breakfast' as they say in Ireland. The teapot is always on the hearth. One scrapes a bit of peat apart from the main lot and sits the teapot on that, so that it faintly sizzles and keeps piping hot all day! Auntie Minnie dons a print cap and busies herself with the churn, a huge wooden one that stands on the ground. Auntie Lizzie mixes flat soda bread and bakes it on the griddle that hangs over the fire and then the iron pot is put on, full of potatoes. Dinner was a plateful of potatoes in their jackets, smothered in butter and a glass of buttermilk. It is food for the Gods! My increasing waistline fills me with a slight, just a slight, spasm of alarm. Went for a walk and bought some 'baccy for Uncle Fred in a little shop that sells humbugs, pins, boiled bacon and boot polish in glorious confusion. Home along a real rough narrow country road—always fruit on the ground from overhanging trees and blackberries. By every small farm house a stone wall behind which a pig grunts over her litter. At one cottage a group of children stand and smile a shy friendly smile. 'You've a lot of brothers and sisters' I say to one little soul with Irish eyes and a long faded frock 'how many are there?' 'Eleven' she said and a little chap with a mass of curls and the face of a 'Bubbles' toddled up to thrust an incredibly dirty little fist into mine.

A quiet night with the old lamp light dancing on the walls. Auntie Lizzie breaks the turf with her strong hands. The battery set speaks of war—always war. It means so little in Kilmore. Washed in rainwater—beautifully soft but strangely brown—obviously off the thatch. No water laid on in the cottage.

11 October 1939

At 5.45 p.m. caught the train for Dublin and a jolly crowd in the carriage—a woman journalist and two students. One poor boy to go up for his exam tomorrow. Usual black-out lights in the train just the merest glimmer and he peers at his maths book standing up. We cross the border and are now in Eire. Everything is printed twice in Irish (Gaelic) and English, even the street names and the train notices. The women journalist tells the story of the Robin Red Breast. How he picked the thorns from Our Lord's head and caught the blood on his breast as he fell. I mentioned that they had the Robin Red Breast in England too but the one of the legend it would appear was of strictly Irish parentage! Edmund C. was there to meet me at the station. As we walk to the Hostel we see Dublin at night—rows and rows of hostels, big houses whose former glory has departed leaving them slummy tenements.   Women, with black shawls over their heads, carry their babies under the shawls and idle past leaving a smell of vinegared fish and chips. Children play about in the darkness and Edmund steers me clear of a little cart full of stale bread propelled by two incredibly dirty little boys. He apologises for bringing me this way but if I want to see all over Dublin—well this is part of it and I might as well get it over. A little old woman in a shawl murmurs softly in my ear as I pass. I stop and beg her pardon but she seems a long time in talking again so I catch up to Edmund who hasn't noticed I still wasn't with him. Ponder on this strange happening and fully a street away realise she was begging! It is going to be a revelation this Dublin. The Youth Hostel is a big old house with wide stairs and painted ceilings. There are not many Youth Hostels in Southern Ireland. The powers that be are only testing them out. They are a little shocked that men and women should tramp and house together albeit in separate dormitories. Ireland, so the warden's wife tells me, suffers from the three P's—Poverty, Politics and Priests but she may be prejudiced in some way. Ten, half past ten, eleven still the children play in the streets—don't they ever go to bed!

12 October 1939

First to the Post Office. In 1916 it was the headquarters of the Irish Volunteers. Here the Irish tricolour was hoisted and the Republic proclaimed. There was a week of fighting and the G.P.O. was shelled by a gunboat in the Liffey. Underneath a statue is a eulogy to the freedom of Ireland from its oppressors. I nod sympathetically for my host is from Donegal and is truly Irish. Besides I admit to not going very deeply into this Irish trouble. I have few opinions. Perhaps it would be as well not to form any until I am safely back in England.

For whereas I was at home in Ulster I feel a stranger here. Not that Ed doesn't do his level best to welcome me—not that we do not meet smiling friendly faces in the shops. But they are so bitter against the English. It is not a recent bitterness like that of the Italians—it is so deep-rooted and so deliberately bred in the schools. Gaelic is taught as well as English and prizes given profusely to encourage study. Follow Edmund's huge strides down O'Connell Street and into Cleary's. I tremble for the delicate pieces of Beleek china in his huge fist. It is such delicate stuff and seems to be a speciality of Ireland. It is expensive even here. Into Trinity College to see the almost exquisite beauty of the Book of Kells and then we walk down O'Connell Street again. Old Flower Women gossip by the 'Pillar' hugging their shawls round them in the sharp bright air. The 'Pillar' is another Nelson on a column as high as the one in Trafalgar Square. In Parnell Street a barrel organ grinds out 'The Rose Of Tralee'—a real barrel organ on a little handcart. The turner of the handle is so pitifully thin and threadbare. I do not purposely fly from suffering in the world but I was much happier when the mournful wails had died away into the distance.

It is strange that while the world was endeavouring to foster international friendship (excluding of course the warring forces of Germany) by means of Youth Hostels and cheap rates of travel, endeavouring to promote an international language and to break down racial barriers of mistrust—little Eire was making herself as aloof as possible—striving for a separate language, trying to become self-supporting to live a proud aloofness albeit in poverty. It is a blind patriotism—it would seem that they are trying to start by going back instead of forward—one can only wait and see how it will all turn out. They are neutral and boastfully unafraid yet they darken the streets of Dublin against raids! Why? Or rather with delightful Irish inconsistency they leave them flaring on until there is a raid in the North of Scotland and the next night they are dark until the scare has passed.

We had seats for the Abbey Theatre in the evening. Who has not heard of the Abbey? The quaint little theatre that needs no plush seats nor ornate walls. In 1907 it suddenly became famous with 'The Playboy of the Western World'. It produced Synge's 'Riders to the Sea' and many a play of Sean O'Casey. They do quite a number of George Bernard Shaw's plays and relish them—never realised before that G.B.S. was born here. How I have loved tonight in the little cramped Abbey. It is fitting that I should have come here so soon after Yeats' death. I can see him in the early days criticising the smallest prop, visiting old furniture shops in Dublin for period furniture and curling the wigs with the aid of Lady Gregory.

13 October 1939

Friday the 13th but I forgot so it wasn't unlucky. We hurry to Player's cigarette factory. The manager beams. He'd be delighted to show us through but orders from Head Office since the war are 'no visitors'. God forbid that spies should get in and the Germans drop a bomb and deprive us of our cigarettes! There are so many priests in the street that Edmund's little recognition becomes perfunctory and slightly automatic. A friar passes in brown habit—a jolly fat friar his fat little toes peeping out blue from his toeless sandals. Two nuns pass with the huge white hats. Out to Phoenix Park—a lovely spot with the smell of the nearby zoo.   The massive Wellington monument is set on a base of broad steps around which small boys play at 'hurling'. This seems to be a national Irish game and is played with a sort of hockey stick flattened out. Unlike hockey it is quite permissible to wave the stick round above one's head which makes it about the roughest game in the world. In the zoo gazed at the Tuatara Lizard—'A very rare specimen from New Zealand'. It is said she (or maybe he) has lived in Dublin for 28 years. It didn't look one bit homesick. Possibly it realised that in Dublin it was 'somebody', a rare specimen to be looked at. In New Zealand it was just a lizard.

Cut through some streets where the less fortunate members of Dublin society live. Every other house a little shop exhibiting for sale a bag of potatoes, a few mouldering carrots or rotting apples. A cat sits on the potatoes and a baby, its nether extremities entirely unclothed, sits with an expressionless face in the corner of a doorway. It is coming evening and shopping has begun. Round about six seems to be a popular time to shop. Possibly many of the women work and have to wait till then. There are stalls in the street—sometimes the women leave them for a while to run home and their daughters take their place, shrieking out like old professional women the merits of their wares. Have I mentioned before the fleas in Dublin? After a visit to the pictures, in the most fashionable seats, I look as if I've got the measles and am far past enduring them without a scratch. After a ride in the tram I am covered in them but then if I will go walking through slums no doubt this is one of the penalties.

14 October 1939

The train at 9 for Cork and in the carriage a real old Kerry man who hates the English, talks Gaelic and slips away for a wee nip of whiskey at intervals. The Irish are charming but only after a while one finds their weaknesses. They are spoilt. Not in the possession of this world's goods but in the knowledge of their own 'delightfulness'. The world has told them they are delightful until they come to believe it. They tell you so straight out, play up to it and pile it on like a child 'showing off' and, of course, the charm goes. He told me a long story about St Patrick and the devil but I couldn't understand a word of it. In the opposite corner a little Irish girl with a New York hat sniffed in disgust. Ten years ago, so she informed me, she left her native land to be a nurse in America and had become naturalised. Ireland, she said, lighting her cigarette, was getting worse. The old man withdrew his gaze from her scarlet nails, glowered under bushy brows, and let forth a stream of Gaelic—a dissertation on Irish politics and profound contempt for traitors in general. She eyed him coolly and resumed her book but the Irish in her won and they went at it hammer and tongs. Eventually the old warrior got out. I gathered up his bag, his newspaper and his flask and deposited him trembling and furiously patriotic on the platform. The Irish-American shrugged and lit up. 'They make me mad' she said simply. 'I guess I'm going back to little old New York as soon as I can get'.

The carriage filled up again. A honeymoon couple and a man going home from a day in town. We steered clear of politics and all finished up on the floor playing with a mechanical soldier on horseback which the old man was taking back for his little grandson. We passed through County Kildare, Tipperary and Limerick. There were many beet growing fields and factories for extracting sugar. This seems to be a new industry under the Free State. There were miles of bog lands where the peat had been cut out. Kissed the Blarney Stone and then back to Cork to stop at Mrs Murphy's. And so to bed—heaven forbid there must be fleas in Blarney Castle too.

15 October 1939

Out to Cobh or Queenstown as it used to be called. A gorgeous day and it is good to be alive. Walked for a while in the Old Church Cemetery. Here are buried hundreds of the victims who perished in the Lusitania and the grave too of Wolfe—the author of The Burial of Sir John Moore. Met the Canadian woman as arranged and we decide on a jaunting car—everyone in Cork is going to the hurling match. Sit on a wooden seat facing outwards and clung to the Canadian woman like grim death. I've been in a rickshaw almost at dusk in the Cinnamon Gardens in Ceylon, I've been on a camel along the long road to the ageless pyramids, I've been on an elephant but I've never been so downright scared like I was in a jaunting car in Ireland. We alight warily at the match. It was the Rockies against the Glen—the match of the season. The little Irishman on one side of me breathed prayers into my ear. 'Mary, Mother of Jesus, help the Glen now' he muttered. At that moment the Glen scored and his tenseness subsided. The man in front chewed his little sandy moustache and muttered imprecations. He was a 'Rocky-ite'. 'It's a dirty game they're playin' he said. The little Irishman spat in sheer amazement. 'And it is ye that 'ud say the Glen play dirty! I'll tear any man apart limb from limb that dares to say that the Glen play dirty!' Sandy moustache stuck his face forward belligerently 'Then by St Patrick I'm saying it now'. 'And by St Patrick you'll niver say it any more. Sure an' ye won't'. And with that they let fly. 'A bob on the man with the blue shirt' hissed a woman at my side. 'Goal' roared the crowd. Sandy moustache spun round. 'One for the Rockies by the grace of God!' Nobody thought about the fight again. All the first half just one casualty after the other. To play hurling surely one needs a cast iron head. In the first half the actual play has been ten minutes. The rest was employed in treating casualties. 'Do you understand it, miss?' A fatherly-looking individual gazed intently into my eyes the way the Irish have. I disclaimed any knowledge whatsoever and he was in his element. 'And you see miss there's O'Reilly. He's the Rock's only hope, now he...... Arrah the divil himself made him miss that goal!' Never have I felt on such a friendly footing with the Deity and the Devil. And at a hurling match in October in Ireland I got sun-burnt. Glen won overwhelmingly for the sixth year.

There was a dance to celebrate the victory of the Glen. It is called a Ceilidh. The huge floor covered with dancers—not a soul in evening dress. Some of the older folk stamp in time. There is an occasional Irish whoop. Both the Canadian woman and I learned to do a jig. We learned the thrill of dancing to the pipes—and believe me it is a bigger thrill than any wailing saxophone ever blown!

18 October 1939

Onwards, ever onwards, towards Killarney. Stopped in Kenmare last night with the Cousins family. For the hundredth time I listen to the Constitution of Ireland and how they hate the English. Being New Zealand I am presumably not English. Doesn't New Zealand want Home Rule too? They are sure we are a poor oppressed people and isn't it nice now I am in Ireland and can be free for a while. Chase mountain goats up and down hills to get a photo. They've such funny faces. Two tattered and torn farmers, complete with tattered and torn dogs, take a great interest in the proceedings. 'Sure now and you're a journalist, Miss?' Nodded vaguely well out of breath and asked 'Why?' 'Well it's only people loike that who'd be doing such a daft thing as trying to photograph a goat'. But oh how like New Zealand all those hills, brown bracken-covered craggy hills, and waving pampas grass are. The air is soft and warm, the mist drifting silently, shapelessly. And then suddenly I see for the first time the Lakes of Killarney. Soft silent stretching into the hills one lake opening into another. On past the Half

Way house drinking in the glory of those holly bushes bright with berries. A car stops and I get a lift. The owner of the car, a seller of homespun tweed etc. has the sense to keep silent when the beauty was great.

Killarney is only a little place—the actual town with funny bewildering little streets. Somehow I had thought it bigger. It has a population of only 5,500—though it increased to 5,501 with me. Somehow Killarney's not as I expected but she is lovely. After all what did I expect; I hardly know. Stayed at Mrs Cahill and on her advice walked out to Ross Castle. Return to sit in the sitting room by a gorgeous fire and listened to Mr Cahill expounding—a dark, long-haired Irish Pole. The Irish in him loathes the English and the Pole in him forbids him to love the Germans.

19 October 1939

There were six of us to go to the Gap of Dunloe. An Englishman with one ear perpetually cocked listening for a phone call from his bank 'don't you know'—his wife with a new perm that she was scared to comb. There is as young student from Belfast who eyes the Southerners as if they were from Venezuela or some such outlandish place. He announces in a stage whisper that 'They're not fit to be called human don't you know'. Resolve to keep away from him. If there's any assassinations going on they'll be well deserved. The fourth member of the party was a young girl. She recited the Irish constitution to me before we started and I looked wildly round for escape. There was no one to escape to but the obviously retired school-mistress with the shirt-blouse and tie. Then the ancient wagonette arrives with a more ancient driver. The Belfast student said 'God' and the Irish colleen looked as though she might kill him. I grinned tentatively at the retired schoolteacher and was rewarded by a 'Come and sit by me dear'. The wagonette may have had springs at one time but they wore out in the gay nineties. We jogged along country roads that were little more than lanes. We came to Kate Kearney's Cottage and left the wagonette and proceed on ponies. The wind whistled in our ears and the R.S. and I rode ahead towards the pass. It is a wild looking valley around here. 'We'll come to the bandits soon' she said and sure enough, almost at that very minute, there leapt out from behind a rock a fantastically dressed individual who raised to his lips what looked like a flute, he puffed his cheeks and blew. The sound came, a thin miserable little trickle. But he made no attempt to toot again, he waited with one finger upraised. Then the sound came back a thousand times magnified. It is the most magnificent echo I have ever heard. One hates to think that there mightn't be poteen stills hidden away in the wilderness. It was late when we returned to Killarney. I have much to dream of tonight and I don't quite know which way to lie.

Gwennie returns to Dublin and then spends a few days more in Northern Ireland stopping with a variety of acquaintances. 28 October finds her stopping in Armagh.

28 October 1939

I work the pump in the back yard energetically feeling that the exercise is good. It's market day in Armagh and I'm let loose amongst the linens. I escape with a tablecloth with shamrocks on. In Scotch Street a man sells herrings from a barrel and a big sow and her piglets wander down the main street. I look over the Roman Catholic Cathedral this afternoon, a lovely place that took, they say, 64 years to build. There is a chill in the air. Soon I think my wanderings will have to end. When winter comes I will return to my people— those dear ones in Yorkshire. It is strange how humans, even the gypsy ones, have homing instincts. The town is full of soldiers. Their feet sound hollowly down the street. Tramp, tramp to the sound of pipes. Men come out of the Protestant Cathedral looking very pleased so doubtless they have been celebrating something. I venture in and a positive blast of heat meets me. It is beautiful in its ruggedness. Religion in Ulster is terribly serious and the feeling between the Roman Catholics and Protestants is very, very hard and bitter. We of New Zealand, who are so tolerant, so apathetic, find it hard to understand. To me it seems horrible that one should harbour such hatred towards one's fellow man even if he is born to worship in another way. I do not think anything has shocked me more than this bitter hatred. Annie and I went to the cobbler's in the afternoon and we sat beside Mr. C.'s fire until my shoes were mended. Poor little man he hadn't been to Belfast for ten years but with an air of triumph he hastens to add 'I was at Portadown six years ago don't you know'. And Portadown is five miles away.

The days finish soon now. It is dark and we are in Grandma's room chatting and doing our knitting and fancy work. Lizzie puts a stone water bottle in our beds directly after tea and a fresh one at nine. It is as well she does for the sheets are linen and there is a hard white frost.

Gwennie returns to Liverpool on 5 November and spends some time in Lancashire and Cheshire visiting and staying with people with a New Zealand connection to her family.

November 1939

Liverpool, Ashton-under-Lyne, Manchester, Openshaw, Darwen,
Spring Vale, Blackpool, Macclesfield, Rotherham.

11 November 1939

It was Armistice Day—a little ironical. Should we thank God for the peace of the last war or curse the present strife? Most people forget, either purposefully or accidently according to their various temperaments, the two minutes silence. It seems so long now that last armistice. The tripe shop has 'chittlings' on exhibition. Seem to be a favourite here. On enquiry find they are pigs' intestines thoroughly cleaned and boiled. I'll try them but.... And these same people look as if they'll be ill when I tell them of the frogs and snails I had in France! They seem to sell every single part of the pig including the lungs or lights and the trotters. It makes me wonder what we do with all those parts in New Zealand. One certainly never sees them. They are delicately and tactfully removed before the pig is presented to the public.

15 November 1939

Ashton-under-Lyne quite a nice little town with a fair number of shops. Called on a friend of Mrs Milton's with a little confectionery shop. The daughter doing up a parcel for her husband in France. What a dreary war this is— a carting round of gas masks, a cold calculating calling up of men in their age groups. Almost as many deaths in the black-out as from the enemy. To Manchester to collect camera and bag and then Openshaw to be greeted riotously by Mr. and Mrs. Lockwood. The dears thought the I.R.A. had got me in Ireland. The said I.R.A. playing up a great deal just now putting bombs in letter boxes etc. Walked through Lewis's and Afflick and Brown's. It is delightfully Christmassy—all snow and holly and red-coated Father Christmases. Skating skirts and sweaters on view and such mufflers and fur gloves as I've never seen. It almost makes me feel afraid. This winter is going to be The Great Adventure. It is hard to make them realise that, except for my short stay in Switzerland, I've never seen snow except once when I was a small girl and a few flakes fell.

19 November 1939

Had a spot of dinner and then off again to Darwen. I have heard people complain at having to see friends of their friends in New Zealand but I think it is a marvellous opportunity. After all what is a country if you don't know its people? The carriage full of smoke and evacuees' mothers visiting their children on cheap day trips. I have always felt sorry for evacuees and their people but here right before my eyes was like a play and the other side of the question. 'Will you have a cigarette' says a little woman whose short legs failed to reach the floor and whose turned-up nose and little round brown eyes stood out brazenly from under a halo hat. But the woman opposite—a big mountain of flesh in a black coat and frock smelling faintly of chips, produced her own packet. 'I can't stand Woodbines' she sniffed 'unless I've nothing else. I must have a bit of summat good even if I have just gone bankrupt'. The others clicked sympathetically and the little women with the short legs leaned so far forward that she fell off and had to be helped back.

There are so many of these bankruptcies in England now, of little shops in areas that have been condemned as slums and pulled down. Why can't they move the little shops along with them into new shops, the same as the people get new houses? But the stout woman admitted she was doing quite well. She knew all the Charitable Aids off by heart and her daughter would soon be on 'Lloyd George'. Must go into this Lloyd George business. There seems to be a complicated system of national insurance here. For illness 12/6 a week for a woman and 15/- for a man. Maternity allowance for an insured person is £2, husband £2, that is of course if the wife works.

On we rush through Salford and Blackburn. Mill chimneys everywhere. The stout woman hitches her gas mask box more securely on to her ample but sliding lap, lights another cigarette and tells of her trip to the Isle of Man. 'Ah goes down into th' cabin room and ah asks our Liza what all t' little boxes were for but bai gum Ah knew what they were for before long. Ah sez to our Liza 'ere lass get outer t'way them baskets ain't big enough for me; and they weren't. Ah'd taken a leg of mutton and some fruit pies and coming home a man says to me, sez he 'Eh lass what's tha got in t'basket?' and Ah sez 'It's me lunch and Ah don't want no more as long as I live. Ah never went away again. Ah haven't been outer Manchester for ten year and ah don't know as Ah want to go'. The woman with the short legs lit another Woodbine. 'Gosh I couldn't do wi' being where my kids are but Ah'd be a fool to tak them away. She gives them a bath every Saturday neeght. They're in Darrin (Darwen), that's where Ah'm getting out. I came last Saturday and before Ah went Ah called at t'Bay Horse. There was an old top theer playing dominos and he treat me to a Guinness. Our Albert says he won't come home and my husband Ernest says he doesn't want t'kids at home again ever. But as I sez to him 'They're his kids and they that's got them won't want them for ever'. Ernest sez 'She's got to 'ave 'em for t'duration and any more wot we has too'. And I sez to him 'Coom off it lad…' So many of these mothers look alike—a little perched-up hat that has been sat on a few times on an oily black head, a black coat, black dress and grubby hands. Woolworths' rings and Woodbines.

And then Spring Vale and Annie Morris becomes a personality instead of a name. The two girls, Annie and Bee, work in the Mill in their clogs, shawls and curlers, just like the girls I saw in Oldham. It is a spotless home and it is always 'Come nearer to the fire' even though I'm already glowing like the last rose of summer. Now I know the Lancashire mill girl. As straight as a die, intolerant of weakness, no one dare be weak in the Mills. Casual, one might say almost offhand, but once they accept you you're a friend for life. Off to Blackpool at night with a crowd of girls in a big bus. In a body to the shops as soon as we reached Blackpool—Woolworth's, Marks and Spencer's, Hill's to buy rock to suck, ice cream and souvenirs. Then to the Tower and into the Ballroom. I could see some of the girls giving me a look as we took off our coats. This was where I'd be a nuisance. We sat down and my guardian angel guided the best looking Air Force man in the whole room to my side. I admit to swinging away triumphantly—I gloated at being the first up, I'd put it across the whole lot of them—and they admired me for it. I was one of them after that, I'd got my man and earned their respect. Although what particular credit there is in 'getting your man' I don't know. As far as I can see I just sat and he came. Having got one's man it seems one stays with him for the rest of the evening—that is if one's technique is right. One visits the aquarium as I did with Ted F. and one wanders round the zoo and then back to the ballroom. Most of the other girls have collected the Army and Navy and the Air Force by this time and they never fail to greet you as they pass. We romp through the Lambeth Walk, Boomps-a-Daisy and the Palais Glide. We drift into Little Sir Echo and rumba to something Mexican. Then on to supper on the roof garden.

Ted F. is half Irish and half Lancashire and a bit of quick wit comes easily to him. This repartee business that the Lancashire people love so is very easy when one gets hold of a few catch phrases. Ted tells me of the clumsy member of his battalion who, when all are on parade, is sent for a ladder. He comes back with one of great length over his shoulder. The sergeant-major roars 'What the so-and-so did you bring that damned thing for?' 'S —s —s sorry sir—I—I—I –.' The unfortunate man swung round knocking over the end man of the row with the ladder. Dismayed he spun the other way and knocked the sergeant flying with the other end. 'Put that ladder down' roared the officer. 'S—s—sorry sir –,' stammers the poor man again and dropped the ladder on the officer's toe. We finished up at 11. Goodbyes said and exchanged photographs and souvenirs like everyone else seemed to be doing. Home with the girls on the bus and we sing, joke and sleep. A huge slab of tripe and vinegar for supper and sit over the fire and pop into bed. Did I report that we dress and undress in the warmth of the big linen press in which our nightdresses are warming all day.

28 November 1939

Auntie Lizzie came over from Rotherham yesterday and we stopped at cousin Susie's. What expensive toys they buy for children here. Susie's not supposed to be well off and is proud of paying £2 for a doll's pram for little Bessie aged three. Last year she bought the two boys bicycles £10 each. There seems to be a different standard of living here altogether. Not so much thought or money spent on education—much more on pleasure and show. But Susie is so thin! She has a good breakfast ready for us. Then to the farm to see the evacuated boys. What a journey, first a bus to Stockport and then a bus to Macclesfield before a four mile walk. The boys look alright—red cheeks and as fat as butter.

30 November 1939

Auntie and I on the train to Rotherham at 5. Both asleep and wakened only at the last minute when a guard flashed a dimmed torch under the blind and a wee small voice reached us announcing it was Rotherham. Rotherham is not one of those 'taxi' places either. If one wants a taxi, particularly in these days of 6 gallons a month, one orders it days beforehand. The blackness so complete that we could only see a yard ahead, if that. Staggered to the bus with case, carrier bag, gas mask, purse, umbrella and a few other odds and ends dangling and dropping on the way. Stagger into the bus in the teeming rain and the carrier bag bursting at the critical moment. Got the giggles so that we couldn't even walk properly. Off at the tram sheds and Auntie goes on ahead. Struggle along in the blackness and presently hear dear old Malcolm's voice 'Wheer are thee, Gwennie?' Home again and laughing and joking, being kissed and hugged and warmed. It seems ages since I left—it was before I went to Ireland.

December 1939

Rawmarsh, Greasbrough, Sheffield, Rotherham.

1 December 1939

Unpacked and sorted out—what a job! Had a good wash up and all those vital things that must be done after two months moving. Might have got on better if we hadn't talked so much. Kept running downstairs to say a bit more and then up again. Then Bessie ran up to tell me a bit and down again. Then we both ran and met half way. Weather rainy and cold but house so warm I need only a short-sleeved woolly jumper. To Rotherham market to buy chestnuts to roast on the hob at night. I love trailing round markets gazing at 'pots' especially. This in England means the crockery cups, saucers, basins, plates and vases—many manufacturers' rejects with an imperceptible blemish. No very high class stuff but we get chestnuts and brussels sprouts at a penny ha'penny a pound. Walter and Betty to the pictures but I take one look at t' fire and stick where I am. Must record that English children call lollies 'spice', the adults say 'sweets' just as the Americans say 'candy'. Fruit cake is spice cake though it hasn't ever seen a speck of spice.

3 December 1939

And I run round to see folk. To Uncle John's where Auntie Polly hugs me as if she'll never let me go again. Then to Auntie Bella's to hear all about Elsie's wedding to be on Boxing Day. Uncle Dick, Uncle John, Betty, Jim and I for a walk round Haugh Lane. A frosty morning but fur coat on, hands in pockets and stepping it out. Come back in time to find Malcolm taking Bessie, the Bedlington terrier, out so go with him. Home to Yorkshire pudding and roast beef dinner with a drink of dandelion and burdock. Round to Auntie Bella's for tea—teeming with rain but we play darts and I beat George (chalk it up!). Have an uneasy suspicion that he let me win and lecture him on the subject. Albert comes in. It's one of the nights when he doesn't like anyone or anything. Doesn't like salmon and Auntie Bella has to give him the ham she has for George's 'snap'.

At night to the Club to renew old acquaintances. Quite a good turn on—an imitation of Nellie Wallace and a sprightly little dancer worthy of a better cause. On to the Crown to meet Auntie Bella. Win the 1d in for cigarette numbers and collect 2/-. To Auntie Bella's for supper. A little celebration with some champagne and afterwards go round the dartboard, bulls eye and all, without a miss! Met Sam Towers with his whippet. He wanted to know all about Mother. No wonder whippets need little coats they're so skinny. This one with the dearest little coat of some warm stuff with red braid.

4 December 1939

Go on 'days' to work as diary is far far behind and hundreds of letters to write. Typed letters to New Zealand steadily. Must get them done as I won't have a chance once I start travelling again. If people only knew how hard it is to get them written. Walt and Bessie to the pictures again and Walt with bad eyes! Slipped over to Annie's, her rheumatoid not much better. Children back at school after three months and many a mother puts up a Te Deum.

5 December 1939

Letters solidly all morning. In the afternoon Auntie and I to Mrs Watkinson's, Grandma's old friend, who badly wanted to see me again. She's really a dear and read our tea cups seriously and effectively. Advised me earnestly to stop flirting and settle down. Told me I drew the men on to push them back. So I promised to mend my ways. They would mend she said confidently. She heard a tune, an old fashioned waltz or hymn that would make all the difference in my life. Could almost imagine myself settling down to extreme and dreary goodness with the echo of Rock of Ages in my ear. Told me my guide still watched over me and would always get me out of harm's way whatever I did. Began to wonder what terrible things she suspected me of doing. My guide she said was a little old lady who walked—so. She imitated her and spoke of her dress. She was always reading she said in days when women didn't read so much. Auntie Lizzie is sure it's Mrs Foster, the people with whom Mother came out to New Zealand. But it is comforting to know one has a sort of all-cover insurance and whatever she is doing for me I really appreciate it. All joking apart I'm convinced it's true! I think there's something looks after me. We had a typical North Country tea, and could one have a better,—crab, tin of fruit, cake, bread and butter and teacake. The two men bathing in the kitchen when we got there as they do in the older houses every night when they come back from the mine.

6 December 1939

Sat and typed and typed and typed. What a week of work. Little Mum's red jumper arrived made from the pattern I sent her from Aunt Eliza's. A perfect fit and I'm dying to wear it. Played darts at night but Malcolm too good. I roasted chestnuts and just as the wireless reported planes over Sheffield they went off pop in the oven scaring everyone out of their wits. Auntie and I sat in alone at night. Walt and Bessie to the pictures again. Malcolm on 'nights'.

8 December 1939

Moved to Arthur's in Roundwood Grove, Rawmarsh. I'm going to like being at Arthur's. Winnie is a dear comfortable soul, not too strong, but gets along nicely at her own pace—troubled with her heart. Joan is a modern miss of seventeen—a generous little soul with 'tidied' eyebrows, vivid lipstick and brilliant nail polish—she'll tone down as she gets older. Just at present it's great fun being seventeen. Round to Alice's in the afternoon and Albert's piano pupils still playing 'The Swallow's Return'. Home to tea and to sit before a big fire. A darkish day and the light on nearly all the time—there's a peculiar stillness in the air. Went to bed late and talked till later. Heard all about the boy friends—Ernest, Harry and Fred.

9 December 1939

Woke at 10 and stretched luxuriously in the feather bed that Winnie brought from Lincolnshire. Trotted downstairs and sat in pyjamas for a cup of tea. Morning just melted away in talk. Afternoon and walked with Arthur to Greasbrough to see Mr. and Mrs. Senior (Leah Causer). Dear Mr Senior says he's been waiting for his sweetheart to come back. Do admire Mr. Senior still teaching at the little Congregational Chapel as he did about 35 years ago. They've ceased to be Mr. and Mrs. Senior and will in future be Auntie

Leah and Uncle George. Bet and Mr Meeks to tea. Rather incomprehensible Plymouth Brethren. Mr. M. won't let Bet play the piano on Sundays or read novels but beams indulgently on scarlet nails and permed hair. Such a pretty girl and a marvellous little housekeeper for her father. Into bed to whisper till 2. Ernest proving difficult so I give a little advice from the depths of my superior? experience.

10 December 1939

Another day nearer Xmas. Went into Rotherham. Joan, who doesn't work at present, signs on at Labour and they tell her if she keeps going she'll have to go to cookery and gym classes every afternoon. Joan, the sophisticated seventeen, going back to school! We sweep out of the office with ruffled dignity. Shops all Christmassy. Leonard Schonhut waves a cheery greeting and Miss. C. glares through the window. Home to a huge dinner. Winnie the best possible cook. With Winnie to her Aunt, Mrs. Kennings. in Netherfield Lane—a delicate soul who knew Grandma Turner. 'T'owd lass she was allus a good 'un' she says in her broad dialect. Home in the blackout to stub our toes on kerbstones and giggle. Dark outside now at 4. Bought more chestnuts to roast and roast we did—all sitting round the fire and 'calling' till one o'clock. (Calling by the way, which is pronounced with a short 'a' like pal, means talking—mostly gossiping).

11 December 1939

How the days slip by. Call on Mrs Brown (Lucy Machin) and just talked and talked again. If by talking I could summon Mother here she'd have arrived long ago. Mary Brown one of the loveliest girls I've ever seen. In every household there are mighty and intricate preparations for Xmas. Everyone whitewashing, papering, scrubbing and tired out. What will they be like by Xmas? Suggest that surely it would be better to do the Xmas cleaning after Xmas when all the visitors and mess were over. But that's not the idea at all. Visitors must find everything spotless. If anyone could find dirt in any of these homes they must have a magnifying glass. Never have I seen so much cleaning going on and polishing of linoleums and brass. They cherish things which we discarded years ago as causing too much work, copper kettles and brass fire-irons. Saw Alice May again with Joan and home to a most satisfactory night with a box of Black Magic chocolates. Joan a dear girl and I like her more and more each day. Arthur they say is like Granddad Turner, stocky, strong and hard-working but such an easy soul to get on with. No one could help but like him.

12 December 1939

Got up eventually and had a cup of tea by the fire. Did I really ever rouse myself in the wee small hours and tramp incredible miles? This is gorgeously lazy—just good sharp walks from one hot fire to another, no wonder I'm not feeling the cold in England. Another dark day but they tell me in warning tones winter hasn't started yet. From the refuge of all the firesides of the family I'm awaiting it fearfully and with baited breath—rather with the Who's Afraid of the Big Bad Wolf attitude.

Tea at Alice May's and Alec plays for me. Thoroughly enjoyed himself with songs of twelve years ago. Funny how one can always date a person's marriage by the last popular songs they remember. Have noticed it repeatedly. Suppose it is because with marriage they stop going to dances and such like frivolities. It is funny how married people always get me alone and confide that they'd have done great things if they hadn't married and all the women who married young are convinced that they would have been raving beauties or frantically successful businesswomen if they'd kept out of the matrimonial market. Try to convince them all that the having of children and bringing them up is the most marvellous work in the world, and leave them mightily consoled. Albert comes in and plays for me the Merry Widow. Walked home in the black-out and sang. No-one knew who we were if they did hear us so what did it matter? Walked into a wall, tripped over a garbage can and crept into the feather bed.

13 December 1939

And to Bet's for tea. Sit, knit and gossip and I learn the psychology of life as modern seventeen knows it. It doesn't really matter they explain whether one loves a man or not, the great point is to be clear of the restraint of one's parents—to grow up and be one's own mistress and that can only be successfully achieved by marriage. You can do all the most marvellous things in the world and yet if you're not married, people always pity you and wonder why. And I'm hanged if they're not right! Might have explained that sometimes there was so much one wanted to do first but it hardly seemed worthwhile. Their life's so much simpler as it is.

15 December 1939

Raced to Parkgate to bank Auntie Molly's cheque (last day). Bet, Joan and I to Rotherham to buy Joan a frock. The seventeens in their newest swagger coats with accessories to match. Neither go to work. Perhaps for their father's sake they should marry young! A cheerful shopping and the man in the cake shop says paternally 'I'd take this one, luv, it's fresher'. Took dinner frock into dressmaker to be let out. Dressmaker just took one look and said in genuine amazement 'Was this yours?' Pronounced it hopeless so gave it to Ruth. Got weighed in fright but still only 9 stone. Xmas presents, of course and 'thank you' presents. Bought Auntie Lizzie an ash tray on an oak stand, Jack Roe a cigarette lighter (also a 21st birthday), Elsie a wedding present of a Pyrex dish and I've bought George shamrock cuff-links from Ireland so he's set. The crowd in Woolworth's stupendous and we faded breathlessly into Rotherham Regal to see 'Four Feathers'. Relaxed with a box of chocolates. Home to Auntie Bella's at 7 and Albert giving Jim his lesson. A slight argument as to whether I should go with A. for a walk or with the family to the Club. Club won. All want to know of Susannah Turner and wish she were with me—I've got to bring her some day. Left the crowd singing and then home. Sat till 1.30 and talked, nearly all of us nodding but just wouldn't go to bed. Tried to fire George with enthusiasm to save to go to America.

16 December 1939

A great day. We go en masse to the maggot factory! What is a maggot factory? Ah! There's the rub! At last I feel unique as if I have seen something that the average world explorer has never seen. It is here they breed the maggots used for the famous canal fishing. Off we go at 11, Uncle Dick striding ahead, young Jim with his hair plastered sleek trying to look like the men, Uncle John—all soldierly—shoulders square and marching step, Teddy Perkins in cap and scarf beaming as usual and Arthur square, solid and comforting looking. And myself in fur coat, woollen gloves and woollen socks in my shoes. Through Swinton and the village melts into farmland. There is a big white boar at stud. He eyes us with little red piggy eyes and the fence seems so inadequate. Not quite certain whether boars bite, kick or butt but I'm sure that one would do something dreadful if it got out. Then the slaughter house for the old crocks and finally as a natural sequence the maggots. Fortunately I always keep a pocket-sized bottle of lavender in my purse. Never have I needed it so vitally. Uncle John and Arthur renege. Uncle pokes his head round the door says 'Come on Arthur' and the two melt away. The rest of us in bravely with maggots on the right, maggots on the left. It is not a pretty story. Carcasses black as ink hang on hooks and from them fall a curtain of white maggots. They fall into a concrete trough and the manager proudly tells us that they have to do the concrete wall quite often as the squirming mass of maggots break it down. Mixed with them are the brown shells left behind when the maggots have turned into blow flies. For some blow flies are deliberately bred. These are introduced to the fresh meat as it hung. Great clouds of ammonia come from the putrefying meat—livers, lights, cows, tails and whole sides. In another room are barrels—a tail droops over the edge of one and a hoof over another. The smell is simply awful to be perfectly candid. My fur coat is over my nose, a handkerchief over that, but I can feel it irritating the lining of my nose. But the maggots—they would be any fisherman's pride and joy. They are A1 at Lloyds. There are pink maggots, yellow maggots and red maggots but strangely enough no one has ever been able to dye a maggot a permanent green—somehow it always comes off in the water. The manager assured me there's a fortune for anyone who can produce a permanently green maggot. Assures me also that the business is a little gold mine. The odour they say is not unhealthy. I don't disagree but... Outside five sleek cats preen themselves in the sun. I emerge from the fur coat and breathe cautiously.

In the afternoon to Mrs Brown's (Lucy Machin). Took Mr Brown a white scarf as a present—a marvellous little man, a deputy in the mine. No education whatsoever when he was young having lost his parents and been dragged up first at one house and then another. Poor Mrs Brown has such a bad heart. Uncle George and Auntie Leah for tea—a real jolly party.

17 December 1939

Got a really early start to go to Sheffield but talked to Auntie Lizzie till 12. Walked to Rotherham and then the long ride by tram, almost 7 miles for 3*d*. We rattle along for half an hour. The shops more gay than ever with holly and cotton wool and tinsel. Bought a teapot for Winnie and a cup and saucer for Little Barbara. A brush set for the hearth for Auntie Polly and Uncle John. That's a few more! Emerge from a shop away down the Moor at 4 to find it pitch dark and black-out. Prowl all through the town to where the Rotherham tram goes from, enquiring from dim shapes on the way—never knew the world could be so dark. But the shops brilliant once one is inside. Noticed an absence of North Country accents amongst the people here—possibly because strangers come up from the South on holiday. Home at 7.30 to warm my back by a big fire and laugh with Winnie and Arthur. Chitterlings for supper. Did I report chitterlings were pigs' intestines—thoroughly cleaned and boiled of course—but somehow I never feel quite happy about them.

19 December 1939

Just pottered—washed my hair and helped generally. After dinner to Bet's and Mr. Meeks who made us stay. Sure Mr. Meeks will marry again. One is inclined to call him a dear old soul but he is only 53. Somehow men look older here.

A Plymouth Brethren of the most exclusive circle. Joan arrives home in tears after a tangle between the boyfriend and a girlfriend and an appointment not kept. Got her a cup of tea and made her a welsh rarebit for supper. Advised her never to have girl friends to whom one told everything and to keep her boyfriends and her doings to herself in the future. Poor little 17. How I'd hate to go back. Much rather be my age when there's still thrills in life but you've learned enough to put an armour on against the sorrows. Poor Arthur and Winnie rather bewildered and no wonder. Winnie said she never went on so in her day and Arthur said he never had time for such nonsense. He courted Winnie when he was 16 and in between times he had to work too hard.

Today I go to Auntie Bella's and I'll miss Winnie, Arthur and Joan so much. Miss the problems and confidences of 17 whispered in bed and the quiet talks with Winnie and Arthur by the fire. Wonder rather vaguely what's the matter with me? Never confided in anyone at 17 and wouldn't now.

20 December 1939

Back at Auntie Bella's and out at night to see Uncle Dick's sisters—Polly and Gladys. Hard frosts now. It freezes all day—not like it does in New Zealand, freeze at night and then thaw out in the day. IT NEVER THAWS—the streets are white and the trees stick out frosty brittle arms like ghosts. Yet somehow I don't feel the cold. I don't have time in between sitting before gorgeous fires. George comes with me—sure he's never done so much visiting in his life. It is really noble of him. Glady's Ruby is a marvellous pianist, one of Albert's pupils—there's no doubt about it he can teach. Aunt Polly's daughter Betty as thin as a lathe—weighs what I used to when I left home (decided I'd rather be nine stone). Got home at 11.20 too late even for fish for supper. Sat till 2 and saw the fire out. Strange how each place seems like home now.

21 December 1939

Into Rotherham to change a cheque and do more Xmas shopping. Some cuff-links like playing cards for Malcolm, a pixie ring for little Betty and a cigarette case for Joan. Home with coat collar up, laden with parcels and covered in frost, looking all the world like Father Xmas. The whole crowd cheer when I got in, poked up the already blazing fire. Uncle Dick gets me a cup of tea quick—George shoots a little 'something' into it just in case I'll get cold and all's well with the world. Helped Auntie Bella in the morning with a spot of scrubbing and waxing. Mighty and intricate are the preparations for the wedding. Everything is being 'turned out' and washed and polished.

A frosty night but gorgeously clear. To Mr. and Mrs. Norman Colclough (Spalton Road, Parkgate) to collect chocolates and biscuits from the 'Chocolate Club' and here I start on the mince pie campaign with a glass of port. For every fresh mince pie one has one is assured of another happy month, so this is the first. A Xmas tree too all glittery with lights and toys—and all for Mr. and Mrs. and the dog! Such a neat tiny home and such a prim little Xmas tree. We'd really set off to go to George Turner's but too late when we left so home at about 11 and to supper round the table, everyone talking at once and Auntie Bella at the loaf buttering and cutting. A quiet sit before the fire with Auntie and Uncle and so to bed beside Betty. Frank arrived today—the first of the 'guests'.

22 December 1939

How near it is to Xmas—an English Xmas! Feel excited all the time, every single minute of the day. Frank and Uncle Dick eat a huge breakfast to sustain them and then march off to Sheffield to meet Elsie coming up from London. Auntie Bella and I go for the lick of our lives polishing and fixing generally. Elsie arrives forlorn and alone—about two hours afterwards Frank and Uncle Dick. Spent about two hours more arguing as to how they could have missed each other. The dishes after each meal grow more and more and I attack them vigorously. At night George and I to George Turner's again but meet Mr. and Mrs. Tom Hansen (Annie Turner's sister) and off we go with them to his mother, a dear old soul in bed with neuritis. Chattered with her and her daughter and a husband. Thought the latter belonged to the mother and then found he was the daughter's. Easily old enough to be her father. Must be losing my diplomatic training to nearly put my foot in it like that. Must be more careful in the future. Another mince pie and another happy month next year. Mrs Hansen and I walk home arm in arm talking of Uncle Sam and family. Too late again to go to George Turner's. Beautiful nights and the streets so slippery one must tread warily. Some say snow for Xmas and some say not. Waited in fish shop while George dealt with the intricacies of 'a pennoth and a fish twice'.

23 December 1939

Uncle Dick arises early and goes to Misterton (30 miles away) for the goose. Many months ago he went to the same farm and selected it to be specially fattened up. Feel a mass of energy. Have supper things washed—two fireplaces cleaned out and breakfast ready when Auntie comes down. Took in from

Schonhut's lad vast quantities of pork and bacon and pork pies. George and I to Sheffield about 10.30, rocking on the top of the old tram as we sat in the front pretending it was the 'Rolls'. A long, long ride past factories and foundries—men in caps and scarves with snap tins. And in the market it was the Xmas of the story-books—rows and rows of turkeys, some hanging, some trussed and at 1/2, 1/4 and 1/6 per lb. Women poke and prod and argue over the price. Some shops hang the turkeys outside, right from the upper windows to the ground floor are turkeys in the clean cold air. Everything is white and crisp. Piles of fish are slapped around, and as I pass, from out of a pile of beef of old England, a cheery butcher with a face as red as one of his own joints yells 'Best New Zealand lamb, lady'. George buys me a little Sheffield fruit knife as a souvenir. We push our way through the chestnuts, the turkeys and the geese, to push again through Woolworth's to buy Xmas decorations and balloons. We giggle like a couple of kids ramming things into our carrier bag. Then through Walsh's where Father Xmas reigns in magnificent splendour. Admire particularly a carved bedroom suite and the shop walker beams benevolently 'Can be supplied with either single or double beds, sir'. We melt away to find ourselves to George's embarrassment in the ladies' underclothing! Then through Atkinson's—another Father Xmas. Bought a cigarette lighter for Uncle Dick and staggered into a café for toast and tea-cake. Two women at the next table order strawberry ice. Good heavens! Out again and into Littlewood's and Home and Colonial Store and gazed into frock shops and at things we couldn't afford. Stared like typical tourists at the City Hall. Bought a mouth organ for young Jim and a companion set of brush, shovel etc. for Auntie Bella. A scarf for Teddy—a tartan one.

Into the markets again, the streets gay with flower sellers and everyone carrying holly and mistletoe. Dark now, almost 4.30, we queue up for the Rotherham tram. Flop down thankfully on a piece of holly! Prowled about Rotherham into shops and at last walked home to eat a huge tea. Frank's Mother and Dad arrived from Spennymoor and Jack, typical soldier now, blustering and forever marching up and down to show us how they do it in camp. 'They do it like this sitthee' he says and 'left-rights' into Uncle Dick carrying the teapot. 'Ah doan't want that thing' he says sweeping away his bread and butter plate. 'We doan't have none of these in t' barracks'. Has to be forcibly reminded that 105, Middle Avenue is not the barracks. Frank's father a dear with twinkly eyes and his mother a quiet, shy soul. At night to the Club to be greeted vociferously by all. Ate more mince pies. George burned a hole in his pants with a cigarette. Everyone thought it was my fur coat and we had a frantic time trying to locate it. Children 'Good King Wenceslas-ing' from door to door—a trifle hoarse after a week of it. But it is lovely to hear them. What if I'd come to England and there hadn't been any carols! The rest to bed and George and I trim up the rooms for Xmas. Never have I giggled so much. I never could blow up balloons. It always seems as if the balloon gets the better of the situation and tries to blow me up! Then the precious drawing pins—such a shortage of them that one must account for every single pin. Sprigs of holly over the pictures and mistletoe over the door. I get my first kiss at 3 a.m. There are two big flags over the mirror for we've the York and Lancs Regiment and the RAF in the family. At 3.30 we 'mash' a pot of tea and find some parkin. Have promised to draw a turkey for Annie. Have never seen anything 'drawn'. All our poultry at home has come decently from the shop. Peer inquisitively and even as I do so the innards come out—over me! To bed feeling slightly ill. There's something 'funny' about innards!

24 December 1939

Up about 10 to get ready the roast beef and Yorkshire. Everything still white with frost. Stiffly white as I have never seen it before. Somehow it is queerly silent outside—the traffic makes no sound and there is no wind. We just have 'five minutes' after dinner and then to Greasbrough to see Mr. and Mrs. Bradder. Right plonk into a Xmas party, trifles, more mince pies, iced cake, crackers and fancy hats. A gorgeous Xmas tree with little lights flashing in and out. I know now that we don't have a Xmas at all in New Zealand. How can we in mid-summer? Our's is just a poor little pretence. It isn't really Xmas with a dish of lamb and green peas and mint sauce on Christmas Day and the cold lamb and salad and fruit sitting on the beach on Boxing Day. Xmas is as I saw it at Greasbrough tonight, the little lights on the tree flashing in and out, almost as if they could speak 'A Merry Xmas', 'A Merry Xmas'. And this is a Merry Xmas whatever the next one may be. Laughing, joking sitting round the fire roasting chestnuts and at 9 with the rest to the British Legion Club. Into the warmth and smoke of a holly-filled room. We drink to the New Year and with a wee bit of Scotch still in our hands we sing carols, the good old carols, 'While Shepherds Watch Their Flocks By Night' and the woman in the little black hat has her baby asleep in her arms. 'Christ Was Born in Bethlehem' roared the man in the spotted red scarf. 'Peace on Earth, goodwill to all men'. Somewhere they're fighting one against the other with guns and bayonets. Someday we'll be rationed more severely than now—who knows if we'll all be together ever again.

And at 12, the magic hour of Xmas Eve, we stood on Greasbrough Tops. It was black except for the great golden full moon. The shadows of the big guns on the hill—the bells sing of peace and in the silence that follows the owl hoots 'To Woo-wo'. It struck a mournful, almost a warning, note for a moment and then it was gone. We went arm in arm, laughing down the queerly silent streets that looked like a Xmas card. At home the fire burns red as it does in the frost, chestnuts crack. We sit a long time sipping a glass of hot rum and there was many a toast to my two dears whose photographs sit on the mantelpiece. More guests arrive and I creep up to bed—Auntie, Elsie, Bet and I in one bed.

25 December 1939

And Xmas Day in Yorkshire. Was there ever such a day? Like something out of Dickens, except for the snow. For in spite of my prayers snow has not come. But it is frosty and everything glistens white. How good the goose smells in the oven—an eighteen pounder. He's fat and stuffed full to his gaping gizzard. Everywhere you look is food—all the conversation is of food—I have become food conscious as never before. A piece of pork on an O.S. dish, frizzling and savoury, brussels sprouts, potatoes and apple sauce. Our plates are piled high, not once but twice. Auntie Bella with the carving knife, Uncle Dick exhorting us to further, almost impossible, efforts. Young Jack tucked in as only a soldier knows how. Jim and Bet clamouring for more goose. Pop Robinson twinkled more than ever. Mrs. Robinson, her shyness waning under the mellowing influence of good English ale. Frank shows that it being the eve of his wedding didn't spoil his appetite. Elsie carving more pork in great generous slices. George silently supplying my every need before it comes a need. And then the pudding! The blackest ever—steaming and sizzling hot. Over goes the rum and I strike the light. She flares up with a mystical blue flame that wavers down the side. There's a cheer and the holly is stuck on top. There's more rum in that sauce than a cookery book ever called for. And there's more fun in the assembled company than Dickens ever portrayed. A long sit while the toasts go round.

To Uncle John's in the afternoon to eat mince pies for another happy month and then to sit in the front room roasting chestnuts and cracking nuts, chatting spasmodically and dozing. At intervals one of us drifts to the piano. It's a funny thing but I play better now than I've ever done. Everyone is so encouraging, so entirely uncritical. It doesn't matter if you don't play correctly, it's just wonderful that you play at all. Young Jim plays anything by ear. Awake from a particularly sound sleep to hear the assembled company 'Hanging the Washing on the Siegfried Line'. Tea time and we manage a cup of tea and a pork sandwich then to the Crown. How did I become acquainted with so many people! They are so genuine in their good wishes and their fun. Teddy beams—his new scarf firmly round his neck in spite of the heat of the room. George exhibits his shamrock cuff-links and Uncle Dick his cigarette lighter to all and sundry. Home to sit over the fire and when it is well on into the morning to bed. Outside it is still cold and white and the carollers' voices clear in the frosty air. I must put curlers in for the wedding—a bridesmaid with straggly 'ends' is unthinkable, am kissed under the mistletoe for the hundred and fiftieth time.

26 December 1939

Somehow it seems that night and morning are indescribably mixed. There is a pleasant bustle and work for all. A great pan of bacon to be cooked to which each one adds their egg and takes what they want and when they want it. There's dear Aunt Eliza to welcome and Uncle Herbert. Mammy Tonge comes in and takes charge. People from all round the district appear to help. We're barely ready when Freddy White comes with the car. Backwards and forwards the car goes. Six times, seven times to Rawmarsh Church on the hill. There is no surplus of cars these days with petrol restrictions. We stand at last in the porch waiting for the bride. She must be just the merest fraction late. Not late enough to admit of any hitch or early enough to admit to haste. Just at the right minute, just when a little flutter of apprehension of delay is rustling through the relations, she comes. She looks so nice in her musquash[23] coat, navy hat and veil and chrysanthemum bouquet. Uncle Dick, his fringe of silky hair brushed to one side, stands stiff. Uncle John is there with Frank. Little Betty is in a fever of excitement as to whether she looks nice and smooths down her blue velvet frock. She looks sweet in the little blue cap and anemone bouquet. We stand at the altar, Frank and Elsie, Uncle John and I, Betty and young Jim. It is all so indelibly stamped in my memory—the ceremony and the little appropriate talk afterwards—carefully appropriate to the R.A.F. All the relations are there in their best. They whisper and rustle. I am conscious of them behind and wonder rather inconsistently, just as Elsie murmurs 'I do', if my seam stitches are straight. George grabs me as soon as it is over. He has a new suit, the shamrock cuff-links and a white heather button hole. A box of confetti descends on us by mistake and we run breathless into the car. To the photographer's then in traditional style to go through the ordeal. It is a terrifying business—the photographer, one of the old school, who cautions one to 'Smile please' and 'look up'. George raises his eyes to Heaven and I break into a retained grin that finishes in an uncontrollable quivering of the upper lip.

It is over and everyone emerges much happier. Back to the house and the breakfast. How can one describe the excited, laughing, and chattering folk—the great plates of ham and tongue and beef—the cakes and trifles and fruit salads. We sang till we were hoarse. Twenty dozen bottles vanished as if by magic and more magically made their appearance. A few who find it overpowering collect in the kitchen to munch meat sandwiches and buns. The company come and go. George and I for a little run to Swinton with Freddie White. Freddie makes those huge galleons as a hobby. Then round to Pharo's for some cigarettes. We take Uncle John and ourselves for a very necessary walk in the fresh air and call at Auntie Lizzie's. Pop Robinson has everyone in hysterics with his monologues in broad Durham twang. Always the fires burn big and red. Olga and Albert play the piano until they drop and Teddy falls asleep in the dining room. Fred Brown sings his last song and sups his last glass of ale reluctantly. Susie has given up 'Smiling through' and gone back to Manchester. Albert has gone home—or at least we hope he got there. Until tonight even one glass was foreign to him. The crowd is thinning at 3 a.. The house guests are trailing off to bed. It is fourteen hours after the wedding. The fires are built up. Mr. and Mrs. Robinson Snr. snore peacefully in the little bedroom. Aunt Eliza and Uncle Herbert creak in the bed in the front bedroom. Bet and a long line of other small guests turn in unison on a mattress on the floor. Jim and a long line of male small guests fling their arms and hands across each other's chests. Every room was full. We wander vaguely round scraping up bits from the carpet and collecting glasses; laugh over the memory of Auntie Polly with the goose bone. Wander into the kitchen to find Uncle Dick and Teddy asleep in the big chairs with the fire out and an unknown with his head on the sofa. Find we'd forgotten to enquire where we're to go to bed. Couldn't find a space anywhere so got blankets down from the cupboard and settled ourselves in the drawing room on a chesterfield and two chairs respectively. I was trying to remember what we did at Fred White's at Swinton—had an uneasy suspicion I'd asked him to make me a galleon. What on earth should I do with it!

27 December 1939

Begins at 10. The blanketed ghosts open their eyes cautiously. Teddy comes in to rouse us out, towelling his fat face vigorously. Uncle Dick resolutely pulls down the black-outs. One by one or pair by pair the house comes to life. James Willy comes round, Uncle John, Walter Brown and numerous distant, not so distant or totally remote relations. George and I wash up. Ye Gods what a wash up! We sweep the confetti as best we can. It is all cheerful bustle—always someone coming and going. One lone bottle is found among the empties—how it escaped no one knows—and a new lot brought in. Find an inventory of the original supply: 20 dozen bottles of ale, 1 quart of red port, I quart of white port, 1 quart of sherry, 1 quart of whiskey, 2 bottles of rum, a case of cider, twelve loaves of bread, twelve pounds of pork, a huge ham and a three tiered wedding cake with a cute little aeroplane on top. Lost count long ago of what had been brought in since. Let the men go to the Club thankfully, had a bath and a sleep and a quiet talk to Uncle Herbert. I do like him. We think over all the events of yesterday. Pop Robinson's bit about miners being like birds because they go down in a cage and have to pick for a living. And then as he says what they get is only fit to burn! A tea 'offs' the remains of everything. Arrange for fresh supplies for the morrow and to the pantomime.

Will the charm of Cinderella never fade? The warmth of the theatre makes us tingle after our walk into Rotherham in the hard white frost. On comes the traditional fairy Godmother, the glittering coach and the dear little ponies. The ugly sisters are as ugly as even I could wish, the fairy as dainty a fairy as ever came out of fairy story tales. The clowns tumble and the mummers fool in good old style. We walk home down the Wentworth Coach Road where the puddles are frozen hard so that I can slide. The moon is big, golden and alive. It would seem that the whole world is electrified that night. Our footsteps are hushed on the hoar frost but I was warm, all except my nose. It has a perpetual drip that freezes. I think I'll have to make a little bag for it. Supper good old English cheese and bread. George has an onion and they tease me into having one too against my better judgement.

28 December 1939

Frank goes back to camp. One of the little pitiful episodes of war brought right to our home. Elsie is a brave little lass but there are tears after the last embrace as the car disappears in the distance. They knew they would only have two days. It's a thing I couldn't do. Round to Auntie Lizzie's for a chat and find them having five minutes before the fire eating breakfast at 11 0'clock. Walt looks grumpy. He has overlaid and had a score of things to do. In the afternoon to the Baths to the children's Carnival dance. All the kiddies had pretty party frocks. Jack still cleaning his buttons religiously every time you look at him and demonstrates how they march but there's so little room for marching in the kitchen and we could scream at him. Yet we miss his shouting when he's not there. Jim has borrowed George's gloves and lost them and they argue until we bang their heads together. We get to George Turner's at last. Poor man has been thinking he was the black sheep of the family. He's taken on an auxiliary fireman's work—has a helmet that is the pride and joy of all the family. Confide my fears to George that I had ordered a galleon on the wedding night. George can't remember either so we go out to make sure. Fred says I might have ordered it but he wasn't quite in a condition to register the order at the time so all is well. A walk to the fish shop at 10 p.m. and a jolly supper.

30 December 1939

Elsie regretfully back to Bicester. Around to the photographers to see the proofs.
On the whole they're good and everyone is relieved. George certainly obeyed
instructions by 'looking up' and my grin, if not elegant, is at least cheerful. To
the Club to be very nice to the Deputy who is to take me down the mine. Seem
to attract the attention of all the Irish people by my bright green georgette
scarf round my hair. Talk a long time to an old friend of Granddad Turner's.
'If th' Grandfather could sitthee, lassie! He'd be fair flummoxed wi' pride he
would'. The singer warbles 'The Holy City' and the comedian, who is a friend
of Jack's, does a first class turn. Realise that wherever I go someone tells me
what a fine 'young women' I am. Am getting hopelessly spoilt. Whatever will
I do when I get home and all my faults get shown up again! It's not the Irish
alone who have a touch of the blarney. And the funny part of it is I'm not a
fine 'young woman' at all. I'm just revelling in all the attention and getting
hopelessly fat. Of course I'm pleasant; I'm sleek, fat and no one to cross me.
Who wouldn't be pleasant!

31 December 1939

The last day of the old year. There's no dinner today. We all pick a bit and
concentrate on tea. Sit in the room for a while and we roast chestnuts and
pop them. We pop corn too and munch 'spice'. Feel vaguely that after New
Year I must slim. Threatened with dire penalties if I start doing any such
thing while I'm in England. It's a hard frost still but it may snow. Someone
reports a few flakes and I rush to the door but it is a false alarm. George
and I get ourselves round to Norcliffes about seven with difficulty and meet
two garden enthusiasts. We talk and argue over bulbs, seeds and plants. Wade
through catalogues and I order seeds for a blue poppy and a golden tomato.
The Norcliffes have what they call a bungalow. Everything that isn't upstairs
is called a bungalow here. Join Auntie Bella at the Club. Can hardly get away
from the crowd. Have an invulnerable armour of Good Wishes to last me all
the year, whether I cross the seas in peace or war. Amidst a cheer of Happy
New Years we wend our black-out way down the snicket and up the steps to
Dale Road.

Back home we sit quietly round the big Yule Log on the fire. Maybe we'll
see the New Year in just by ourselves, maybe more will come. It is so funny
waiting and then comes the rings at the door. Uncle John, Auntie Polly, Walter,
James, Irene, Teddy, Donald, Malcolm, Annie; how many drift in and drift out
I don't know. It was an endless procession of red shining faces emerging from
scarves and coats. But we carve the poor carcass of the ducks to their limit.

We eat trifle until the bottom of the dishes are shining and at twelve we stand and drink to 1940—to what? To a year of war and devastation—to a year of bravery that means just carrying on—to a year of sorrows for some and joys for others. We none of us know. Someone whispers in a strained unhappy voice 'Don't let them sing Auld Lang Syne' but someone has started up and we link arms. Auntie Bella wipes her eyes and wonders where 'our lass' will be next year. 'Our lass' looks at the photograph of Mother and Daddy and knows where she will be. Auntie Polly cries and Uncle John looks positively miserable. Then I laugh and tell them that I'm still here and the unhappy little moment passes. Time enough when I have to go. I hate to think of it. It is bad enough now even when I go away to stay in another town. Don't let's think about it. Think only of them all piling out of the door into the cold frosty air, of the warmth of the colliers' fires and the warmth of their hearts.

January 1940

Rawmarsh, Greasbrough, Leeds, Aldwarke, Bakewell, Rowsley

1 January 1940

It's the New Year and 'the morning after'. 'Wesh up pots' and do a hasty sweep round. Albert comes in with Mary Ellen—a sweet girl with large placid eyes. Everything about Mary Ellen is placid. She says 'Yes' and 'no' dutifully but no more. Albert and I spar as we often do and he always comes back for more. Root George out of bed with difficulty at 1 o'clock—we have to go to the Norcliffes for flowers. It's a cold still day. The trees look for all the world like a little girl in her stiffly starched party frock. It would seem the world was dead—that we had no right to be walking the streets. Call at Uncle John's to find him drooping over the fire. Upstairs Auntie Polly and little John lie weakly on her bed side by side. Maurice in the next room gives me a sweet angelic smile like a martyr and then rushes with undignified haste for the bathroom. No one knows what it is they have eaten. Can it be the salmon? No, because Maurice didn't have any and he's no better than the rest. We all sit round and wonder. We sympathise, stroke their heads and go. It's all we can do. A bright fire at the Norcliffes and a fire burns in the greenhouse too but the outsides of the glass is patterned with silver. There are still chrysanthemums in the glass house.

At night to Aunt Gladys (Uncle Dick's sister) to a jolly party. Here in England parlour games still survive—all the old postman's knocks and forfeits that I thought had happily passed away when I was a child. Then to the piano to roar out 'Park Parade', 'The Man with the Mandolin', 'Till the Lights of London Shine Again' and, over and over again just when anyone thought of it, 'There'll Always Be an England'. It is strange to think how in the years to come these songs will mean 1939–1940 to me. Enjoyed thoroughly a selection of the classics. Ruby passed the Piano Senior Exam with honours. She is Albert's pupil. He can evidently teach. Says he'd even undertake to put me through my exams but he doesn't know me!

A marvellous tea and an equally marvellous supper. Never in all my life have I thought so much about food. Everyone seats me with my back to a roasting fire in deference to my thin New Zealand blood. Begin to wonder if I have any N.Z. blood in me—it's so renewed and replenished with the roast beef and Yorkshire pudding of old England. Never cold now. Not even when we walked from Aunt Gladys's in a cold, still, dead world. Life is lovely here on holiday with all these dear ones around me.

2 January 1940

Uncle Dick and George to work again and most of the 'staying' visitors gone. Ponder on a little jealousy on the part of certain members of the family and decide on a tactful course. Round to Auntie Lizzie's to chat then to Uncle John's to find out how they all are there. I find Grandma Glossop kneading bread and old Aunt Lizzie, her sister, crooning over the fire. Uncle John to work but Donald home with the trouble now. Little John much better, his button of a nose as red as mine. Round to Arthur's to find Joan and Winnie thoroughly turning out in good old English style. Chairs up on the table, the whole place reeking of wax and soapsuds. Then to Rotherham. First to find the Food Control Office to get ration book changed for a travellers (rationing of sugar, bacon and meat begins on Monday next). Then to buy a tea-pot for Auntie Bella and a pair of stockings. Got Auntie Lizzie some bacon and chitterlings and call at the hairdressers for Joan. Buy Betty a fairy tale book. Home to find Uncle Dick getting in the coal. Set to and shovel for him while he takes the sacks round the back. The streets still white and slippery, the whole path a sheet of ice. The red jumper is marvellously warm.

At night to the pantomime again—'Jack and The Beanstalk' and walk to Rotherham. It's pitch dark; the chemical works send up an unearthly glow. The trolley buses glide by visible only by the red sign at the front. A cigarette glows in the distance and an odd torch is flicked on and off. 'There'll Always Be an England' sang the chorus girls outside the stage castle and Jack, in his glittering tights, strutted in front. We dive into the Top Hat chocolate box and the special Chocolate Brazils. The beanstalk grew and grew and the hind and fore parts of Minnie the Cow did antics that surpassed all expectations. 'The dame' was as fat and fair as ever but best of all were the performing dogs. Girlie that went dead until picked up by two little paws, limply slung into an ambulance and wheeled off by Spot on his hind legs. Then followed Baby with her head sadly hung carrying a bunch of flowers. 'Roll Out The Barrel' struck up the orchestra and on came Scamp rolling on a barrel as fast as his little legs would carry her. Some people behind recognise George and we hear them whisper along the row, 'That's Georgie Roe—see he's courting'. We do a little giggle and they add 'And she's got a fur coat too'. Feel like turning round and informing them I'm only his cousin but they don't live in Rawmarsh and most likely they wouldn't believe us anyway.

It's blacker than ever coming home and the paths like glass. Call at the fish shop for two fish and a pennoth. I've learned to love the quiet sits over the fire after supper seeing the fire grow less and less, turning over the coals and finally banking it up to keep the room warm till morning.

4 January 1940

Here at Mrs. Senior's and awake out of a delicious slumber on a feather bed. One lot of hot water bottles put into bed about seven and renewed at half past nine. I can help so easily here, it is much more like home than the other families I've stayed with. Uncle George and I talk mostly about religion. I thought out similar problems, working out similar theories in those difficult days of extreme youth. In the afternoon to Chapel. The same little Congregational Chapel that Mother used to go to. Nearly all the women remember Mother as a girl. Mrs. Hutchinson is the first to kiss and greet me. She was Miss Marland and by the look of her one would think she was 'Miss' still despite three children. She is prim but so kindly. Mrs. Cooke (Lucy Cottrill) is there and wanted to know when I'm going to tea. Mrs Bacon—one of the Dysons from Victoria Road—is there and Mrs Merrills who was a Goodison. Her sister Annie went to school with Mum. Several elderly ladies also who knew Grandma Turner. Grandma must have been a wonderful woman, there are so many who are grateful for what she had done for them, for help given in time of sickness. Many of them try to find some resemblance but none can. I'm not like the Turners at all. I'm afraid I'm just pure Northern Ireland. Mrs Brown's sister, Emily Machin, asks specially about our home and New Zealand in general. We have a prayer, a hymn, a solo and then I have to speak. Haven't the faintest idea what on but after all I have a lot to tell them. Wake up to the fact that I've gone on for twenty minutes after I should have stopped. They're such dears no one has even shuffled. A cup of tea and a chat. I can see little Mum in the Chapel and afterwards, on the Pleasant Sunday Afternoons, walking with Auntie Leah to have a cup of tea with the old ladies in the alms houses or to sing at Greasbrough church after taking tea at the Minister's. It is strange that all the years I've heard about Mother going to sing at other churches I never knew it was Greasbrough she went to with its quaint little stone cottages—never knew the beauty of Greasbrough Tops on which I stood at Xmas Eve.

From Chapel to Mrs Brown's for tea. Such a jolly tea with a Mary and her friend Milly.   Mary is 25 and everyone is so curious to know when she's getting married—almost past hope according to Yorkshire standards. Home in the black-out to play Lexicon and dive into the liquorice allsorts until our tongues are black. Xmas lasts just as long as does Xmas cake, mince pies and sweets. It's the holiday spirit in England to the last nut.

5 January 1940

Pottering in the morning and into Rotherham to the market. The frost has gone, it is almost warm—surely it must rain? Bought some tulips. They're forced of course. Lovely daffodils there are too, golden yellow with a sweet fresh scent. I buy some anemones too for Auntie Leah's basket—little buds that will open. There are Channel Island tomatoes at 5d per lb! When I think of the price we pay in New Zealand for early tomatoes! A walk with Uncle George to the Stores and we play Lexicon and have 'Beetle' afterwards. My beetle with such a curly tale it looks like some prehistoric animal. Xmas fare still on, have had so many mince pies that I've exhausted all the months in this year to be happy in and started on next year. Some houses have a great idea of putting a string across the mantelpiece and hanging the cards on that. Crumpets for tea (they call them pikelets here) and fish cakes. It is good to toast them sitting on the little stool reddening one's face at the fire. Played Lexicon again at night and chewed nuts and reminisced—especially of Mr. Parkes, whose photograph is in the little chapel. A worthy man and earnest. Auntie Leah remembers how he used to energetically sing 'tiling on' for the old hymn 'Toiling on'. We sang it on Thursday just for old time sake.

8 January 1940

With Uncle George for a wee walk to Aunt Jinny's—an energetic little woman whose daughter is a missionary. We're to go to tea on Tuesday. Greasbrough is a pretty little village. They still keep up the Feast here in their own particular style. First everyone cuts their hedges and puts up clean curtains. Then they all invite their relatives to come to see them. On Feast Day they all repair to the village common where the Band plays. It has a village benefactor too. A kindly man who knows his own importance. Having made some money he proceeds to give some of it away with a loud booming voice, making sure everyone knows just who's given it. In the afternoon an orgy of visitors. First Aunt Kitty (Mrs. Nurse) then Auntie Jinny and finally Mrs. Dunkeley and her daughter Margaret. Poor little Margaret, so precise and delicately natured! So fearful of ever being 'Yorkshire' that her speech is almost unrecognisable. They stay till 10.30 and I've nearly talked myself hoarse. I get lazier and lazier. I love every minute of life.

9 January 1940

And we're going to Auntie Jinny's for tea. This is Horace Causer's wife. Mum will remember Horace. He's a school teacher and for thirty years he has taught in Greasbrough school. What is more he hopes to teach there for thirty years more! Has absolutely no desire to change. The weather quite different—a strange phenomenon—a sunshiney day with an almost cloudless sky. No one can understand it for January. Snow alas seems further off than ever. Poor Horace has influenza and has to retire with his germs to the front room while we laugh and chat in the 'house'. Auntie Jinny, a bustling soul who reads tea cups, delivers me a special warning about falling down stairs. Daughter Connie is a school teacher and frankly admits that she hates to soil her hands. Their car is in the garage with a tarpaulin cover over it to keep it from freezing!

10 January 1940

Up late and pack. Played a little patience with Uncle and we talk again about many things. He gave me a beautiful bound Bible. It is something I can cherish for always to remind me of the two dears. And then reluctantly the bus to Rawmarsh. Only reluctant until I get there. One couldn't possibly be reluctant afterwards. Stopping with Annie and Herbert. Annie has a sharp-featured face with the most gorgeous pair of blue eyes I've ever seen. Never been known to miss a joke. Just loves to cook and peer into the stew pot stirring, ecstatically sniffing the rich gravy. Her hair isn't golden or platinum like her sisters but just brown like mine. We've got that in common and moan about it. Herbert comes home—dear old Herbert as slow as Annie is quick. He takes me round to Auntie Bella's (next door but one) to say 'Hallo' and then to Auntie Lizzie's to get little Mum's letters. Home in the pitch black over ground white and silent. I seem to be alone and say 'Herbert, where are you?' A voice comes from well in front 'I'm here, aren't you?' He had strode ahead in the blackness and was talking to me thinking I was still by his side. So I grab hold of his arm.

11 January 1940

Up very late. We sit on two little stools talking and talking. Scurry round and do a bit of work—strange how the upstairs rooms in these houses aren't cold even with a white world outside. Then round to Auntie Lizzie's—Uncle Albert beams as he lies on the sofa. He's had a haircut and it is a haircut an' all! Bessie and I to Cathie Wannop's (Miss Hague's daughter—Miss Hague was Mum's teacher at school). Although in strict fairness to Miss Hague, now deceased, I should add that she was Mrs Wannop when she had Cathie. (See private diary No. 2 re Cathie). We sit for an hour in Cypress Villa (in Green Lane) and freeze. We are shown the big house, admire the china cabinet and marble fireplaces and take our leave as soon as possible. Fly home to a marvellous fire.

12 January 1940

Turn out to see Auntie Miriam at Canklow. Mr. Potts (the lodger) and Herbert sitting over huge steaming bowls of soup. Both awfully decent to me and I sit and rock in Grandma's old rocking chair. The five cages of canaries sing their heads off, the black leaded lambs, rams and antelopes on the hearth shine and the two little wise birds in the sixth cage sit like Darby and Joan side by side immobile. Aunt Mid's (Miriam) chest very bad. Nights foggy and buses often not running but I get there and back safely in spite of the warnings. Must record that all rice puddings here are made with condensed milk—in fact very little fresh is used and seeing it I don't wonder. It appears that a certain percentage of added water is actually allowed! Then to the pictures to see 'summat' about the North West in colour. We take Auntie Lizzie and she sits munching brazil chocolate muttering at intervals 'mm ah mmm' as the picture progresses according to her liking. Still a white frost but it's grand.

13 January 1940

And I walk to Kilnhurst Stores with Ruth and Auntie Lizzie. Never have I known it freeze so hard or so thick a fog. We follow the path but there's nothing to see but stiff white trees like white ghosts. Icicles hang from the hedges and one from my nose. All wrapped up in my fur coat and I can't truthfully say I'm cold, except my feet. Something funny has happened to them. First they go numb, then ache, then get so sore that I feel as if I'm walking on peas. Hobble home and warm them in my hands till the feeling returns. That great white world—it almost frightens me. They say it will snow. Uncle Dick calls round to take me to the Meadows. We call first at Aldwarke Pit for his pay. The men don't get paid on the job, they have to go in their time off. There is a queue of men and a shift has just come up. Seem to be introduced to at least half. A smiling black face turns out to be cousin George Turner.   George Roe is with us too, 'laiking' as they call it, because it's freezing too hard to work down the quarry. Then the Meadows frozen hard inches thick, the ice cut into powder by the sharp skates. I'm dying to try but Uncle Dick shakes his head 'Tha'll brak thy ankle sithee if tha goas on those things' so I must perforce be content to be held on either side while skating. Back past Aldwarke Hall—the sun a great golden ball through the fog. The trees hold out their ghostly arms and a red-breasted robin hops from bough to bough. It is an Xmas card scene. In the afternoon to meet Annie in Rotherham after she's had treatment for her feet. She's late and I stand outside Woolworth's and freeze. Inside all is warm. We perch on high stools and drink Bovril and biscuits—a shop gaze and then home. I'm so thankful these days for the rug the firm gave to me. I think of them so often—how the time has flown.

15 January 1940

To the Greasbrough Dam to see more skating. The ice is like thick glass. Days getting longer now, not dark till about five, but it is dusk and the skaters fly round like ghosts. Went round to Jack Senior's, another brother of Auntie Annie Turner. Another W.E.A. man and a communist they say but found a great deal in common in the poetry line—especially de la Mare and Robert Bridges—rather a surprise here where the only poetry they know is the rattle of coal against steel, the sizzle of a good Yorkshire in the oven and maybe 'It was the schooner Hesperus'. Stayed rather longer than I thought discussing old favourites. It was like something from another world. I seem to have become so steeped in the pit and the forge, the satisfaction of good 'snap' and Gracie singing to the troops. There are still people who love the delicacies of Francis Thompson[24]—I'd almost forgotten.

Dream to the bus to go to Auntie Miriam's and stand thinking and then— IT SNOWED! Thin fairy flakes tumbling, tossing and dancing on my coat. I stared and stared. A man near me buttoned up his coat. I looked up at him 'Is it snowing?' He gave me a curious glance and said it was, curse it. Faster and faster it came and a light breeze swept it down the street but it came thicker, playfully almost, until, as I ran home, I ploughed through it white and fluffy. My hair was white, my hat heavy and my coat like a polar bear. I laughed aloud as the kerb-stones vanished under the white soft pile. The shapes of everything vanished, everything was levelled up. A car shot past and a voice called 'Gwennie! How do you like this? Don't forget tea tonight'.

It was Arthur Hague. I shouted back and ran on. An old soul coming up the Titanic steps shouted from his snow-filled beard 'Nah then tha's got snaw at last'.

Into Auntie Lizzie's breathless. They were all there ready to take my coat and shake the snow. It is inches deep now. Round to Auntie Bella's to tell them it was snowing. They were expecting me and all laugh and talk at once. Then up the steps to Annie's door—all the neighbours calling out asking me how I like it. To Rotherham with Annie, we have our rubber boots on and plough through it disdainfully. It is warm in Woolworth's—it is always warm in Woolworth's. Bought a record of Gracie singing to the troops 'Cheerio As You Wave Me Goodbye' and 'They'll Always Be an England'. Annie has a gorgeous radiogram. We fly home and just about wear the records out. We sit up late that night, Annie and I talking about all sorts. It's 2.30 when we creep upstairs. Now England is complete. Spring flowers, little violets and sweet wild lilac—summer roses and white hawthorn, autumn holly and red hips on the hedges, and now winter snow and a robin with the reddest breast bob-bob-bobbin' along.

17 January 1940

Round post-haste to Auntie Lizzie's. A gorgeous sunny day with the snow thick on the ground. In the winter nothing can be dried outside. A big fire is made up both in the kitchen and the house-place and everything dried inside on the racks that let up and down to the ceiling. George came round in the afternoon—got a new job. Long hours but twice as much money. If he saves it will be the hardest day's work he ever did. Flew into Mrs. Wileman's for tea. Mrs. Wileman is one of the few who bake brown bread. Mr. Wileman working at the Forge as a furnace man. His face is permanently red like sunburn from the heat. 'He works right hard' whispers Mrs. Wileman, her mouth working expressively. 'He does these sorts', she pushes an imaginary poker into a furnace energetically 'but he's always kept his looks, Bill 'as'. Bill looks as if he could murder her and mutters he's alright. Sybil comes in—a pretty dark girl who works a book-keeping machine. She flings her coat and hat down, which her mother carefully puts away. I've noticed it here; if a girl goes to work she does absolutely nothing at home—her mother washes stockings, puts things away and even makes her bed. Slip through the fence at 10.30. 'Don't forget to tell your mother' she said 'that you had tea with me. Tell her you've had some real good 'snap' all made of the best—the very best'. Sybil says 'Oh, Mother. . .' and we wave a cheery good-night.

18 January 1940

Up at 11.30. In the afternoon to the little Chapel to tea. Mrs Hutchinson is
there and she brings the old school register for 1890. There is little Mum's
name, Susan Turner, next to Leah Causer, Grace Kirk, Betsy Gwynne and
Frances Allcock. Methinks she was absent more than she was there but they
assure me that was when she went to sing and recite at other churches. A nice
little service and a speaker then tea at a long trestle table. Dear Auntie Leah
addresses the meeting, gently advocating a jumble sale for the missionaries.
Would Mother still be doing this if she hadn't gone away to New Zealand? A
christening too of a wee one, Blanche Elizabeth. Mrs Hutchinson performs the
ceremony. The mother looks a mere girl but she has another two, older. Call
at George Turner's on the way home. The snow freezing now and like glass on
the steps. Men outside shops chip it away for safety. Everyone is in the kitchen,
it is full of airing clothes. Seems there's been some good training here, all the
children never forget their 'Please may I leave the table' and 'please' and 'thank
you'. Have found the Yorkshire folk like you to keep popping in. Run home in
a blacked-out white world to find Uncle Dick visiting Annie, who gasps. He's
only ever been once before. We listen to war news and a good variety.

19 January 1940

Snowing again—the light powdery snow falling on the old snow that has been
trodden into ice. Have a good wash up, clean my skirt and do bits of mending.
The hours flee by. Dumplings for tea and tonight to the pictures. I think as I
gaze into the fire how few know England like this—know the heat of the fires
or the sparkle of the sun on the snow. I think of Teddy Perkins' father. How
he lost his waistcoat at the pit and was searching for it. His mates seeing him
enquired 'Heigh oop what's tha' looking for?' 'Ah'm looking for th' westcut'.
'Then tha's a fool for tha's got it on lad'. Teddy's father took an amazed look
under his coat. 'Eh well nah' he replies nodding his head. 'If tha hadn't a towd
me ah'd a gone home wi'out it'. There is a quaint story too of his returning
from the pit when he had only got half way there. He passed others of his
shift just going. As he passed them they naturally asked why he was returning
home. It was the strap or rope on his water bottle that had broken and, not
being fussy whether or not he worked that day, decided to go home and mend
it and miss the shift. But he was a man of few words. All he answered to
their enquiry was 'Rope's brok'. The men thinking it was the rope at the pit
turned tail and went home. There were few men turned up for that particular
shift—those who did go thought there was a strike and went home too. And
all because the strap on Perkins' water bottle had broken.

20 January 1940

And another ambition realised. I've seen a really big pantomime at Leeds, the home of the panto. Tumble out of bed reluctantly, feeling as if it's the middle of the night. It's 7.30 really and at 8.30 we race through crisp crackly snow to the bus. All warm but our feet which slowly but surely freeze. The windows are covered with thick frost and we scratch them to see through. Everywhere is a white world—Wath upon-Dearne, Wombwell and Barnsley. Cleared portion of the window freezes over again. At Leeds we tumble out thinking of warm shops and dinners. A great building faces us with 'Tarrens' sprawled across its walls. It's a good landmark for the bus depot. Dive into the first likely-looking place to get out of the cold and find it's the markets. They're going strong on all sorts of goods especially fish packed in ice! We fly after the first shuddering glance. Then to locate the Empire and to book the panto. Thawed out in Marks and Spencer's and then Lewis's. Once in Lewis's there's no need to go further. There's everything at Lewis's'. Hot lunch seems to be the next thing we're wanting. Round all the departments—up the escalator and down in the lift. Bessie just as nervous as I was on escalators and has to be initiated.

Two o'clock and we rush to the land of Dick Whittington. There is the cat, grey, shaggy and with green eyes and there is the Dame true to tradition, the girl friend of Idle Jack, and Idle Jack is George Formby himself. Little eyes that twinkle, a big toothy smile and a casual manner. He comes on dressed in a sort of pyjama suit of big brown and white squares. He has a pile of banjos and ukuleles which he uses instead of stopping to tune up. His usual strum is fast and furious. He takes his uke and plays 'My Little Stick of Blackpool Rock'. Somehow I've never really appreciated George Formby until I see him in his natural setting. The crowd bring him back again and again. There's a fairy too resplendent in white and silver and Father Neptune roaring his deep-throated displeasure. There's a scene under the sea with hanging seaweed beautifully coloured. The ballets are perfect, dancing and kicking with mechanical precision. There lies Dick by the famous stone and the bells chime 'Turn again Whittington, Lord Mayor of London'. On comes the acrobatic dancer in little silver panties and a silver star on her middle—cymbals clash and drums boom. It is half past five when Bessie and I come out—three hours laughing at George Formby with his risqué (not quite so much as usual because after all it is a children's pantomime) jokes—risqué but with his fatuous grin, just priceless. We hear him say for the last time 'are you alright kids?' and all the kids shout 'O.K. Jack!' He can get the crowd roaring 'Run Rabbit Run'. It was a little harder to get them started than I thought it would be in England but once going the place shook.

Out into the black-out to visit a few shoe shops in search of Wellingtons for the children to wear to school. There's a shortage on account of them being made of rubber. Then back to Lewis's to stand in a queue with the pantomime girls off duty to get a plateful of fish and chips and trifle and coffee. Still with their grease paint on, they 'snaffle' a bit of tea before the early house at 6.30. Wander through the store again and fly at five to seven to catch the bus at seven. At Barnsley the bus stops and I ask the conductor if we have time to get out. Conductor says quite without embarrassment that if we only want to go to the lavatory we have. Poor Bessie blushes—that's the worst of having such a milk and roses complexion. At ten o'clock two frozen people face through the snow, home to a blazing fire. Herbert having a day off on his own. He works every day, Sunday included, but occasionally 'laiks'. If he earns too much his income tax is too high. The coldest night they say for 25 years!!

21 January 1940

And everything frozen. Even the hot water bottle which I popped out of bed in the early hours is frozen when I come to empty it, it won't run until the ice is poked away. The wash basin is stopped up with ice and the hot water won't run. Must let the fire out or the boiler will 'bust'. We light a fire to cook the dinner and sit in fear and trembling but nothing happens. Uncle Dick comes in 'Get the fire lighted sithee' he orders 'nowt'll happen' but we don't fancy being blown up by boilers like Steamboat Bill. In the afternoon to George Turner's for tea where boilers are fortunately still intact. Forgot to report Frank over for the weekend. Says camp is freezing—the poor chaps, no fire and they can't keep walking for ever to stay warm.

23 January 1940

Up at 10.30. Getting worse. The days much longer now—no need to light up till close to five. Great consternation at Uncle John's—burst pipes and flooded out. Tried Ruth's, then Annie's, then Auntie Lizzie's and finally Auntie Bella's to find a toilet that would work. Fortunately they all live round about so everyone ran to Auntie Bella's. Don't think it got time to freeze. Back to Ruth's—met Malcolm looking for an unfrozen one and directed him to Auntie Bella's. George and I out to celebrate his new job at the variety. Ice thick down Willowgarth, freezing now not snowing and everyone putting salt down to try and melt the ice. Rump steak for dinner 2/0d per lb. Meat is about the only thing that is as dear as New Zealand, except butter. That's 1/6d per lb. just as at home. Across the fields to Walter's in the hard crispy snow. Olga's washing. Walt is at home. Looked at his ferret—a strange dreamy tan rat-like little animal. Find they're used for getting rabbits. Repulsive-looking little thing but it can't help it and it seemed such a shame to keep it cooped up. A marvellous new radiogram here. Plays records through the radio, five being put on at once and as one finishes it automatically starts the next. Mechanics a positive mystery but seems to be fool-proof.

Sometimes I have to laugh when I think how my days are made up of these little visits to people I've grown to love. Sometimes I feel frightened because some day I'll go away—not because I want to but because I have to go away, and I may never see them ever again. We have so much in common—I know all their hopes, their fears, their ambitions. There is such a welcome wherever I go. Anyone upstairs is called down as soon as I get in and all the bits of news related. I am going to miss it all so much. Outside the weather changes, the rain falls.

25 January 1940

This is the greatest day since I left home. I have had other great days which I thought were the greatest but there can be none so memorable as this. For today I followed in the footsteps of Granddad Turner and went down the mine, down into the depths of Aldwarke Colliery. Into Rotherham first to do a spot of shopping for nearly every member of the family. 'If you're going into Rotherham could you bring me…' is the cry everywhere I go. Back at one and Willowgarth just a solid block of ice where the rain has washed the snow away. Put on old tramping shoes and woollen dress, Mr. Tong's overalls and an old blue raincoat of Auntie Bella's, tie a scarf over my head and away. Meet Walter Brown and Joe Peverley at the pit top. Hang up my coat in the office, tie up my hair under a tin hat and off we go. Bend my head obligingly to let Mr. Peverley fix on the lamp and find I can't lift it again so must perforce carry the lamp in one hand and a stout stick in the other.

Into the cage and we're going down—'down to the sixth floor, fifth floor' fourth floor…'. It drops suddenly—one has a vision of huge ventilating fans whizzing by. Our hearts stay at the top and catch us up about half-way. It is just as the miners say, about half way down you get the impression of going up again. We pass several old seams until we have gone 400 yards. It is here that the 'doings' begin. The cages are loaded with trucks of coal from an upper and a lower deck—four tubs on each deck, each tub contains 9 cwt. Up they go with monotonous regularity. The passages here are through rock which it is said extends right through the land from Co. Durham. We walk along a narrow path 2 ft wide by the side of trucks coming and going. The two sets of rails have the same gauge between so that the two centre ones can be used as a pair if necessary. Every now and then, when the rattle of trucks behind us is heard, we have to run for a refuge hole. These are in the wall every ten

feet and I believe are compulsory, and well they might be unless one wanted
to go careering through the mine chased by rattling, barging, relentless trucks.
Through the engine house where all the haulage of the trucks is controlled
and to the top of Dalton drift. Here boys unhook the tubs which slow down
over creepers and then disappear into the depths. Then through the doors
which control the ventilation of the pit and into the return airway. Here comes
the biggest thrill of all. We get into one of the tubs, lie down for the roof is
low, give the signal and down into the depths we go, into what seems like an
unfathomable blackness—a hell made more hellish by the rattle and bang of
the trucks. One is lost in a world of blackness and noise. The gradient is 1 in 3
and the breaks negligible. I cling to Walt. It seems as if we're racing and rattling
into eternity. Walt doesn't look so good either when we get out. He hasn't
been down before. Have to laugh when we find we're fearfully following Mr.
Peverley hand in hand like a couple of children. We've negotiated Dalton drift
and the miners do it every shift! It is 98 degrees Fahrenheit down here, the
hottest district in the Yorkshire coalfield. Through doors then to the bottom
of the main drift with huge arched girders and along the light haulage road to
the loader. A cheer greets us from Uncle John—a black Uncle John and some
cheerful black faces that Uncle assures me I know quite well. He hauls me
delightedly over the rails in between the trucks, puts gloves on my hands, and
I tip over a dozen or so trucks sending them on their way.

From then on the coal is not in trucks but on conveyor belts from which it is
tipped into trucks. All along the conveyor road are the big rubber and canvas
conveyor belts full of coal. The road is up to our ankles in water with a burst
pipe. The air is hot and stuffy, slightly gaseous. The roof gets lower until it is
only 3 ft 6 ins high. We take a drink from the water bottles. Did I report I had
my Dudley moon round my neck like the men? And down we go practically
on our hands and knees. There are props now, huge blocks of wood shaped at
the end like pencils. This sharpening is not to make them sink into the ground
as one would suppose but to enable them to spread out like a mushroom
when the pressure came, otherwise the props would break in the middle. In
some cases they have broken, not through pressure from the roof, but through
the rising of the ground owing to wall pressure. Sometimes the ground rises
and more roof has to be blown away. There are holes in the rock ready for
the gelammonite.[25] They say fir wood is best for props. And then the coal face
220 yards by 4 ft high of solid black coal with twenty six men at work with
automatic picks. Twenty six men coal-black men stripped except for shorts,
sweating, toiling and shaking in every rippling muscle with the vibration of
the drills. We are stooping, half crawling all the time now and when we stop
to talk just squat in the dirt. The men all have a nod and a flash of white teeth
against the black of their faces as we pass. One of these black forms is Uncle
Dick, his sinewy legs braced against the drill. A huge lump of black shining

coal falls at his feet narrowly missing his shins. We sit on the job for a while and I have a drink out of his water bottle. Nearby is a great machine which the men call 'Samson'. It is a Mavor and Coulson coal cutter. No shots of explosive are put into the coal, it is undercut by Samson which rips a piece from the base and makes it easier to pick down. As we go many a man comes forward to greet me. The air is getting heavier and we are coughing more frequently. The men stop the Deputy 'Be careful of the little lady, Joe'. 'Little lady' indeed, sitting on Samson as black as the ace of spades, pouring water into me from a Dudley, the black sweat pouring out of every pore as quickly as I poured the water into me. I think a lot of them for that compliment and solicitude.

They work a seven and half hour shift on a 5 ft cut along a 220 yd face. The tubs of coal hold 9 cwt. and it is said 1,100 to 1,200 tubs are filled off each cut every day. In filling the coal each man has a stint 10 ft long to clear. For this he gets 13/-. If he clears more than 10 ft he gets 1/- a foot for each additional foot. This is a bonus system and Mr. Peverley assures me it is working out fairly well. The coal does not gradually peter out into the rock as I thought it would. It stops suddenly as it meets the rock. We come back along the bottom tail gate, a narrow passage used to convey timber, and through doors to the main conveyor road. All through the mine, where there is coal or coal dust, is a fine white powder of non-combustible material such as stone dust. This is to minimise the danger of explosion. If the percentage of this powder was not sufficient the coal dust in the air would ignite. We tramp along—it seems miles and miles. Mr. Peverley first, then myself and then Walt, sitting down at intervals in the gloom to have things explained. It is pitch dark apart from our lamps. As we sit Mr. Peverley argues in favour of atheism and continues as we walk. 'Who was Christ anyway?' floats back and 'look at Russia..' I tried so hard to look at Russia but all I could see was the toiling, sweating men at the coal face, and all I was aware of was the gaseous, choking feeling in the air. Walter, contrary to all precedents, was silent and I felt as if I should say something. Get enough voice to shout occasionally above the roar of the trucks 'Uh, uh' or 'well what do you expect' or something that I vaguely hoped would fit in with anything. We ride on the conveyor belt—quite against the law but Walt drags me on. Then he announces quite casually to hop off. One leg hopped off but the rest of me stayed. Dragged off just in time by an agitated Joe and Walter to prevent being tipped into a truck or tub as they are called. Couldn't help thinking what a surprise Uncle John would have got if I'd turned up in one of the tubs.

We reach the cage at last and sit for some 'snap' and a drink for half an hour. We discuss atheism, anti-Jewism and many other 'isms'. Don't know much about some of them but cover up discreetly what I don't know and blare forth something, be it ever so small, that I'm dead certain of. The men come up, Uncle John amongst them, and up we go. I sit at Joe's desk and write this very report, push the tin hat on the back of my head and put on the old blue raincoat. Uncle John gets a mirror. An 'object' looking back at me, an object dead black with red lips and white teeth and glaring eyes that seemed all white. Then Walter, being Walter, dared me to finish the day as I should. 'The miners' he says with a nonchalant air 'always go to the Station Hotel'. Uncle John expostulates but he's much too nice to be an uncle, and he expostulates in vain. 'What'll your Auntie Polly think' he finally argues weakly. 'She won't know if you don't tell her' I whispered confidentially. 'Come on'. And so in we went, into the 'little room with a big fire'. Drinks are ordered. The barmaid serves three and shakes her head 'I can't serve th' lad' she says firmly. 'You can't tell me he's over fourteen'. We all look round vaguely for th' lad and then Walter's eyes rest on me. 'Gie the lad a drink' he says 'he's worked a shift. Coom on nah be a sport' but she shakes her head firmly and, what is more, launches into a scathing lecture on the folly of men such as Walt and the poor innocent Uncle John bringing a mere lad in for a drink. They ought to be ashamed of themselves they should. 'That lad's a lass' says Uncle John and she comes round the table to look. I get the drink. We argue a bit about politics. It is fun to argue with a tin hat on the back of your head and your hands in the pockets of overalls and your face so black no one knows you. A real old timer comes in. His eyes seek out my modest whisky. He nods 'Yon lad's got plenty to splash hasn't he, drinking that stuff. Now when Ah was a lad Ah was lucky if ah got a gill or a sup arter someone else's pint'. Everyone turns to look at th' lad who's supping whisky and the game's up. They all come round and shake hands and say 'Well tha's got some pluck my lass. There's never another gal been down where tha's bin today'. To finish up I rode home in the bus at half fare as a pit boy and no one knew! Not even Auntie Polly!

Round to Auntie Lizzie's first to tell the tale and Uncle Albert shakes as he lies on the sofa and looks at me. Round to Auntie Bella's where everyone is hauled out of bed to look. Into the bath at last to wash every particle of me including hair. The water swims in black. Come downstairs and Uncle Dick is waiting for me. 'Ah thought tha'd washed thisen' he says and hands me a mirror. The wretch he knew what I'd look like. In spite of all the scrubbing all around my eyes was black. It takes Vaseline to get that off. It's twelve o'clock when Ruth and I creep into bed—hair not quite dry. But sleep…

26 January 1940

Spent all morning getting clean. Eyes still black and hair, despite of washing, still black. Rubbed cold cream all over my skin and another good wash and I wasn't so bad. Ran round again to see everyone and talk it over. The world is white again, it's coming down hard. I can still see that black hole. We were so far down that there was another mine on top of us. That is where Uncle Dick goes when he says 'Good morning' so many times. I must try to return his 'Good morning'. He must feel sometimes as if maybe he won't ever come back. And in Granddad's day it was even worse, there was more danger—what men must do for bread. I would move heaven and earth to keep anyone of mine out of the pit. Snow deeper and there are dire forebodings about when it thaws. We're to be flooded out but there's no sign yet only snow and more snow. At night with George to first house at the Regent. A good variety programme and rather a good joke. We're going to double-cross Hitler. 'We'll give him Ireland!' A splendid impersonator of farmyard animals—a car going through a flock of sheep, the horn tooting, the sheep baa-ing and the dog yelping.

28 January 1940

No one up till 11. Out to snowball—conditions just right for good hard dry ones. Build a snowman all complete with old hat and pipe. There's naturally only one name for snowmen now and afterwards we take great and vicious delight in knocking him down with the hardest of hard snowballs. Ruth had New Zealand lamb for dinner. Pack up and back to Auntie Lizzie's to take a ticket in Temple Gates. Since professional football and horse racing stopped this particular popular form of wholesale gambling has come in. One draws certain letters for each day of the week and if the first letters of the first two words in the headlines of the daily paper happen to be yours well you've won. (P.S. I never have). It is done quite seriously amongst all the recognised bookies. Round with Auntie Bella to pay various clubs and meet Mr. Peverley. Try to talk mining as technically as possible. Finish up at the Club, it is warm and cheerfully noisy. The chief turn a man impersonating a woman with a magnificent bosom! It would have delighted the heart of Titian himself. 'Eh lad' says one old soul to another 'that lassie's been down th' pit reeght to coal face. I wish owd Jimmy Turner had been alive I do an' all'.

29 January 1940

Into Auntie Bella's bed for a half hour chat and then to pack for Bakewell. Snow deeper than ever. There never was such a winter for twenty five years. The cream is frozen on top of the milk when we bring it in. Bessie terribly disappointed— thought she'd get a house, only the third offering in five years, and then missed. Such a bustle to find a phone to ring the station. No buses running, roads all blocked with snow. Reports that roads from Ambergate to

Bakewell closed but decide to take the risk and leave Rotherham at 4.30. They turn us off at Ambergate. It is difficult to find out if the train can go further or not but the station is a cheerful place with a big fire. There's a group of officers going to Rowsley to camp but none of us know when we'll get there. Maybe tonight, maybe tomorrow — it feels uncannily like something out of Dickens. It is easy to imagine that we're waiting for the stage-coach instead of the train. With the officers is a Major, a courteous helpful Major who guarantees that with the assistance of his entire company I'll get to Rowsley eventually. A dozen men click to attention and salute and in the middle of all the fun the train pulls in. We are hours getting to Rowsley. It gets dark. The Major with one officer insists on seeing me safely to Picory Corner, near my destination. Was rather relieved to see the others turn towards the camp. A military escort of two was nice but about a dozen and people would have thought I was under arrest. Half way between Rowsley and Picory Corner the bus comes. 'The military escort' sees me on and standing back salutes smartly. I get out at Picory Corner at 8.30 and presumably the journey was at an end. But I hadn't reckoned on the little lane of say 200 yards or more. It had not been cleared, the snow it seemed was about two feet deep. There was only one thing to do. I threw the suitcase and scrambled after it. Occasionally I got into drifts and lay helpless with laughter buried in soft yielding snow. It was an hour later when I knocked at the little arched door. The little grey stone Lodge was silhouetted against the sky and a bright light in one small latticed window. They'd put it there in spite of the black-out just in case I came. The fire glows red and Dolly and Billie are just the same as before.

30 January 1940

Up comes Dolly with a cup of tea and perches on the end of the bed for a chat. The pipes are frozen here too only more so than anywhere else. There's not only no hot water but no cold water — no 'nuffin'. We don woollen socks and rubber boots and plough through the snow to the river for water. The trees are weighed down and breaking under the snow, the great slopes of the Derbyshire hills an unbroken white sheet. In Rowsley the shopkeepers remember me from last July! Old Mrs. Groome mumbles over her papers. There's only the day before yesterday's. They're held up on account of the snow. According to the woman at the grocer's shop it is mortal bad weather for cold. 'And you know Miss there are only three degrees of a cold, 'Cold — cough — coffin'. Coal is scarce on account of the trains not being able to run so there's a can of oil to take home for the stove. Also a can of milk, a bag of groceries and papers. A great silent Rolls slithers by. It stops. The door opens and a figure with a short, fierce beard looks out unbending. It doesn't smile but enquires in a studious, courteous accent if they can give me a lift. A pair of immaculate lavender gloves picks up the oil can and the milk can and the chauffeur, by this time round to help, deposits the groceries and the papers in front. The old gentleman arranges the fur rug over my knees and sitting bolt upright, with his hands on his silver-headed cane, looks straight ahead. I have never seen anything quite like him before. He is a product of a past age and when he dies there will never be any more. He is so absolutely correct. Not for one moment did he allow me to feel conscious of the can of oil! At Picory Corner he leans forward to the speaking tube. 'Stop here, Micky boy' he orders. We slow down. 'Micky boy', who is at least fifty five, opens the door. He bows his little pointed beard into the depths of his fawn coat and glides away. Today too I went tobogganing with the family from the first farm. We raced down slopes clinging to each other wildly and 'hurrahing' all the way. Then we toiled up to the top again and then, like all tobogganers sooner or later, we fell over, rolled in the white powdery snow, a mixture of toboggan wheels, arms and legs. It was good to come back by the oil stove, the room is stifling hot, and after the cold one's nose goes scarlet.

February 1940

Matlock, Rawmarsh, Greasbrough, Bradford, Haworth, Huddersfield

3 February 1940

To Matlock to buy the Blue John stone ring that Frank and Elsie are giving me as a bridesmaid's present. A lift most of the way in Mr. Davies' car. The chauffeur a kindly man with teeth exactly like the hare in Walt Disney's 'Tortoise and The Hare'. At every bus stop are groups of grumpy men lugging home half sacks of coal which they've had to fetch from the Railway Station themselves. They carry a bag of golf clubs cheerfully but a sack of coal...! In Matlock the shops are warm and outside it's thawing and dire are the predictions. Floods are in the air. We open a tin of salmon for dinner and chop up the door of the outside toilet to boil the kettle! Tomorrow the coal will be here. It's thawing and a steady drip drip comes off the roof. The river is a raging torrent.

5 February 1940

It's a sad parting. I pretend it isn't a parting, that I can spare another weekend, but I know I can't. Two hours to wait in Rowsley—train held up in the snow—and another wait at Ambergate. Sheffield is yellow with a dense fog. There is always such a welcome at Auntie Lizzie's. As soon as I get in Auntie seizes the poker and stirs the fire to fresh and frenzied efforts. Auntie and I to the Variety at night. A good show—one rather good Vicar story. Not usually in favour of these Vicar jokes but these quickly done and not unduly stressing the Vicar part. 'The lighting system to the church has failed and the Vicar announces "The meeting of the young unmarried women of the parish will be taken by myself in the vestry as usual. Although the lights have failed I have been carrying on with them in the dark!" More performing dogs too, a dear little Peke puppy pulling a little cart with a baby monkey in it and a huge Borzoi pranced with a monkey jockey.

7 February 1940

Stopping with James and Bertha in Greasbrough. A dear little cottage this. Bertha and I to Rotherham to visit the chiropodist. Poor Bertha has a verruca—not a musical instrument as I imagined but a germ picked up in Blackpool that gets into the feet. A spot of shopping and the hunt begins for an old English muffin. Find out that the tea-cake things I've had are definitely not muffins. All the shops used to make them but don't now. Back to chat with Mrs Sanderson. She is still talking quickly in little jerks but I'm sort of getting prepared for what she is likely to say and ready for her little jokes. She is really a marvellous old lady—never been to school and can't read and write, but a great worker. She has lived in this very house since she was married. James is reading his eternal travel books. James! who will not bestir himself to travel to Sheffield, revels in travel tales of the Islands, of pidgin English and scalping cannibals. The family decide to try and makes some muffins. Mighty and intricate are the preparations, first to the Store for a few things and we chat to two energetic maiden ladies for an hour and a half. All hang over the recipe—the only one we can find is headed 'German Muffins'. It doesn't seem quite patriotic but we go ahead. They turn out well—like you'd expect German muffins to turn out, slightly tough and heavy but no one would dream of mentioning it.

9 February 1940

Forgot to mention the 6th was Pancake Day and before I left Auntie Lizzie's she made me some pancakes. Everyone eats them maybe with treacle, maybe with orange juice. Tackle another lot at Bertha's. It is top-spinning time for the children. They have a whip and top here such as I've never seen in New Zealand, they set the top going with some string and then flick it round with a whip. Round to Jim's today, who lives with his wife's parents. Mr. Hardy is a great carver. Has a big box full of the most complicated carver's tools. James and I over the fields to the dam. Betty, the dog, skates over the ice after sticks, her little legs straddling as she struggles to regain her balance. Over frosty stiles through drifts and we walk to the cemetery to see angels carved by Mr. Hardy. Rather nice lady-like angels.

The toilet in the yard still blocked up, as Mrs. Sanderson says 'Frozzen up' and we have to run out equipped with key and a bucket of water. It is marvellous how these English people can stand the cold. Bertha wears 'Locknit' silk knickers and vest throughout the winter. Over to Rawmarsh. A man coming out of the Horse and Jockey slips and sits down suddenly. Bertha and I burst out laughing—feel a bit guilty about it but he did look surprised. Went on a few yards and Bertha sits down just as suddenly. Hear a roar of laughter from behind. Bertha indignant but you can't really blame the man for laughing. The street so slippery we cling to Jim and tread like cats on hot bricks.

12 February 1940

Snowing hard. Will the weather never act according to schedule. The snow shifters who have put away their shovels, take them out again. Old Mrs. Watson comes in. 'The young people nowadays' she says 'are too fond of themselves. You can't do nowt these days wi'out them saying "Oh mother". They call you daft if you 'ave a bit o' fun'. Old Mrs Sanderson nods and rocks. Trotted down to the local snobs[26] to get my shoes heeled and viewed his machines as I sat in my stockinged feet. 'Eh lass' he says 'how did tha' coom to knaw abaht snobbing?' Informed him that my paternal ancestors for generations had made boots and he made his way round the counter to shake hands. 'So 'ave mine, lass' he says 'and I do an' all and my boy atter me'. Left Bertha to call on Mr. and Mrs. Cooper at Herringthorpe Valley Road. Exchanged all the news. Packed up again tonight and all of us round to Auntie Lizzie's to take me home.

14 February 1940

A year today since I left home. A glorious year of freedom, of warm-hearted friends and relations who really and truly want one, of dear folk whom I'll never forget and of a war the horror of which has scarcely yet dawned. I have sought and I have found. I have finished with dreams because dreams have become reality. In Auntie Bella's fire I'm seeing a little girl running to school and dreaming of all the countries she's going to visit when she's a big woman. I'm seeing a bigger girl thrilled to bits when she published her first story and pretending to be casual about it. And then a grown up girl struggling with an impossible pile of work and typing frantically against time—and then the ship sails away and the adventure starts. Soon it will be all over, I'll be home again and it will be as if a page has been turned and a fresh chapter started.

George gives me a pally slap on the back 'Homesick, old girl?' No I've never for a moment been homesick. How could I with all these dear people about me, but George is not convinced. He hauls me off to the Variety with a huge box of chocolates. We have to carry our gas masks everywhere—no place of entertainment will let anyone in without it. The mail brings six Valentines! The shops are full of Valentine cards—gorgeous things tied up with ribbon.

15 February 1940

Awake at 5.30 to Uncle Dick's boom as he goes to work, 'Good morning, mother' 'good morning all'. Reply weakly and fade away into oblivion. Forgot that yesterday I had tea with Aunt Mildred. Aunt Mildred's mother, Mrs. Allen, is the driving force of the household. Uncle Albert by the way didn't die playing football. He'd finished playing and was running off the field. He tripped and fell, hitting his head and becoming temporarily unconscious. Unfortunately he fell with his nose and mouth in quite a small pool of water and was drowned.

On the bus at last for Bradford. The whole is just as white as ever. Arrive and Aunt Eliza's is all 'frozen up' and we have to get water from next door and conserve it carefully. I can see me amongst the great unwashed as I was in Bakewell! It is good to see them all again, Hilda, little Shirley and Celia in their pixie caps and Clem. Meet the young football pro. who boards with Auntie. No football now so he's in the police force. The poor soul is such a doleful member of the police force—he has just had two teeth out and a dose of influenza. Such a talk at night at Auntie's and I sit over the fire. Uncle Herbert breaks his silence to tell me that Mother used to say he'd get T.B. He gave a little chuckle and at the end of another silence suddenly looked up and says 'I haven't got it yet'. The dear eats vast quantities of bread and butter and is as thin as a lathe but presumably ails nothing.

20 February 1940

Aunt Eliza down with the flu, just like Fred, the footballer, before her. Make hash for dinner and rhubarb and custard. Make coffee too—no one seems to have it here very much but all enjoy it. Fred having medicine now and Auntie the lemon drinks. The cupboard by the side of the fireplace looks like a dispensary. The vegetables at this time of year are perpetually potatoes, peas (dried) and Brussels sprouts. Poor Fred—the idol of all the girls! All I'll ever remember of him is sitting drooping beside the fire, his eyes dull and his fair waves standing up all straggly. Rather disappointing from my point of view too—after all he's the first professional player I've ever met.

21 February 1940

Got up and was violently ill. Fred cooked his own bacon and egg. Asked me if I wanted any and I was promptly ill again. Auntie staggers down and we bake amid groans. Hilda comes round—does a bit of cleaning and seemingly a lot of banging around. We hold our aching heads and pray for her to go and leave us in the dirt. The coal man comes and I precipitate dangerously and dizzily down the cellar steps. He is a pompous little man who has things to say to me about not hurrying sufficiently to open the door for him. I open fire verbally to my own surprise and he backs up the stairs in haste followed by a few unpleasant truths about British coalmen in general, especially ones with tobacco-stained walrus moustaches.

24 February 1940

Auntie still without a voice. Beginning to peck a bit now. Sampled some Stork margarine today and just couldn't tell it from butter. Of course it's the same price as butter but won't be so bad if butter gets even scarcer than it is now. Still 'corfing' but take the risk of going to Haworth to see Charlotte Brontë's home. Clem and I change buses at Keighley where Mother used to live before she came to New Zealand. Haworth is a lovely little village with grey stone houses bordering winding cobbled streets. The main street winds up to the Black Bull where Bramwell Brontë spent so much of his time. Call at a little village shop to buy some Carter's Liver Pills and ask the way to the Parsonage. The little old woman in curling pins hobbles out into the street to point the way. There is the old old church and behind the famous parsonage. Contrary to what I expected it is quite a pleasant place. As soon as one enters the doors the nineteenth century enfolds one. The walls are painted a clean pale cream. The caretaker was an odd soul—a scout master, a nature lover and a great student of the American Indians. He talks avidly on the Indians for half an hour before I could tactfully bring the conversation round to the Brontës. But he has a sense of humour and sees the funny side to the little village and village life. His love of nature is a constant surprise to the natives. He gets up to watch the herons getting trout from the stream before, as they say, 'God wakkens'. Then we see the little relics of the Brontë household, the harpsichord that tinkles still and a cabinet with paintings of the twelve apostles on it. The cabinet is mentioned in *Jane Eyre*. There is Emily Brontë's mug and a comb used by her when she died. It is burned just as it fell into the fire when she collapsed. But most astounding of all are the tiny little books containing ten pages written microscopically. There are the writings of Charlotte Brontë in 1830. It must have been a strange life bound up by all the Victorian conventions. Perhaps because of these very restrictions, buds that grew inward tightly instead of blossoming out loosely and beautifully.

A cold wind blows over the moors and I feel that if I don't hurry home I'll soon go the way of the Brontës. At the foot of the hill I meet what must surely be the oldest inhabitant. He is toiling up with a huge basket of eggs. The wind is buffeting and biting. I offer to carry the basket for him at least as far as the top of the hill. He stops, takes a firmer hold on the basket, but says not a word. Then he frowns at me from under bushy brows 'Ah've known my eggs longer than ah've known thee young woman' he says, and with that cryptic remark he toils off up the hill without a backward glance. An extra moorland blast almost blows us out of Haworth and home.

28 February 1940

Met an old man who remembers the Brontë family, his father knew the old Reverend gentleman. Doesn't know 'what these 'ere tourists come to look at 'aworth for'. His father had said 'T'owd gentleman was alreight but he thowt nowt about him'. The plumber came and we get water again. Just about embrace the poor man. A dark dismal bus to Huddersfield with the windows all blued out to stop with Bertha Allcock. Introduced to Arnold Appleby. Never have I seen anything quite like Arnold Appleby. He is a curate. I know now from where spring all the 'curate' jokes. He lodges next door to Bertha and the landlady's 16-year-old daughter, Mary, is playing havoc with his heart. She's a little, well-developed huzzy for 16 but with a certain florid beauty. He is a small man and bald and from the back view the seat of his pants look as if they want filling up. He calls to her as he comes home and she coyly waits his arrival in the drawing room window. 'Ma-a-ary' he positively bleats waving a flabby hand. And Arnold knits! There he sat bolt upright on a high chair, his toes turned in, shrouded in a positive cloud of lolly-pink knitting. He explains the pattern and exhibits his work proudly. He's knitting a bed-jacket for Mary! One wonders what his parish will say if he turns up complete with a sixteen year old bride, for Mary's mother has intentions as well as he!

March 1940

11 March 1940

This is definitely a red-letter day. It is hard to say 'goodbye' to all the people I have visited in Lancashire but the old feeling is coming back. I'm travelling again! And it's Spring! It is a different feeling from visiting and staying with people. There is the adventure—one never quite knows what one might do or where one might go. After the long winter rest it is like the start of a new trip. Saw a shop on my way to the station with the notice 'Horse flesh sold here'. Meat dark and yellow fat just as it looked in the shop in Versailles. Whoever buys it? We're certainly rationed but not that badly.

Chimneys—a town of chimneys, thousands in a row like soldiers. Canals with barges—an old woman undoing a lock for a barge to pass through—a patient tow horse plodding along the little path by the canal. These are everyday sights to those who pass through Stoke, Birmingham or Crewe. A dirty day and there's black mud everywhere. Shown the way to the bus for Hanley and hopped straight off to the Newcastle-under-Lyme bus. At the Canal Bridge one gets off at Etruria. One cannot miss Wedgwood. It is a big building with 'Wedgwood' in huge letters on the roof and the inevitable canal by the side. The show room is full of the most gorgeous pottery—sets delivered to the Royal Family and the famous blue and white figures. All fairly and, I must say, justly expensive. Find that kaolin is china clay—surely it is advertised as being part of some of the famous stomach powders? What on earth has china clay to do with indigestion, unless it forms a sort of protective porcelain lining to one's stomach! Everywhere there were cups and not all samples either. It would seem that tea was in great demand in the Wedgwood factory! Never have I seen so much beauty or so much dirt at Stoke-on-Trent, and to think the very beauty is made out of the dirt.

Tonight I meant to go to Warwick. Somehow I had an idea it came before Kenilworth. When I saw the little Kenilworth station I fell off all in a hurry. Left the case at the station and walked up Castle Hill. Through the trees the castle showed—mellow red sandstone in the lovely green. But even ruins have 'hours' and the castle was closed so that's that for tonight. Just opposite the Castle are some quaint little tea shops and one of them promised to find room for me for the night. Back to the station where a loquacious porter offered to wheel the case up on his bike. And so destiny took me to Miss Moth. I sleep again in a tester bed with all the family portraits hanging round. We sit by the family fire and talk to Miss Moth's aunt. She is a rather marvellous old lady crippled up hopelessly with rheumatoid but she reads and thinks and talks, the kind of person who uplifts one mentally instead of depressing. Indeed it is strange to find her here with the twittery, slightly vacuous, Miss Moth.

12 March 1940

The castle is lovely in the early morning—perhaps all the more lovely because I have a rather nice guide. In the kitchens are grooves in the floor to let the blood of slaughtered animals run away. One can almost see them being roasted whole on the spit. In the dark deep dungeons, which narrowed towards the top in a sort of bottle neck were poked prisoners—they could get in but owing to the shape of the room it was impossible to get out. We stood on a stone ledge and talked—a soft rain, almost a friendly rain, was falling. The stone ledge was narrow and what is more it was high. Suddenly I became aware of its narrowness, I had an uncontrollable desire to cling hold of the Very Nice Guide. Perhaps if I had been anywhere else I might have done spontaneously but in Ye Castell of Kylingworth the proprieties just shrieked to be observed. Instead the Very Nice Guide talked seriously about stone architecture for a very long time and I stood rooted to the spot praying that when the time came to move I wouldn't be faced with the alternative of going crashing to my doom or grabbing him round the neck. There was no one else looking over Kenilworth. Tourists seemed to vanish like a dream since the war. At night I stayed in Warwick.

13 March 1940

Warwick is an ancient town with gates and timbered houses. Now Warwick is not an old castle. I have come to 'sniff' at castles that are not old, the present building dates from the thirteenth century at the very earliest and some built in the year 1770! Here too Queen Elizabeth was entertained by the Dudley family on her way to the famous Kenilworth celebrations. What an expensive person she was. Surely she didn't have to be entertained twice in a distance of barely ten miles! The best place to view the castle is the bridge. From here it has a massive dignity. An aeroplane drones overhead—just suppose it was an enemy one, that it saw the castle and, out of sheer spite for the loveliness of it, dropped a bomb. Will there be any of England left when it is all over? This England I have grown to love. I went late to Stratford-on-Avon. I dived into the first little house I saw who 'took' people. It had a Shakespeare knocker over the door. The bard looked gravely down at me while I slept.

14 March 1940

I'm glad it is wartime and Stratford-on-Avon is practically empty. What must it be like in peacetime this little bit of England to which every tourist flies? One can tell they do because nothing is left to the imagination. It caters admirably to the 'look and run' variety.   Everything is so blatantly marked. The streets are full of notices 'To the birthplace', 'To Ann Hathaway's Cottage'. There is no need to say whose birthplace. Some of our poets have left a bit of themselves in many places with just some little corner that they call their own but not Shakespeare. He is whole-heartedly Stratford-on-Avon. But even if there had not been a Shakespeare, which is in itself unthinkable, Stratford-on-Avon is beautiful. Downstream, mellowed a little by distance is the Memorial Theatre. It is not a lovely building—a clear cut modern pile of red brick and stone, slightly incongruous here, and suggestive of anyone but Shakespeare. But no doubt it is admirably built and perhaps inside more suited to its purpose than if it had a more sympathetically exterior. One can wander about Stratford for it doesn't matter where one looks there is something that must not be missed but the notices 'to the Birthplace' have a fatal attraction. 'The Birthplace' is a very picturesque, timbered and gabled house right on the road. It has such tiny rooms—this unpretentious house and a little wiggly staircase. It was from this house that Shakespeare went to the Grammar School. (In spite of the popular custom here I resolutely refuse to call the poor dear 'The Bard'. It is merely sententious and I feel about it exactly as I used to in Standard 1 at school when the teacher put a sample composition up on the blackboard for us to copy. I didn't like the way she'd written it and refused to copy it. Not being capable of doing any better I just went without doing any). Even the boy leaning on his bike knew his job. 'That's the Shakespeare Hotel, Miss' he volunteered. I could see it was and wondered vaguely if he wanted me to 'shout' him a drink. But his shining morning face decried any such intentions.

He had some information to impart but he wasn't giving it all at once. So I admired his bike, obviously a new one and his pride and joy, and then in one burst of confidence he said 'The rooms in that hotel have funny names—the bar is called "Measure for Measure" and the "little room" it's "As You Like It". The 'little room' turned out to be the coffee room.

In Church Street is Holy Trinity Church and it is Shakespeare's grave and monument that make it famous. Bells were ringing pleasantly through the avenue of limes. At one time there were elms standing near the porch but these were cut down in 1871 to provide wood for mementoes! Slept again at Stratford with one eye on the clock—tomorrow is an early, a very early, start.

15 March 1940

On the way to Oxford and then to Bicester to stop with Elsie. It was good to see Elsie who worked at The King's Arms. The hotel's full so I share Elsie's room—a pretty place with her own wireless and radiator. The hotel kitchen is a huge one and at the long table the young girls sit preparing some food. There is no mistress or housekeeper at the King's Arms. When the wife of the proprietor died he never put in another supervisor of the kitchen. The staff, like Elsie, have been there for years and just carried on as they always did. Everything is delightfully free and natural. We eat fresh salmon for lunch. Strange how one can always get it here. What happened to all the trout in New Zealand? Never ever have I seen any in the shops. At night to the pictures, afterwards to sit before the big fire and when in bed to whisper and talk with Elsie until we reluctantly, but quite uncontrollably, fell asleep. Elsie such a dear compact little thing. There is a certain compact roundness about some English girls that is entirely absent in Colonials. We are too angular somehow unless we're fat. She is just round and neat and in proportion. There is money in Bicester. One can see it in the big cars that are parked in the market square. Why do some men just ooze prosperity—red faces above rough tweeds?

16 March 1940

Somehow I wanted to get back to London and yet I didn't for London meant booking to go home and even if there weren't a boat for ages and ages I'd still be booked. I had a temptation to stay at Oxford but I came to London. A teeming wet day. There might be letters and things so straight up to New Zealand House. Could I leave one small case while I attended to a few things in town? The very superior woman in the reception room looked a cross between indignation and fright. She shook her head and eyed my case as if it might contain a bomb. They had no place for keeping luggage. Pointed out rather tartly that my 'luggage' as she called it, was only one small case and I didn't want her to 'keep' it only to leave it for an hour. Finally picked up the offending case and marched from the room as full of dignity as a dripping, flapping raincoat would allow. Felt injured and slightly offended. So this was my welcome from New Zealand, my return after I'd been wandering, a stranger in a strange land, for ten months. Became conscious of the woman catching me up. 'Perhaps the girls in the communications room might be able to...' 'It doesn't matter' I said frigidly 'I will make other arrangements'. But there were letters and I read them there and then.

Next up to the Bank in Berkeley Square. The good old London smell is in my nostrils, after all it is New Zealand that offended me not London. Have an appointment so am ushered into the presence of a Very Important Person. I am sure he was important. He was Mr.T in a very big office with a very solid desk and a discreet carpet. One reached him in a mysterious way being passed from one to another like a ball. I was announced. Mr.T looked up with keen eyes under bushy brows. 'Ah' he said and opened a drawer at the side of the table, drew forth my letter and, strangely enough, the envelope. I sat and waited. He referred to the letter, looked in the envelope, and looked at me again. Then he spoke. 'And to think' he said 'you led me to believe you were a blonde'. I just stared. Had he really said blonde? Maybe he said 'bond' and it had something to do with my going home. Then from the envelope he drew a curl of pure golden hair. Even then I just said 'Oh', a weak but comprehending little 'oh'. So that's where the envelope had gone! I remembered at Susie's, cutting off a curl of that lovely golden hair to take back to Mother and putting it in a new envelope. Scratching round for an envelope when I had written the letter to the Bank I found one—the one with the curl. 'It's Susie's' I gasped. But the man with the bushy brows had a sense of fun. He kept a tight hand on the curl even when I explained all about it. I wanted it back—what possible use could an unknown curl be to him? 'I'll give it back to you' he said 'in exchange for Susie's address!' But it put him in good humour. We got on admirably after that. I wanted a boat but I didn't want one in a hurry, I couldn't uproot in a hurry. My conscience and better judgment told me I must get a boat but if all the boats were full or there weren't many... 'I think you'd better go pretty soon little lady'. The bushy brows drew closer together. 'Things are going to happen soon'.

Together we planned out boats and trains for the journey home. It won't be like the rest of my trip that has been delightfully leisurely, I'll have to keep a certain amount to a schedule. It's wartime and one must book right through by specified trains and boats. I haven't thought so concisely for a long time. There'll be the boat across the Atlantic, the rail across taking so many days, the Lurline to Honolulu and the Niagara home. Suddenly it seemed so vivid and real that it was almost as if I were going tomorrow. I felt that I hated the man for starting it all. I was actually booked. However long it was before the boat went, I'd always know I was booked. Called again at the offending New Zealand House. I had left word that I was expecting a letter. Gave her strict instructions that until further notice I was in London and no mail was to be forwarded to Yorkshire. She looked at me blankly on my re-arrival two hours afterwards and asked 'Name?' 'Oh' she said 'a letter came for you a little while ago and I've just send it up to Yorkshire as usual'. I left. I didn't feel responsible for what I might do. So off to Dartmouth Park Road in Highgate to be smoothed into place by Mrs.C. It was good to see her again.

18 March 1940

London is so weird in the black-out but it doesn't keep people at home. To Greenford to find Mrs Ness with the bike shop on the verge of closing up. All the young lads away in camp and no one to buy bicycles. But we sit outside on the long low chair, only for a little while but it proves spring has come. Mrs. N. says long ago she attended a meeting of New Zealanders to look after the N.Z. troops as they come over but so far hasn't heard any more about it. Australia and Canada have a marvellous organisation. Related the story of my case and pitied the soldiers. Learnt a bit more rhyming slang—'Jam jar' or merely 'Jam' stands for car. This is the last time I will see Mr. and Mrs. Ness. Aeroplanes drone always overhead. It sounds ominous and yet we have only heard the rumbles of war. Take messages back for their people in New Zealand. This afternoon to the 'Duchess', that little 'intimate' theatre in Aldwych to see 'The Corn Is Green'. It is a comedy and yet there is much more in it than that. Sybil Thorndike acts superbly—her acting is finished. She _is_ Miss Moffat, just as Emlyn Williams is Morgan Evans. Rather a remarkable person this Emlyn Williams. It seems that he wrote the play too. As the young inarticulate miner he was so true to type. He must have known them so well—the truculence that is bred of an inability to express themselves— the turbulent young face that refuses to accept things as they were. The calm strong face of Sybil Thorndike on which was written sympathy and patience. We had afternoon tea brought round on a little tray with chocolate cakes. It is only a little theatre. It seemed more as if we were guests in a big salon.

20 March 1940

Decided to go to Canterbury. If one wants picture postcard quaintness one should go to Canterbury, walk down the High Street where beetle-browed houses bulge out over the road. The long low lattice windows bulge out further still, and the carved beams still more until every house looks as if it were leaning forward, all angles, corners, carvings and mouldings. I walked up the street to the Cathedral. More than any other Cathedral I have seen this one seems to be at rest. It has been great with a magnificent greatness and it is content now to remain as it is. Once there was treasure at Canterbury but that was despoiled by the 'Professional Widower'.[27] There was the tomb of Thomas a' Becket, it was magnificent with gold plating and jewels. Now nothing remains of the shrine but the memory. It was small wonder that it was covered with jewels if stories are to be believed for it is recorded that Louis VII was reluctant to part with a magnificent carbuncle ring, and the stone, as soon as it reached the shrine, flew of its own accord out of its setting and stuck into the wall. One wonders, perhaps a little blasphemously, if that wall were not magnetised. Perhaps it could be done today—what a harvest one could gather amongst the war-time engagement rings!

Thinking of Becket's murder I shivered, even 1170 can come terribly near in Canterbury Cathedral. 'Thinking about Thomas Becket' a little lady in a non-descript black frock looked at me with piercing black eyes. I admitted I was. 'He was a bit of a nuisance you know', she regarded me quizzically. I hated to admit that I'd really forgotten what Becket ever did apart from the fact that he was murdered. So the little lady explained emphatically 'For instance he believed in a different law for the clergy from that for common people. If a member of the clergy murdered anyone he was only unfrocked and he had to commit another murder before he was hanged. That's not right is it?' I shook my head weakly. It didn't sound right but then I hadn't ever remotely considered the prospect of a Bishop of anywhere committing a murder. Then came the excommunication by Becket of the bishops who had taken sides with Roger, The Archbishop of York. 'And' continued the little woman 'he was justly killed'. I believe the little woman would have been the first to drag him from the altar itself if she had lived in 1170. I looked at her fierce little face and wondered if there was not something in reincarnation after all. We wandered on to the tomb of Edward Black Prince in Trinity Chapel—under a hanging canopy a life-like effigy lies clad in full armour. We walked for a while in the cloisters but the little woman was getting back vehemently to Becket again and I hurried her out; after all murders have been re-enacted and I didn't want to find a bit of my scalp go sailing into the air. I left her telling a girl with long straight hair and a history book all the ghastly details and made my escape.

There is such a quaintness about Canterbury—the Weavers' Houses with the window boxes bright with flowers right on the river, the sluggish Stour, that seems overcome with the weight of ages. Walked up the steps and round the walls. One could see the city as she really is—red roofs nestling hospitably round the Cathedral. I am no longer sorry I didn't walk as the pilgrims did along the Pilgrim's Way, for it would not have been a pilgrimage. I cannot raise one atom of sympathy for Thomas a' Becket or one atom of antipathy for that matter. It is all so long ago. What can we of 1940 know of the intrigue of 1170—not know but understand?

Did I ever record the rather surprising—well shall we say—advertisements which decorate the walls of the Underground which move slowly past as one ascends or descends on an escalator? Amongst all the theatre advertisements is an attractive young lady and the words 'It's unnatural not to eat potatoes'. Has this homely vegetable fallen into such disfavour?

21 March 1940

Beryl has the measles but we think probably by ignoring the fact we won't get them. How sand-bagged everything is in London and evidently has been for a long time as some of the bags are beginning to burst. The windows criss-crossed with paper here too. Today at lunch with Mr. Beckett. We go to Gennaro's and hear the latest reports of the factory—going on war work as hard as they can. We have minestrone soup and a rich red Burgundy with our steak. There is a delicious dessert of the trifle variety and afterwards Gennaro himself comes round—pours more wine. His waxed moustache is the essence of smartness and his immaculately tailored rotundity suggests ample repletion and complete satisfaction. He leaves a small bunch of violets on my plate—English violets that have a scent suggestive of cool mossy woods. One lingers a long time at lunch at Gennaro's and then took leave of Mr. Beckett. Sometimes he would like to go back to Yorkshire to live but then on the other hand, he waved his hand vaguely, he would miss all this. I knew what he meant. Later Mrs. C. and I to the Strand Theatre. Just in the right mood to laugh at Ben Travers.

23 March 1940

Up very, very late and walked with Bob past Hilly Fields. Everyone Digging for Victory—straightening up unaccustomed backs. To think that the velvet lawns of old England should have to produce cabbages. All the trees are white-ringed to show up in the dark. Concrete gun emplacements are being built—England is preparing as she has never prepared before. Stopping at Bob's in Brockley, getting here by devious ways of buses and trains. Now South London is definitely not North London—it knows nothing whatsoever about North London and doesn't want to. To live in North London one is as remote from South London as if one lived say in Edinburgh. Bob's is a friendly flat with lots and lots of books about. The air-raid shelter in the back garden is full of water—whatever will they do in a raid? At night Bob and I to the Gaumont Theatre in Lewisham, a suburb as big as one of our cities. For

1/6*d* we get four hours. Felt as though I become one with the seat when we eventually rose stiffly to go. But a good programme. Deanna Durbin, whom Bob strangely enough candidly admires, in First Love, an extravagant and exotic romance in Jungle Fury and a variety programme. Taken again by the dog act—even a Scottie in a kilt.

24 March 1940

Teeming with rain so not much good arranging anything much so we walk to One Tree Hill. Go past the Horniman's Museum. Would like to have seen in this. Surely it is the one mentioned by Trader Horn to which he sent many of his specimens? Through Dulwich where is the last surviving toll-gate in the county of London. Nearly all the ground at Dulwich is owned by the College—a series of red brick buildings. Originally it was called Alleyn's Gift of God for the sons of poor people but in view of the high fees it has become discreet to be known as Alleyn's Gift of God College! Up College Road are big houses rather of the type of our more expensive places in New Zealand. A nice amount of ground and pleasant 'Old English' gardens. Dulwich is a quiet suburb now. In the times of Dickens it was an old village out of London through which the Coach passed. Up Stony Hill and along Sydenham Hill. (Bob awfully interested in the fact that I was born in Sydenham, N.Z. and went to Sydenham Methodist Church and Sunday School).On Sydenham Hill is the Crystal Palace or rather its remains. Somehow I had always had a childish idea that it was made entirely of glass. How I ever expected it to stand up without any frames I don't know.   It is strange how it has burned—the entire part of the middle buildings gone and the two towers left standing. One can see that they were a mass of little windows. It was only in 1936 that it was destroyed. Bob says the fire was a quarter of a mile of sheer flame and water was brought from as far away as a mile and a half. It would seem that the road along the old Crystal Palace site is where there is a church parade on Sunday mornings. The Salvation Army is out—a famous band frequently heard broadcast.

27 March 1940

I can take London easily this second time of coming. I think I am mellower in myself, not less keen but knowing that I have seen so much I need no longer be afraid that something will happen before I can see all those things which I longed to see. A feeling of completion of England is creeping over me—not satiation, that is different. Shopped and gazed at the new spring fashions. I am warier now about those pretty Jewish girls who hover in the doorways of the guinea shops. Took walks round many familiar places so that I shan't forget them. Hyde Park Corner, Trafalgar Square. In Buckingham Palace grounds a huge barrage balloon was down. Dying to take a photograph but every time I focus my camera a policeman looks with a twinkle in his eye. When I lower it he looks away. There was a man 'had up' the other day for taking photographs of interest to the enemy so perhaps I'd better not risk it.

28 March 1940

We go to Regent's Park and the Zoo. It is prettily laid out. The Zoo Gardens are intersected by the Outer Circle road and the Grand Union Canal, three divisions thus being formed, known respectively as the North Garden, the Middle Garden and the South Garden. The three portions are connected by tunnels under the Outer Circle and by the two bridges over the Canal. The tunnels are all sand-bagged now with tiny entrances in readiness for use as air raid shelters. But the animals are cared for in war time. Each one has a little plate over the cage. Private individuals have undertaken to supply the food for their particular 'pet' for the duration. It is said that every animal has thus been catered for. Some have a peculiar affection for snakes, others for ant-eaters, some evidently delight in the thought that at least the rat family will not go without. But whatever their tastes the British public has responded nobly and after the War the kiddies will still have a Zoo to come to. The animals know nothing of the War. It is rather a kindly Zoo. In many cases the animals are retained purely with deep ditches and walls. Somehow it is much better than the awful prison-like look of bars. The polar bears are behind glass. One really wonders why. Surely those of all animals can stand the cold. Stayed for a long time looking at Monkey Hill. It looks so natural but it is decidedly less natural than it looks for the caves are heated on cold days while in dull weather they are bathed in ultra-violet artificial sunlight by means of electric lamps. Walking round the Zoo is definitely tiring. We crept home and took our shoes off thankfully before the fire.

30 March 1940

Back to Bob's. Phyllis already in her tweeds. Whoever in England goes walking without tweeds? Somehow English girls 'carry off' their tweeds. I definitely don't—only succeed in looking dumpy, plain, uninteresting and 'serviceable'. The three of us by train to Sevenoaks. It is to Sevenoaks that Bob's firm is evacuated, the entire set of offices being accommodated in a lovely old house, the staff being accommodated with local residents. What a commotion that must have caused. All terribly keen about it all and seemingly like one big family with their picnics and dances and whist drives. There are antique shops in Sevenoaks, gorgeous 'muddly' ones in which one can spend hours. Everyone in England seems to conspire against me in the matter of buying antiques. They all rush me past hurriedly with the comforting reflection 'You won't want that when you get home'. Knole Park is lovely surrounding Knole House with, they say, 365 rooms. It is strange how these Tudor manor houses, built about the 15th Century, seemed so fond of exactly 365 rooms or windows. If there are 365 rooms surely there are 365 chimneys too? Never have I seen so many chimneys in either house or palace. It is owned by Lord Sackville. That gentleman is chiefly famous for having knocked down Norman's (Bob's particular friend) brother with his car. We wandered about picking primroses and shy white violets. Surely this is what I came to England for? I have seen England in its every mood for a year now—have completed the cycle of a year. We cross over fields by means of real old-fashioned stiles to Shipbourne and then by road to Hildenborough. Was there ever a more delightful place for an office? The house it would appear was owned by one Dr. Fish, a dentist, who has let it to the insurance company. Surely the old house has never known such strange days when files hung on its august walls and filing cabinets desecrated its halls.

We nearly called at the Green Dragon but the bus came. All remember the old joke about the St George and Dragon Inn. 'A weary traveller arrived late at night at the George and Dragon Inn. He hammered on the door but without effect until at length a window was pushed open angrily and a woman appeared "Is this the George and Dragon?" he enquired mildly. "It is" she retorted and proceeded to inform him in no uncertain terms that they weren't open, and he was definitely a nuisance. Then said the mild little man "Could I see George for a minute?"' By bus to Sevenoaks and home to a huge supper at 10 p.m.

31 March 1940

Bob up first again with tea, made the fire and breakfast and agitated until Phyllis and I got up. It's Sunday and we walked round by Crystal Palace. Sure enough there's the Church Parade—I just knew there would be. Dinner at 3. Careered merrily along on the top of an ancient bus to Southborough and set off to find Orpington. Surely this is real suburbia? Every house has a name. There were even a couple of New Zealand ones—Otago and Tainui. Their owners stood on the neat paths and surveyed, with complete satisfaction, neat cars. Small boys on tricycles race up and down from house to gate. It was all so pleasant and 'well-fed' looking.

April 1940

Bromley, Farnborough, Cambridge, Ely, Lincoln, Rawmarsh, Swinton, Rotherham, Bradford, Wentworth, Manchester, Liverpool

1 April 1940

With Norman and Bob to Bromley. Cannot quite get over all the footpaths through the fields. Very seldom needs one to walk on a road. At Hayes Common is a typical 'Bank Holiday' crowd—poor, scruffy, little begging-for-pennies children. It must be a poor district round here. Sat down for lunch and saw a snake wriggle off in the grass. Hunted him out to see him wriggle again. Bob very surprised we have no snakes in New Zealand. Seemed to be under the impression we spent half our time combating mambas. At Holwood is the Wilberforce Oak. Here he sat with Pitt discussing the abolition of slavery. Poor old oak! Surely it would be better to let it die a natural death? I feel so sorry for these propped-up relics. Thoroughly enjoyed wandering along by footpaths through ploughed fields, through little villages, watching a Hurricane plane swoop over the golf course. We went up to Downe House where Darwin worked and thought for forty years. It is a big house with a big garden and a tennis court and a peculiar chattering comes from within. It sounded for all the world like monkeys. The traffic on any road is terrific. Dodged between motor bikes, buses and cars and escaped on to the footpaths through the fields as often as possible. On bus at Farnborough just in time to avoid the rain. Just sat and talked by the fire at night—talked of everything under the sun including centrifugal pumps! How the time has flown. Beyond the day after tomorrow I'll perhaps never see London any more. Must get out of this fatalistic sorrowful state. Of course I'll see London again some day even if I'm old! To bed in the little bed by the fire watching the embers die out.

3 April 1940

Almost the first thing I found in Cambridge was an old, old street or lane leading from the Market Place into King's Parade. It was so narrow that a trade sign hung right across it. I stood and 'gaped' after the time-honoured custom of tourists. An old man with a bald head and a large pipe nodded casually. 'Ever heard of Pepys?' he said (He called it Peeps). 'Well the Three Tuns Inn that he was so fond of used to stand there'. I thanked him for the information and passed on. I had forgotten Pepys' association with Cambridge. Somehow I like to 'find' places and wander into them purely because I myself like the look of them and not just because the guide book says so. I found Trinity because of the effigy of good old Henry VIII at the Great Gate. The Hall has a lovely oriel window and the castellated top was outlined against the sky. For Clare and Pembroke I have a weakness because they were sponsored long, long ago by women. So were some of the others but I've lost my guide book so that fact will forever remain shrouded in mystery. I lost it near the rambling Old Castle Hotel. The owner came out and his language was picturesque too. I listened spell-bound—I doubt if even within their sacred precincts the old Colleges had ever heard a richer vocabulary. But with it all I just loved The Backs, the grounds of the succession of collegiate buildings from the ancient High Street, with sloping lawns. Each College looks lovelier than the last from the Backs. Each is like a jewel in a setting. It is, to use an American phrase 'high, wide and handsome'. A group of young College men in Air-Force uniform are being trained—it might be Cambridge but their Sergeant Major is of the old traditional type!

I do not know if I am 'Oxford' or 'Cambridge' but an overwhelming realisation has come over me. I am just plain 'Colonial' and we 'colonials' are plain. I do not regret it nor am I proud of it, I just realise it. I am as far away from England really as the Poles.

Now I always remember H. V. Morton's description of Ely—'There is nothing at Ely but the Cathedral' he writes. There isn't except about eight thousand people with the queerest accent—it isn't so definite as Lancashire or Yorkshire but just somehow clipped. The country round Ely is an enchanted country. It is not like anything I have seen before. The coconut palms of Ceylon were more familiar to me than the fens of Ely. For miles around the town the fields are actually under water and dim grey mist hovers over all. And yet these fields must sometimes grow and produce for houses on little risings sit like broody hens serenely. The town is towered over, commanded and shadowed by the Cathedral. Morton has said 'The Cathedral is a lady' but No—definitely no—if she is a lady then she is a Grande Dame, a matriarch. Have an unconquerable desire to say Ely giving the 'y' an 'i' sound. A local inhabitant looked pained. 'Elee' she murmured 'You're not English are you?'

Had another unconquerable desire to bring the same local inhabitant to New Zealand and set her down alone and uninstructed before Ngaruawahia! I shall stay at Ely tonight. I want to see the effect of the sunset on the fens.

4 April 1940

The sunset was just a dreary passing of day into night, it was the sunrise that was lovely. It flooded the watery fields with life—a warm coral glow. Ely looked the fairy Isle that she is. This land would be nothing without mist.

The train slugged its way through more sodden country, the pink glow had gone and it was just dead and drear. It was so like Holland in the wet. One wonders how people here can ever be joyous or light-hearted. It was a long wet journey. As we got out of the drowned country the rain ceased—it seemed only natural that it should. There was scaffolding round Lincoln Cathedral. Either they were taking out windows to bury them because of the war or it was just the usual course of events, I do not know. Scaffoldings round Cathedrals in England are as frequent as holes in the road. The Cathedral definitely looks un-English, its twin towers rise from a wide ornate front. Suddenly as I looked the bells rang with a resounding peel—so often they do that. It is almost as if they know... These towns on two levels, like Lincoln, fascinate me. One can go up steep little steps holding on to the rails for grim death. Old men plod up and old women with never a complaint. Possibly they have never lived anywhere else so they never realise that in some cities there are elevators of little cable cars for sudden steep slopes such as these. There are antique shops in Lincoln—but they are not touristy ones. They could easily be waved away as second hand shops. Amongst the little 'souvenirs' the most frequently seen is a 'Lincoln Imp'. He is a wicked looking little imp with big ears.   No one seemed to know the origin of the Lincoln Imp but all told me he was in the Cathedral so back I toiled up the steepest little street that ever came out of a fairy tale. Sure enough there in the stonework was the Imp. Frankly it repulsed me. A quiet old man in one of the antique shops looked over his glasses 'I've heard tell' he said that 'the imp was a small dwarf who found sanctuary in the Cathedral but his brain was as misshapen as his body and he saw fit to mock the very angels who protected him. In the end they could bear it no longer and turned him into stone'. Consequently, for no apparent reason, he's now sold for Good Luck. I bought one but somehow I have an uneasy suspicion about the Imp. What if he doesn't bring Good Luck but Bad...?

Had a belated tea in the High Street and then quite suddenly decided to go home. There was a train and it would be fun to be at No. 42, Park Street tonight. The train beat its endless way into Rotherham. Rotherham is just a black 'blob' in the black-out, the Parish Church looms up like a huge ominous shadow. It's cold too—somehow it seems years since I left London. They were all there! Auntie Lizzie, Uncle Albert, Bessie, Walter and Malcolm. They poked the fire up and shot the kettle on. Somewhere about 2 a.m. to bed. P.S. Up again at 3. Kidneys playing up, first time in the whole trip. Must have overdone it or MAYBE IT'S THE IMP!

6 April 1940

Saturday and it's Uncle John's day with his 'Lit' gel'. Get up early and have a cup of tea, creep back beside Auntie Polly. Off to see Mr. Dudhill.—an old man who always lived next to Granddad Turner. It seems there was a funny little custom between the two. Whenever Granddad bought tripe or udder he bought enough for Mr. Dudhill and the latter when he bought, did the same. He still keeps his whippets and if they're on the chair he sits elsewhere! Old Mrs. Dudhill busy cleaning her fire-irons. They are already shining. The old chap gives my hand many a shake. He always wondered if ever he'd meet Jimmy Turner's daughter's lass from New Zealand. The Yorkshire people say New Zealand peculiarly. Their 'New' is very elongated like 'nee u' (while we have a tendency to shorten it). The Zealand has more emphasis on the 'Zee'. Back to a huge dinner and then Auntie Polly, Uncle John, little John and I to Swinton and back across Piccadilly fields. Patted a Great Dane I would love to have adopted and taken back home but he would be awkward to pack! Met Mr. X. outside the Swinton Hotel. Mr. X appears rather put out and tells a long tale about going out a lot with some married couple but today the husband couldn't come so he and the wife came. Rather a shame we caught them but if he hadn't gone to such great lengths to explain we wouldn't have known she was even there. The whole gang into supper and such a supper, Yorkshire pudding—stew meat and vegetables and rhubarb and fig pie.

7 April 1940

Still alive to go with Uncle John to 'reckon'. Everyone seems to remember me and we meet George Turner, Uncle Dick, Joe Peverley and Arthur. Women selling badges for Children's Home or something and everyone buys. 'Heigh oop John' they say 'is that the young woman that came darn th' pit? I'm proud to know thee lass'. All wish me luck when I go home. Call into the Club to get yellow tomato seeds from Mr. Norcliffe. After supper Auntie Bella and Uncle Dick give me the dearest handbag, like a miniature Gladstone bag. Surely now I'll have room enough for all the 'mess' I carry about. The only bit of mess that's grown less are the traveller's cheques! Traveller's cheques run out at the end of the year so cashed the remaining ones last February. Frankly now that I've paid the remains of the return fare and sent the rest over to America to be picked up there, there's not much to worry about. Under war conditions I am not allowed to take more than £5 in cash out of England! George gave me a chain for my bag key. A most peculiar chain this, worn only by a gang of bookmakers called the Sheffield Toughs. For a walk with Elsie and Frank and it teems. Dry the 'animal' by the fire. I threatened to come home with the remains of one fur coat. I'll be lucky if there's even any remains. Teddy, George and I to the Regent to see a Yorkshire play by Rotherham Playgoers (Storm in Port—James R. Gregson). Perhaps I enjoyed it more than the Yorkshire people. After all I doubt if I'd thoroughly enjoy a comedy of New Zealand people. Being N.Z. they most likely wouldn't seem a bit funny to me. To the White Hart for supper.

10 April 1940

Did a bit more packing—it's becoming a habit. Gave Ruth my dinner frock— fits me like a sausage skin. Took the other evening frock round to a dressmaker who kept looking at it, measuring and repeating in an astounded voice 'Did it really fit you?' Assured her that it did and felt like saying that although I'm over nine stone I'm not a Colossus yet. Supposed to go to Sheffield with Walt but Punch, the dog, just killed nine fowls (P.S. Poultry this week on the table to every scion of the family) and the policeman says he has to be destroyed. A young officious policeman, who never did like Walt anyway, one P.C. Raffles! No one sees anything incongruous about the name but me. To them he was just P.C. Raffles and they have a more wholesome respect for the law than I have. Held a tangi[28] over Punch. Left Auntie Lizzie and Bessie in tears and trailed wearily and reluctantly down to the police station to meet P.C. Raffles at 4. Saw a bus waiting and sat in it for a quarter of an hour talking of Punch. Realised it was a stationary one and not likely to go for hours. Arrived at the station late for P.C. Raffles but the Sergeant was there. Saw a ray of hope in a black sky. He looked a Sympathetic Sergeant. Kicked Walter in the shins to let me try and he took the hint. Punch looked like a woolly lamb, his round eyes full of innocence. Made him sit up and shake a paw. Explained that he was only six months old and we just hadn't realised he'd grown up enough to kill fowls. We'd arranged for him to go to Manchester where there were no fowls but of course if P.C. Raffles' word was final—if he was the one to decide… P.C. Raffles was not the one to decide! The Sympathetic Sergeant bridled, P.C. Raffles had presumed. He—the sergeant—knew nothing of it. 'Then perhaps…' we ventured. We listened to rumbling 'umph umphs' and the suggestion that we take the dog back home. We might get a summons if the farmer insisted. If we did it would be the first time and there'd only be a caution… We gathered up Punch, and his look of injured innocence, and fled before he changed his mind. General rejoicing at No. 42 and Walt and I to the pictures to celebrate.

12 April 1940

Off to stay with Aunt Miriam at Canklow. Uncle Herbert comes home from night shift. How well Aunt Miriam looks after these men. Her hair is black as the raven's still and as shiny. (Rather silly that ravens don't have hair—the correct idiom I believe is raven's wing). Went with Aunt Miriam and Marjorie to see a friend in Alma Road Hospital—a poor soul, paralysed. Difficult talking to one who cannot answer but it is so like Aunt Miriam to be visiting one with whom others cannot be bothered. A bright enough ward but mental cases in another part of the building and quite visible through windows as one enters. Into Rotherham for Aunt Miriam's meat complete with ration cards. Did I report that I turn up everywhere with my little weekly ration of sugar, butter and bacon? Just potter round and chat all day. Aunt Mid tells me all about my childish hero, Uncle George Henry. How he came home from India in his resplendent red coat and never went out of the door. He just sat and shivered. A swashbuckling type Uncle George Henry, a romantic figure when he died young. But while he lived—well no one quite knew what he was going to do next.

14 April 1940

A walk with George and Teddy to see old Mr and Mrs. Sutton who knew Grandma and Granddad Turner well. He's a Norfolk man and clips his words. It's pleasant out and makes one want new clothes. The boys buy some more 'spice'. Everyone teases me about the little locked up bag Auntie Bella and Uncle Dick gave me. They say it's just like the one Nurse Hardy takes to her cases and will slyly enquire if it's twins this time. Go to the Titanic Club for the last time. All the cronies say Goodbye and the singer wails 'Wish Me Luck'. To Mrs Hansen's for tea. They make me so welcome and all send their love.

15 April 1940

Some scrappy bits of diary but that's how the days are going—running round here and there and packing a bit in between. All the Aunties have raked out cases from cellars and attics to get me home. Why buy they say, after all they're not going to be opened, many of them, till I get home. With Auntie Lizzie by train to Bradford to see Aunt Eliza. She hasn't been to Aunt Eliza's for over ten years. The two sisters sit and chat and we run up to Hilda's. Another baby coming soon. Mrs. Smith isn't too optimistic, says she sees an ethereal little creature hovering on the border of this world and the next and slipping away from us. It's so silly really, why do we take notice of these people?

16 April 1940

Back in Rawmarsh. No news yet. Simply must pack just in case the wire comes. Call round at Mrs Glossop's to alter a frock. There are so few sewing machines in Rawmarsh, if anyone has one everyone borrows it to do bits. Flew round to the dressmaker's for the evening dress and she again wonders 'Did it really fit you?' Forgot to report that Auntie Lizzie and I had to walk from Rotherham last night—too late for the last bus. The dim shapes of chimneys outlined in the glow from the Forge and the sounds of work cut uncannily through the still night air.

17 April 1940

A reprieve! No sailing until 26th. We breathe again. Fly round to tell everyone. Into Sheffield to see the Consul and get Permit altered. What a performance to get out of England—much worse than getting in but then it's war time. In London I'd filled in fifty three questions on three foolscap sheets. There is very little of me that remains a mystery! Packed a bit more—even Teddy's china dogs. Dear old Teddy presented me shyly with a lovely scarf and two silk hankies. 'For you, bought them at Spencer's' he says abruptly as he shoves them into my hand. In the midst of it all L. comes and I have to rush to the station at 4. But the family all like L. and doesn't he like their home-made bread. To see 'Spies of the Sky' (so excited I don't even know what it's about). To bed very late.

20 April 1940

Awakened by the early-rising L. at 8.30 and we eat for breakfast the Scotch marmalade he brought, which I point out is made in Manchester. Suggest to L. that it may be better to wear discreet blue pyjamas rather than the bright red and white striped ones, but Malcolm says 'Tha weer what tha wants lad'! A soft morning calm and warm. Think perhaps some of these early spring days are warmer than later ones (memories of tramping in bitter winds in South of England). The hedges across the fields on the way to Wentworth a soft green. Men plough the fields with heavy horses in corduroys and leggings (the men not the horses).The little grey stone village of Wentworth turns out to see L. in his kilt. And then Wentworth Park when the sun comes out for a while and lies softly on the timid deer. A big antlered buck stands for a while and gazes at us. A black-faced sheep 'baas' and from across the path twin lambs come running. They pull and tug at her. The broad façade of Wentworth House stands calm. It seems to stand for old England—an old England that is being swept away. We sit on a fence and chew grass—a hay cart passes. There is a smell of manure in the air. A throstle[29] sings as if its throat would burst. At length Greasbrough and the Milton Arms and tea. On the walls are hunting scenes. Two men who come into the 'Little Room' melt away discreetly on seeing us.

Home to Auntie Lizzie and a good dinner. It is strange how the two seem to go together always! Today Bessie moves into her new house and L. puts his good Scotch sinews to the test getting the furniture downstairs. He is stronger than any here. At night to the Club and rather fun. L. takes off his coat and draping a napkin over his arm puts his other arm over the waiter's shoulder. The latter sprang to it. Together they sing 'Annie Laurie'! Found the Chaperone in the washstand drawer and put him back again—best place for him.

21 April 1940

We fly to the station for L. to catch the 12. Ask the way of a boy who speaks Scotch. L. has to stop and shake hands and form a Caledonian Society. The train pulls out... Get a lift back—a silent mother and father and a sobbing daughter. Her husband has just left for camp. These are the days of partings— we sit each with our own thoughts and each alone knows what they are. George and I 'do' Parkgate. First George and Doreen to say Goodbye to the kiddies. Alice May's next—the poor soul, minus four front teeth, sits before the fire weeping silently—she looks so depressed. Mrs Senior's next to say Goodbye. Have a cup of tea and leave with many messages. Always a few tears at going—waving until we turn the corner. Home for a few minutes for a drink of Gaymer's cider and then for a walk across the fields to talk of things that must be said when the time for parting draws near. It is a night in a thousand with the softness of spring in the air.

23 April 1940

I fly to Greasbrough in the morning to get James and Bertha out of bed to say Goodbye. Dear old Mrs. Sanderson cries and hopes I'll get home alright. Assure her I'm born under a lucky star. Across to Smart's shop with the stove in the centre and then to Mr. Senior's. More messages to take home to Little Mum and another cup of coffee to drink. Bessie's new home is slowly shaping. Before she went in she papered throughout. The houseplace is all smiling and shining with the new three piece suite and sideboard. It is an old house and the bath in the kitchen covered up. It is good to see her settled or as they say here 'Ee but it's champion'! Then to Annie's and buy cakes for tea. We gloat over vanilla slices and creams. There has been a letter from Jack—no word of where he is going but he sent his cap badge back—an agreed sign if ever he went overseas. We pray it won't be Norway. Pop into the White Hart and then to the Star to say Goodbye to Mr and Mrs. Green and arrange for a car for Thursday. It grows horrible near this time of parting and those I am going to leave grow dearer. Stay at Auntie Bella's and creep in beside Betty.

24 April 1940

Into Auntie Bella's bed for a last chat. A rush round to see Mrs. Cooke to say Goodbye. A bit further along to Mary Wright's to thank her for the necklace. Old Mr. Liversedge comes down and she pats him into place. Funny position these housekeepers. Pack frantically for a brief space and run hurriedly to the chemist to get photograph of myself in 'pit muck'. Said Goodbye to Uncle Dick and Betty. Annie comes round with the news that Uncle John and family are awaiting at Auntie Lizzie's. Uncle John on his way to work so he says 'Goodbye' to his 'little gel' and goes out rapidly. He can't stand much, Uncle John can't. Wave the others goodbye in the blackout and stand for a moment in the doorway. I'm tired. Somehow I feel as if the life is going out of me. Walt slips an arm round me and tucks me up for a moment and then in to the party. Such a party—fish, chips, ale, stout, toasts, darts and jokes—Annie making everyone scream with laughter. Little Auntie drinking two glasses of stout. More goodbyes and a walk down the 'backs' with the parting guests.

25 April 1940

Thursday at last and all bustle and rush. Ram things frantically in my case and lick labels. Rush into Fred's to say Goodbye—the taxi at the door—the whole street turns out to wave. The station—fussing with luggage—only a few minutes to wait and then goodbye. George is good on the train—he does not speak for a long time. For the first time in Manchester it is fine. A good dinner and we both feel better. We race to the station just in time to see the train steam out. It's such a relief to see it go but there's another and we can't miss that. And so I wave Goodbye with a man's hankie that smells of cigarettes. Then to Edna's to stay the night. The dears are so glad to see me.

26 April 1940

It's morning before I can turn over. It is impossible that I should be leaving England—somehow my mind won't work. But I'm at Liverpool, I remember vaguely the harassed-looking girl telling me her sister was dying of meningitis. Fix up about luggage and report at the office. Wait interminably to have passports etc. examined. Give up my last link with England—the old gas mask—and on to the boat. We sailed maybe at five—a grey boat drifting into a shadowy distance where grey sea meets grey sky. In years to come I shall laugh at that extreme exhaustion I felt. It will seem like melodrama but it wasn't, it was and is horribly real.

27 April 1940

Very few passengers on the boat but crowds of Canadian soldiers. Some have gone sick in English camps, which they confide are the coldest they have ever experienced. Some have been fighting in France. One or two are going back to train Canadian boys. The decks piled high with aeroplane parts and wings to be assembled in Canada and up on the top the lads are singing as they polish the big gun. It's going to be rather fun this trip. Some are peering out to sea looking for periscopes as the ship runs her zig-zag course. A few timid souls run round hugging their life-belts—they'll get over that. Life boat drill at a given signal and we all dash up to the muster decks. Stand and freeze for an hour and then dismissed. We've no convoy but I've Saint Christopher on my arm, a little black cat in my bag, a Scottish talisman on my chest and a Maori one in my purse so I guess I'll leave it to them. 'Our gang' has formed already with Rene, Mrs Grantham and I with Danny, of the bandaged head and a map of Ireland written all over his face, and Harry, the trapeze artist in private life, who can chew up razor blades as a pastime (he obligingly has a meal of them for my benefit). Harry is a huge chap, easy-going and good-tempered as a Great Dane. Funny little Eddie, the Scot, an idealist with bright blue baby-like eyes and a champion chess player from somewhere.

A wonderful day to be at sea—to stand in the bows amongst the mine sweepers and feel the salt spray on one's face. To rise with the ship and shriek as the wind shrieks. The stolid form of Harry plants itself squarely in my path and we fight our way back to the side. It's a storm alright. The seas grow higher and higher and the wind louder. We can only stay on our feet by clinging to a part of the ship and to each other. This time—surely it has risen never to come down again. She is going down—down into the wicked depths of a wave—surely there will be no rising at all... And then the wave comes—a veritable Colossus of a wave and we scatter defeated. The fur coat drips like a drowned rat. Rene splodges up and down in her water-filled shoes. It takes all day to dry out but it was worth it.

May 1940

Montreal, Ottawa, New York, Coney Island, Toronto, Oshawa, Regina, Vancouver, Seattle, Portland, San Francisco, Los Angeles, Honolulu.

1 May 1940

Up feeling full of beans. Brightly announce that it's May Day but it arouses no response from the lower bunk. Up on deck to find no one. Find I've read my watch wrong and it's only 5.30! Wake Mrs. G. up to apologise for being such a beastly nuisance. Ask an old lady if she's sea sick? She shakes her head sadly 'No dear but I can't sleep you know in all this'. Wondered vaguely what 'all this' was. 'Well I don't take my clothes off at night you know. I just lie down like this. If we were torpedoed and called to meet our Lord...' 'The Lord would like you just as well in your nightdress' I said firmly 'and if we were torpedoed it wouldn't matter anyway'. So I got her downstairs to her cabin, bribed the steward for some brandy and saw her fall asleep. Goodness knows why she worried—her ample flannelette nightie was as covering as any coat.

Did Bill tell me last night that he'd been moose hunting with Errol Flynn? I wonder if the story was true? There is a huge incinerator by the kitchens. In this every speck of rubbish is carefully burned. We have been warned not to throw as much as a cigarette paper overboard in case the enemy should see it and know a ship was in the vicinity. Found out today that we're on the Duchess of Bedford. It's been a deep dark secret but all the souvenirs in the shop are marked thus, so evidently we are. That's why she rolls. The Drunken Duchess is her nickname—she's made flat-bottomed to get up the St. Lawrence! 'Pop' joins 'our gang'—a hardy veteran of the last war who gave his wrong age to enlist again. Looks just about ready to collapse. Most of the Canadians are going back on account of troubles developed by the damp in

England. A walk with Eddie to discuss philosophy, Epstein and the hereafter or the absence of it. Discovered a crowd of little boys on board going out to Vancouver from an orphanage to be taught farming—jolly little kids with skipping ropes and tops—all fitted out splendidly—obviously new 'rigs' for coming away. Women in charge most efficient. One little lone orphan girl who clasps her doll. Cannot help wondering if she going to be taught housekeeping for the little farmer boys.

2 May 1940

How the week is flying. Just can't get up this morning, we have central heating and incredibly soft beds for on board ship. The sea calm now and all sorts of people appear that I've never seen before, but they've appeared too late to be really part of the 'Crowd'. Little Sandy—the Glasgow shipbuilder—runs round getting up games and telling all the funny stories he ever knew—long-winded rambling stories that seem to have no apparent end. 'I can't understand a word, Sandy' I say despairingly. 'Well then my bonnie lassie I'll go slow the noo'. He does but the result is worse. The young Canadian boys are so much younger than Englishmen of the same age—more like our N.Z. boys—not exactly younger but not always trying to pretend they're older like they do in England. They are extremely candid and not afraid to admit things they don't know and can't do. 'Gee wasn't I embarrassed' with a long emphasis in the 'arr' part of it, said young Bill in the course of a story. What Englishman admits frankly to anything embarrassing him?

3 May 1940

We have a farewell dinner, roast turkey and cranberry sauce. All dress up a bit and the soldiers polish their buttons. Afterwards we sat up on deck in the cool quiet air to watch the lights of the St. Lawrence, the first lights any of us have seen since September. This is Canada. Poor little turbulent England so far away. Little farms that are dotted along the shore are still snow-covered—the air is biting with an icy touch. Everywhere are little churches with little steeples. We have a long wait for the immigration officer and then it is too late to go ashore at Quebec, but I've seen the Heights of Abraham. There are little Czech refugee women on board who look longingly at land. One wonders what they have left behind and what they look forward to.

4 May 1940

Discover a train for Ottawa going late tonight but time to look round Montreal first. Locate the Bank in St. James St. and actually get some money. It is one of the strangest towns I've ever seen this Montreal. It is more French than Paris—more like a French seaport, Marseilles perhaps. Three times I asked the way to be met with 'No Inglish'. The fourth time I asked in French. 'I don't speak French, lady' was the reply. There are delightfully old-fashioned, horse-drawn vehicles to go up Mount Royal. They seem to be relics as there were only two—just like the phaetons and barouches used on the Continent. Back rather reluctantly to the city by tram. The driver shouted something that sounded for all the world like 'boiled turnips' and I realised it was McGill (the University). One is lulled into a sense of false security in Montreal. To all intents and purposes one is in an English country and act accordingly and then discover that one is in the heart of France. Looked through Eaton's store. Real Yankee fashions, so different from the English ones. All preparing for summer and I feel suddenly mouldy and shabby. In the Ladies' toilet was a dryer to blow one's hands until they were dry. Must get used to this phrase 'the Continent' here. We always mean Europe but here it obviously refers to America and Canada. Train to Ottawa at 9.15 and a little sleep till we get there at 11. Times are most important, the railways run standard time and the city is daylight saving. It is so easy to turn up just one hour late!

5 May 1940

The little boarding house is a simple place but it is deliciously warm. I'm going to love this central heating that I've always heard about in Canada and America. No shivering in the bedroom or teeth chattering to the bathroom. Got a bit worried when I saw the meagre amount of bed clothes last night and piled on coats etc. which I promptly threw off again. It was just like a summer night. Had a leisurely tea and toast in my room. I think this is the first Sunday I've had abroad that I really feel as if it is a Sunday. In Europe I was still hard at sight-seeing on a Sunday and in Ireland I went to Church so much I felt as if I had done a day's work. In England it was generally a signal for packing up and going to stay with another Auntie. But this morning is definitely Sunday.

Now whichever way one looks Ottawa is dominated by the Parliament building. The whole city is picturesque—a city of roofs, gables, spires and steeples. It reminds me of Lucerne—a grown-up Lucerne full of dignity and beauty. Went with Frank, Dr. and Mrs. Lomar to their home, No. 11 Linden Terrace. It was strangely enough just the sort of place I had hoped to find. It had every degree of comfort and certain antique treasures that made one long to explore. I had a real Canadian dinner starting with tomato juice (it has to be tomato with the 'a' sounded as in 'play'), roast ham, baked pineapple, potatoes in their jackets and asparagus, followed by apple pie and coffee. Whoever in New Zealand would think of baking pineapple and yet how nice it is. The kitchenette is a dream, just like one of those complete, absolutely modern kitchenettes one sees in American magazines.

In the afternoon a long drive. The roads for the most part are marvellous, especially those within the city limits. And of course there is the right hand drive! Frank will never know how I held my breath as cars whizzed at us presumably on the wrong side. There is evidence of cheaper petrol (or gas as they call it here). The cars are all huge Auburns, Hudsons and Packards. Looked in vain for one 'baby' car. Out of town Canada is going to be thoroughly Colonial like New Zealand. The fences are post and wire except for very old ones which are logs laid horizontally. All the farms seem to have an old buggy and a two storey wooden farm house with a veranda all round. Just for all the world like the old homesteads in New Zealand. Ottawa even has its street lights different from anywhere else. The whole place is brilliantly lighted. I can revel in it after poor black England. The streets are so wide and clean, the grass walks and centre squares so clean cut. There is a whisper that Ottawa is preparing for the British Government if things should become very, very serious. What more fitting place could they have for a new beginning.

6 May 1940

I don't want to go to New York a bit. All my life I've wanted to go to New York and now I don't want to. Feel so resentful about the war today. If there were no war I could stay in Ottawa, have another day, two days, three days. If only these war-time restrictions didn't tie me down to a certain boat I could absorb a little more of Ottawa's grace and charm. It's not fair to be rushing through Canada like this. Why cannot I wander through as I wandered through Pisa and Lucerne and Paris without a specified boat looming ahead? I daren't even growl to anyone because they only say 'You're lucky to be here at all'. I am. Someday I'll come back…

The train went at 6.50. It is a soothing air-conditioned train—no noise, no dust, no 'nurthin'. We just glide through the hours. There's a 'commercial' typing his orders in the train, so why can't I do the diary? There's an unacknowledged contest of speed, and I win easily. Our route takes us through the Adirondacks and past Lake Placid—it is well named. We follow the Hudson River all the way, sometimes right on the very edge. There is still ice on the river—great broken-up chunks of it. Then come the lights—the wheels sing 'It's New York—New York'. Huge apartment houses flash by lighted from top to bottom. I feel like the boy from Johnsonville who has come to New York to make good. I have such a little time here—and so much to see! For the first time in my trip I book in at a Y.W.[30] There are hundreds of them in New York. This particular one reminded me of a Hotel Splendide. There was a most superior individual at the desk and on the notice board the lecture booked for the evening is on Birth Control! You have a room, a huge room with a telephone and a private shower. The toilet is shared with the next room by the simple expediency of, when one is using it, locking <u>their</u> door. Of course forgot that and locked my own with the result that Mitzi appeared.

I have never known anyone quite like Mitzi. She loved life from the top of her curled head to the tips of the highest heels I've ever seen in my life. She was frank to a degree. She asked if she could come in and talk to me. 'Gee' she said 'you talk cute'. If anyone 'talked cute' it was Mitzi not I. 'If I was cute like you' she said 'I guess I'd show them'. I never found out whom she'd show, or, for that matter, what. Mitzi was curious about New Zealand—for the country she cared not a hoot but she was interested in the girls. Were they all like me? What were the offices like—did we have any offices? What about our love life? So this is New York, and isn't it hot, from a meteorological point of view I mean! 'You haven't got much time here, have you?' I confessed I had very little time. 'Then' she said calmly, 'we'd better start now'. Mitzi started and I followed. We got a train to Coney Island! The big dippers and the roundabouts were in full swing. Do they never go to bed in New York? There were crowds and crowds and crowds. The main street is lined with stalls and drug stores. Why 'drug stores' I'm positive they never even smelt a drug. There are coconut shies. A lad called Sonny threw something and won a fat negress on a stick which he solemnly presented to me.   His mate took it back to balance on his nose topped by an ice cream cone. Maybe the trick can be done, but he couldn't do it—it landed down Sonny's back and we left in the riot that followed. The beach was beautiful or it was tonight. The sand strangely enough is red. There were coloured lights in the trees. Coney Island is less than two miles long and yet it is said that on a holiday over two million people congregate there. More than the population of New Zealand! I would have liked to have stayed on the beach but Mitzi was inexorable. She phoned someone called Lem, whom we were to meet at Kate and Mike's. Lem was a quiet stolid individual who danced like a dream. He looked at me appraisingly and agreed with Mitzi's suggestion that I was cute and then asked if I'd mind saying it again. 'Say what?' I asked. 'Can't' he said 'you say "carn't"—funny isn't it—like they do in the English pictures'. 'It is "carn't"' I protested. 'Aw come off it' he smiled indulgently. So we drifted off to Kate and Mike's for pancakes, maple syrup and sausages. Eat it first very gingerly, carefully segregating the sausage from the syrup, but once you've braved it together it's really quite good. The lights are very shaded in Kate and Mike's. It is still crowded and suffocatingly hot.

The orchestra wails like a lost soul. A negro, maybe Mike himself, stands under a palm and croons at intervals, but no one listens.

And then I saw Broadway. Dancing, laughing Broadway. I just want to stand the rest of the night and look. There is an extra blaze of lights round Madison Square Garden. Everything seems unreal—the ancients were right there is magic in light. How can these people of New York be quite like the rest of the world amid this artificial radiance? Now I know what is meant by Rockefeller Centre and Radio City. They are blocks of buildings, some of moderate height and perhaps three excessively tall buildings and one gigantic one. There is a vast underground system that ties together all the buildings. Walked back to where we could see the Eternal Light. It's scintillating—a huge star on top of Madison Square Garden, an almost living memorial to the dead of the Great War. And I thought of London—so black.   Have decided that no-one in New York ever sleeps. The heat is terrific and I mentally divest myself of woollen underclothes. Every man we pass mentally divests me of them too. Never had that feeling about men in any other country in the world. But after all if one will prowl in the early hours... We say goodnight to the good-natured Lem. 'Isn't it late to be going in?' I enquired of Mitzi. Her carefully brushed eyelashes open in astonishment. 'It's only four' she says.

7 May 1940

Mitzi I find does work. Her love-life isn't sufficient to keep her entirely. So I have a very early date with the Statue of Liberty. The underground again! How handy they are. There are such a heterogeneous collection of people in New York and frankly I don't like the look of them. A fair sample is found in any underground carriage. Surely they are 90% Jews and the rest mysteries. A voluptuous dark-haired woman leans back in her seat and chews gum with great lazy open-mouthed chews—the girls look so hard and worn. Maybe it's unkind to say it but most of the men look like criminals and a fair percentage of the women aristocratic prostitutes! The Statue of Liberty is huge inside. We reached her hat where we looked out of holes to the Manhattan skyline. There is an atmosphere about New York—one feels so small as one never felt in London. The water danced blue and silver—the skyscrapers rise like a dream city. Back and to Wall Street. Now Wall St. is 'Down town'. It is the most amazing street, one can stand and look down it. It looks merely an alleyway between two tremendous buildings and at the end is the dark spire of Trinity Church. If one did not look too high it was so like England to see this spire in the heart of the city silhouetted against the sky. But then it is New York and it is nearly impossible to look high enough. I walked along Wall St. like a country bumpkin gazing upwards until my eyes developed a definite squint and something happened to the glands in my neck. The men here looked definitely 'Wall St.' They hurried along pre-occupied—all looking as if they were on the verge of making or losing a fortune.

Found my way back to Broadway and sure enough at the corner of 34th St. was Macy's. Here I met Mrs.R. and over a perfectly marvellous salad of every fruit and green under the sun, topped off by a dream of strawberry shortcake, we decided where to go. First to look at the fashions. There is a preponderance of golden fox capes this year. The type of girl who had them on just would wear golden fox! But perhaps I'm misjudging them. England has made me dull, prosaic and unduly suspicious. Out and to Seventh St. which is a peculiar street. At the Time Square end it houses the Opera House and at the far end, the Down town end, it is part of Harlem. We've left Time Sq.—left the shoe-shine boys sitting sleepily besides their little boxes. They are everywhere at every corner, outside every building and in every little recess—negroes whose faces are coal-black and their teeth white. It would seem that everyone in New York shoe-shines away from home. We took our tired way to Harlem. It was stiflingly hot. The crazy tenement houses were packed. At an upstairs window a big negro buried his head in the ample black bosom of his lady love. There are strains of weird tom-tom music and shuffling feet coming from little night clubs. The whole of Harlem that is not dancing or flirting at a window is out walking in a certain section of Central Park. Joe with his bright brown shoes and navy pants and lumber jacket—Dinah with her tiny beflowered hat so absurdly like those I've seen on 5th Avenue at stupendous prices, and between them the 'little un', diminutive in blue denims, scarcely able to toddle, the frizzy head done up in myriads of tiny plaits. There are condemned tenements it would seem by the hundreds but I see no sign of new buildings to take their place. Obviously something should be done about Harlem, crowded together under conditions that make for vice. One would have to be tough to live here.

Dear Mrs. R. decided to stay in town so that we could do a spot more sight-seeing next day, so phoned home to Rye to let her husband know. What a marvellous service the Bell Telephone Co. has. He was trailed from his office to the office of a friend and finally home for no extra fee. If we had been unable to get him then all that would have been charged was a small sort of 'searching fee'.

8 May 1940

A run first of all in the very early morning over Brooklyn Bridge and then we leave the car and make for the Empire State Building. First and foremost you pay a dollar and then you ascend almost to heaven. In the Observatory at the

102nd floor we were so high up that it seemed as if it were another world. It is hard to believe that express cars rise to the 80th floor in a minute but strangely enough I felt none of the choking sensation in spite of the speed. We were 'scraping the sky', higher than all the other sky scrapers. One can pick them out—the Woolworth, the Rockefeller, The Chase National Bank and the Chrysler Building. Perhaps the Tower of Babel was not a myth after all.

We had lunch at an automat. For one has not been to New York if one has never slipped a coin into a slit as in a gas meter and pulled out a ready-made dinner. One can see it all in glass showcases, hover for a long time in an agony of indecision, before finally inserting the coin. I produced corn on the cob and manoeuvred melted butter from running in a greasy stream down my chin. I had water melon and ice cream, and coffee and almost wept because of a limited capacity. It was such fun to see pop out just what you want.

I shall see no more of New York but what I have seen I shall not forget. I caught the train by a split second with Mitzi and Mrs. R. tossing my bag in after me. Talk on the train to a man—a funny, old-fashioned, foreign soul. He bows stiffly and definitely—I've seen that bow before. I put it down mentally to Germany but it seems he is a doctor from Austria who has been visiting his mother in Chicago. The war has broken out and he doesn't quite know what to do about going back. I bring my German into play feeling more than slightly guilty and traitorish. He tells me of Vienna, of his mother, of his wife and family, of the brotherhood of man and the Stock Exchange.

11 May 1940

We travel all night and all night I sleep. Toronto is rather a fine city—a clean spacious city with square buildings. It is strange how the fashions are modified when compared to New York. They are so much more conservative in Canada. The bus to Oshawa bowled along at an alarmingly smooth pace. Here too most of the houses are wooden and upstairs. Haven't seen one house of the single storey bungalow type. A perfect day—Harry at the bus to meet me and we walk down streets that have that peculiar quietness of the middle morning when children and workers are away and women working placidly inside with windows open and curtains blowing gently out.

Now Oshawa _is_ General Motors. Practically everyone runs to in the morning and pours out at night from the huge block of buildings in the centre of the town. Of course such things as looking through the factory are cancelled now that the war is on but I see Colonel Chappell and we talk of New Zealand and of England. Finally he called the Awfully Nice Secretary, under the circumstances I could be shown round. Where is the rush and 'sweated labour' I've heard about in these assembly works? Everyone vows they're busy but all have time to talk. One man certainly does nothing else but fix a few bolts, the A.N.S. explained that he is only on that work for a while and that practically every man of any age in the factory has been through any department as part of their policy. We saw the chassis at the start moving very, very slowly along a belt. The engine was fixed into position, the battery and all the parts, one at a time. It moved so slowly that if theirs was not a big job the men had ample time to stand and chat in between. There seemed to be a complicated social life connected with the Works—the Secretary stops here to remind one of the baseball, another of the Camera Club and certainly without exaggeration they all look happy enough. As we walk on the bodies become more and more complete until they are fully equipped as regards the chassis. Then at a synchronised moment, with five men standing in readiness, the roof opens and down comes a shining body. It lands exactly on the chassis—a few bolts are screwed and lo! a Buick. What impresses one most is the order and lack of mess. It is so tidy! It almost seems they have cleaned up for my coming. Every kind of guard possible is on the machines. About twenty complete cars have already been turned out today. It would seem that large contracts are underway for army trucks etc. with the best of workmanship and materials—in fact there are masses of khaki work of all descriptions in the yards. The G.M.C. and Ford's combine to do this work. Odd jobs the A.N.S. says are found for pensioners. There were a number of them about who didn't look as though their odd jobs troubled them particularly.

Harry and I to Toronto for dinner to eat chop suey at the cleanest-looking shop in Chinatown and I learn, under the charming tutelage of a Chinese, to use chop sticks. It is hard but not impossible. Why is it that Chinatowns, albeit smelly, are always so fascinating? Harry eats like all the Canadians. The business of 'cutting up' is attended to first, the knife put on one side and the dinner eaten with the fork.

15 May 1940

I'm on my way 'out West'! The Prairies, great stretches of flat land, pass by—it is such a pale delicate green just as far as one can see. It is all the same. I'd never dreamt it would be like that. We whizz through hours of it and fall asleep frequently. Arrive at Regina and Rose seemed to make straight for me and explains that I just 'looked foreign' somehow. Have breakfast at the café run by Rose and her brother Louis. Do Americans, or I should say Canadians, do nothing but eat? People consume Coca-Colas on the way to work! Freddie arrives half an hour later from the barracks in a whirl of excitement. I get introduced to, it would seem, thousands of people. It is a casual café, Lee, one of the girls, cooks hamburgers or hot cakes or steaks as customers come in or if she doesn't Rose does. It seems to be a social centre, the same people come day after day in their odd spare moments, sit on their high stools or hang over the counter and talk. The café of the small American town takes the place of the pub in England. It is a meeting place for boys and girls. An automatic record player grinds out prairie songs as it eats up nickels—the whole of Regina seems to live on 'cocs'.[31] We dance for a while and wander 'down town' and into shops. Regina isn't so very big—only about as big as Invercargill I should say, or perhaps Dunedin. And we meet a Mountie! He's Jim. His red coat fits him like a glove—his riding boots are of the softest leather and his wide hat at just the right angle. Perhaps it's just as well I'm not staying in Regina. He has a slow, quiet, almost lazy smile. 'Say how about a show this afternoon?' I really didn't want to go to a show but with a real Canadian Mountie in his red coat... So we all went back to the café for dinner and then a taxi to the barracks. Next week Jim said they'd all have khaki uniforms, so it seems I've seen the last real Canadian Mountie for some time. I didn't dare ask him if he always got his man. It seemed such a banal thing to say. So I asked Rose. Rose wasn't so shy. 'Of course he doesn't' she said 'he's never got anyone in his life'. I looked at Jim for confirmation and his slow smile spoke volumes. It was as much as to say 'That's all she knows'. This big broad-shouldered piece of Canadian efficiency has an inordinate fondness for Walt Disney cartoons. His hearty guffaws mingled with the agitated squawkings of Donald Duck. We took a taxi back to Regina. No one seems to walk at all here. Rose looked horrified when I suggested it. We had tea, the four of us and then to the station and a grand send-off.

16 May 1940

Past Calgary it gets hillier and hillier. We pass 'dude ranches' tucked away in the hills and occasionally are in time to see gates open and the 'dudes' ride out. An Indian hits the trail in his old cart with his squaw and children sitting behind. He looks neither to the right nor to the left, and the old horse plods on. The foothills rise into mountains, fir-clad slopes rise to incredible heights. Snow-capped peaks disappear into the clouds. It is Switzerland on a large scale. There are adjectives that apply to the Rockies that have been dwarfed by common use but their true significance applies to the mountains and canyons of the Rockies—they are magnificent, splendid—colossal. There is no better place to think than in a train. Not planned thinking but a letting of the mind wander wherever it will. Was struck suddenly by the names of places here that are replicas of those in England. Just South of the Great Divide is a Windermere and a Lake Windermere.

18 May 1940

The Lone Star Ranger wakes up with an amazing growth on his face but his grin is cheerful. He fetches my coffee, depositing half in my lap, apologises profusely and sits on my hat. Just a great big rough man from the West. Ask him if he is going to the fiesta at San Francisco to ride bucking broncos. Good Lord No! He's a bank clerk in Buffalo! It's Vancouver and it's the first time I've seen the Pacific since I left home. It is the same sparkling Pacific dancing in the sun just as it does in Waitemata Harbour. It's a perfect day, I can feel the sun eating into my poor English sun-starved English skin. Took a street car out to Stanley Park (they are always street cars here—never trams) and stopped to consume a huge glass of buttermilk. All the shops, that is all the little confectioners and milk bars, sell buttermilk for 5 cents a glass. It has a slightly sour, cheesy taste and is always icy cold.

I can truly say that Stanley Park is the loveliest park I have ever seen. It is a great park, the natural forest has been miraculously preserved. There are firs and cedars as unspoiled as if they were right in the heart of the Rockies I have just passed through. Across the harbour one can see Vancouver—it is so strangely like Auckland as viewed from Northcote or any of the North Shore drives. At the Sunken Garden I chatted for a while with one of the gardeners, for who is more intimately connected with the garden than the gardener? He knew every little English flower that ever grew. We aired our views on the war and won it before I passed on. I shall always remember Canada for the dark pines reaching up to snow-clad hills and yet here in Vancouver they have it all. There are palm trees in Stanley Park. It is all a coastal town should be. It has its own charm and is a promise of what lies behind. Ran into a boy off the train and we eat a chopped steak which turned out to be a sort of hamburger not a steak at all as we know it and then to Chinatown. On the West Coast the Chinatowns are much bigger than in New York or even Toronto. Wails of Chinese music come from dark little shops but the girls are exquisite, their painted faces as immobile as a plaque. We roam into a Persian antique shop full of priceless relics rubbing shoulders with Birmingham junk.

19 May 1940

I got raked out of bed at an unearthly hour by a maid who informed me a young gentleman was waiting for me downstairs. I had promised the boy from the train to be ready early, only it was extra early. He had a car and away we went for a drive around the ocean beaches. English Bay, Kitsilano, Locarno and Jericho. They were deserted except for a few lone figures. There were already yachts on the harbour. I wanted to cry out all the time—how like it is to Auckland. We raced back to the boat by 10.30. I never thought I'd have anyone to see me off in Vancouver, but the Boy Off The Train waved vigorously and set off to conquer new worlds at a great speed in his hired car. The Marguerite is a fairly big boat—it even boasts a magazine of its own. It gives you useful information such as the fact that connections for electric razors are installed in all public washrooms and hot water bottles provided on request. I could have done with the hot water bottle but it was day time and whereas it is perfectly conventional to have one at night it would look extremely odd to ask for one in the day time. We stop for quite a while in Victoria and later I warmed to Seattle. The lights would beat Broadway almost. There are sky-scrapers that scrape just far enough to be thrilling without being ostentatious. It is a vigorous city. I rang up the Ryans whom I met at the Youth Hostel in York. Well they might have thought I got lost on the way.

20 May 1940

The telephone over the bed woke me up. It was Pat Ryan. She and Jack would be over at ten. She was just dying to see me, what had I done since York and did I go the way I said I would through Scotland, and what was the war like and... I wandered down and around the wharves for a while before they came and found the most fascinating shop. There were ships in bottles, Indian pipes, tomahawks, sea horses, dried fish of the weirdest shapes, masses of coral and a huge pair of whale-bones. A little group of religious fanatics were preaching in the streets. There were perhaps a dozen men with longhair, cadaverous faces and long silky beards. They stood with their arms hung by their sides gazing forward with queer expressionless eyes. When the preaching was over they began to sing revival hymns doing little actions all together. After the first line they all put up one forefinger and wagged it backwards and forwards solemnly. At the end of the verse the wagging forefinger ceased and the hands were spread out to the side and finally clasped together. All movements were done exactly together and in exactly the same place in each verse. Their hymn finished and they marched solemnly away.

Jack and Pat arrived, flinging themselves out of the car lustily and healthily. Wanted to know everything—just everything darling, as Pat said, that I've been doing since I left York. So I tried to tell them while we drove at a perilous pace round the shore of Lake Washington. We dashed to their home for lunch and I met Jack and Pat's mother and father. We had chicken, squash, which I find is like pumpkin, a youngberry pie (youngberries it seems are like loganberries) and pineapple juice. The hub of Seattle seems to be at the intersection of Pike St. and 4th Avenue. If it were to grow it would be New York over again but its people have no semblance at all to the New Yorkers. They are a more solid prosperous people—one feels that they only wish their sky-scrapers so high no more—that they only wish their city just so big. Finished up at Woodland Park and buy peanuts for the animals and eat the best part ourselves. Ride on the merry-go-round and take photographs by the Totem Poles. These Totem Poles fascinate me, used as I am to the Maori poles. They are so different with the beaked faces and staring eyes. Possibly the ugly flat faces of the Maori poles fascinate people from Canada just the same.

Turned out a lovely day and I've started to freckle! That's the penalty to pay for having acquired a delicate skin in the mists of England. To a show at night, and the train at 11.30. Have fired Pat and Jack with the New Zealand ambition when the war's over. They're confident 'the brave New World' will never be in it. Assuredly it seems so far away now.

21 May 1940

Came to life in Portland, Oregon. We have passed through some magnificent country. Portland is the city of roses. All these West Coast towns look so thriving, so solidly prosperous. Perhaps too it is the effect of the hills always at the back.

We are nearly in California now and on the left is Mount Shasta. We are near the Sacramento River canyon and far off the Mossbrae Falls shimmer through green foliage. We fight against the darkness but there comes a time when we can peer no more. Even the coffee and doughnut man has ceased to come round with his shiny little coffee container on wheels and doughnuts sealed in cellophane. We will be in San Francisco when it is morning.

22 May 1940

This is the California we always hear about—the sun is soft and warm and the sky smiling. We reach Oakland first and change to a ferry! It appears the trains are not yet running over the bridge. San Francisco has just as distinctive a skyline as the famous Manhattan. The steel supports of Oakland Bridge show it as in a frame. Surely in all the world there are no taxi-men so pushing and persistent as in San Francisco. They try all methods—they are patronising, servile and even fatherly. It is useless to say No however decidedly, to exhibit a minimum amount of luggage and evince a desire to walk up Market St. One just has to extricate oneself and positively flee; just in time to meet everyone going to work. There is no thrill quite like the thrill of having a city to explore.

San Francisco is astoundingly like Auckland. Of course we are not yet grown-up, we have no bridge to the North Shore but when that comes, and our buildings pile higher to the sky, we will be San Francisco—even to Chinatown. San Francisco's speciality seems to be leather goods. Bought Daddy's present in trepidation—the old feminine cry—it is so hard to know what to get for men. For men are so much the same all the world over and they don't want to be different. A woman would love a Chinese coat but give the average New Zealander a sports shirt with gay scenes of Hawaiian revels and it would lie unhonoured and unsung for ever in the drawer. Walked from one end of Market Street to the other. It is a strange thing, something to do with the traffic regulation, that no street crosses Market St. but many start from it. Market St. is easy—it runs straight and true but once out of it San Francisco is a maze. Up Montgomery St. are the skyscrapers. It is the Wall St. of the West. Compared with New York they are mild skyscrapers but they are considerable and quite sufficient to present a respectable sky line. We will always remember the flower stalls along the sidewalks. There were masses and masses of roses. Even the usual city smells were not proof against their fragrance—they were so clean and fresh—but I saw no 'flower women' here, the tenders were all men. It is at the statue in front of the City Hall that visitors are compelled to stop. True the San Franciscans pass it unnoticed but don't we all in our home town? It is Lincoln seated in what may be called a 'characteristic attitude'. It is his face that attracts and his feet. The latter are so naturally placed. As to his face, well frankly I never did like Lincoln's face. I don't say so in public for I would offend my hosts, and he was an admirable man, but the fact remains that if I had lived in the nineteenth century and met Lincoln socially, I'd have given him a wide berth from pure instinct.

Now at Powell and Market Sts. the cable cars start. They are such funny little rattly contraptions that take one to Fisherman's Wharf. At one stage up a particularly steep hill it seemed as if the law of gravitation must win. The conductor smiled he'd seen tourists in difficulties before. 'It's 45 degrees up here, Missy' he said. At Fisherman's Wharf we got out. The motorman and conductor got out too, seized the absurd little car one at each end and spun it round on a turn table, got in and, with a great clanging of bells, rattled off. There are such funny souvenirs at Fisherman's Wharf. Baby tortoises, on which one can have messages engraved, can be sent to any place in the U.S.A. It seems they'll live that long without food or water. Has no one set up a society for the prevention of cruelty to tortoises? If not it's time they did. An enterprising salesman at one of the stalls dangles a huge crab at me as I pass. It is ridiculously cheap and I bought it. I had to do something with it or else cart it round all day so I sat on the wharf, gazed at the Golden Gate Bridge and ate it. It was delicious.

The harbour looked wide and generous. 'San Francisco' may be just a cheap popular song but it is grand, and it belongs here—'San Francisco open your golden gates.' It looks a land of promise. It is too—a land of a thousand promises and a thousand problems. Its people are a little hard and self-centred but you are always their equal. It is every man for himself but there's always a smile. Now just a wee way from Fisherman's Wharf is a ship—an old sailing ship that is calculated to destroy many an illusion. It is the Motion Picture Ship. It has, so the notice on the side says, been used in 'The Mutiny on the Bounty' and similar pictures with settings on an old sailing ship. If one looks closely one can see hanging from the yardarm the figure of a man. It hangs dejectedly in the breeze. He is always there ready, so that when the point in the picture is reached when the villain or the poor unfortunate victim is hanged by the cruel Master of the ship, they have only to shoot the scene without going to the trouble of hanging another figure up each time! Went through Chinatown on the way back. It is said it is the largest Chinese community outside China. The overhanging tops of the shops are shaped like a Chinese temple. A girl like a picture sits at an upstairs window—she poses because it is natural for her to pose. It seems hard to say it but there is no beauty in the English race after studying the exquisite beauty of the Italians and these perfect little Orientals. We may be fresh and pretty but we are not purely exquisite. We are as a full blown rose to an orchid. I climbed the Coit Tower to see Alcatraz. It lies—a solitary island in a vast ocean. There are no little connecting islets and the water seems deep to its very shores. This is the island for the worst of the Public Enemies—that is those of them who are caught!

24 May 1940

The 'Lurline'[32] is a brave white boat—not so big as I had thought, but essentially a 'holiday' boat. A group of Salvationists sing farewell hymns. I am leaving America—and I am not leaving it satisfied as I left England. I haven't seen enough. And then something slid under the door. It was a cable. 'A safe voyage and good luck—Frank'. The dear—he must have known I'd feel like that about leaving. The cabin is full. Mrs. D. comes from Kentucky. The negro influence there must be very great. 'Ah just can't reckon it out' she was saying. I hardly understood one word of what she said. The 'mammies' of her early youth had left a tremendous impression. Her words seemed to have no end, they slithered into one another with a delightful laziness that was musical but entirely incomprehensible. Life on the Lurline began. Lots of girls going to join their husbands in the Navy. We have a dear old soul as table steward—Curly—without a single hair to curl. I love the daily life of a boat—the lounging in deck chairs watching the flying fish and chatting with people who are so different from one another.

26 May 1940

Somehow we dream our way into Los Angeles—or rather Wilmington. Los Angeles lies miles away on a little train. To the shops in Los Angeles and then caught the train to Hollywood. Who has ever wandered up Hollywood Boulevard and can ever forget it—the white modern buildings, the clean wide street and the lavish green palms. There are shops with the latest in Hollywood playsuits. Every little girl up to 17 is an exact replica of Deanna Durbin. Over 20 the Joan Crawford type seems to win. On every corner is an Owl Drug store. As usual the portion devoted to drugs is very, very small. The main portion is devoted to ice-cream sodas, the rest to toiletries and Kodak supplies. There are oddities in Hollywood too as nowhere else in the world. A man at least seven foot tall unwound himself from a drug store stool and bending at the door strode down the pavement. A trio with beards to their waists walked arm in arm down the Boulevard. The streets off the Boulevard and running parallel with it, such as Sunset Avenue, are charming. They are filled for the most part with apartment houses but they are so charming with no fences and little gardens with gaily flowering shrubs. Even the shops do not face the street stolidly and respectably like an ordinary shop. They so often veer off sideways and stand a little back so that one is able to enter them through a little sort of courtyard. Every other apartment block houses a fortune teller. Surely this is their Mecca? Just couldn't help but wander into one. She lay on a divan smoking 'fragrant' scented cigarettes; at least advertisements would have called them 'fragrant'. Some men that I have known would have had another name. 'You will marry' she said. 'It is a pity but you will marry. All men are brutes—quick there's Errol Flynn'. Dashed to the window in time to see a huge roadster and the back of Errol Flynn's head disappearing in the distance. He has a very nice 'back of the head'. She promised me 'an affair on the boat' and then relapsed on the divan and I felt the time had come to tender my payment and go.

A taxi took me to Beverley Hills. We had glimpses of houses and swimming pools. Slick shiny cars containing slick shiny film stars were pointed out to me. Many I didn't know at all. The men were fairly ordinary looking creatures but the women are so over-painted, their hair for the most part lost in a tight-fitting turban and a cigarette between their lips. It is the beauty of Beverley Hills that I loved—the greenness and coolness of it all—the wide clean streets. We saw Deanna Durbin's home of the Spanish type with a quaint little Chinese temple affair nestling in the trees. The film stars can make me a Bolshie where Royalty fails. Why should these exotic over-painted, over-sexed, over-indulged people live in Beverley Hills? I have no desire to be a Queen—I envy no Royal Family. I have no violent desire to fight for equality of man or wipe out Dukes and Duchesses but I feel wickedly covetous about Beverley Hills. To think that all this beauty is the exclusive prerogative of people like that—I felt a wrath as righteous as any Victorian matron against their 'goings-on'.

I was frankly glad when the taxi driver landed me again in Hollywood Boulevard. I was getting all 'het up' with envy—a thing that I'd never done in my life before! But it was Hollywood alright—at one theatre they were doing 'The Mikado' in swing. Opposite, Grauman's Chinese Theatre brought an oriental flavour to the street. Here on the paving stones are signatures of stars done while the concrete is wet. There was even Rin-Tin-Tin's paw mark. I stood on Tom Mix and let a bright youth from the East take my photo. Caught the train back to the boat reluctantly. At San Francisco I felt as though I was leaving America and I was unhappy. I don't feel like that now. I feel as if I am going to Honolulu which is something quite different.

27 May 1940

Lots of new faces today. All the girls in their sun-suits—all anticipating their holiday romances at the Royal Hawaiian to the tune of $12 a day. Some of them look at me rather patronisingly. 'Am I just on holiday?'—Yes. 'Am I staying at the Royal Hawaiian?'—No. They remark 'Oh' in a tone that implies that if one does not stay at the Royal Hawaiian one might as well stay at home. They condescend to explain that they're staying at the Royal Hawaiian for three weeks and pause to see the effect. There isn't any—about a dozen have told me so already and it is no news. So they ask how long I'm on holiday for. I just couldn't help it. I prepared to move 'Well as a matter of fact I've been on holiday for well over a year now' and nonchalantly 'just travelling about you know'. Their 'Oh' was different this time—a most peculiar 'oh' combining surprise, a new respect and a sudden realisation of an error of judgement. I shot down to my cabin furious with myself for having acted so childishly. They deserved it but to talk like that just isn't—well it isn't English!

29 May 1940

We are all in our best. I feel I should have 'prepared' for Honolulu. As I stood by the rail someone, I know not whom, flung a leis round my neck and welcomes me to Hawaii. A blue sea dances about a grey battleship. There is a huge carrier with the planes packed as neatly as sardines. The 'big birds' of the sky boom and swoop overhead, dipping and circling in welcome. I am glad, so glad, that somewhere in that sea of faces waiting for the boat I am watched for. I would hate to come to Hawaii a stranger. And then a cry of recognition—Mr Wills and Grace. Ropes of leis[33] round my neck, a confusing joking about my fur coat, a fussing after luggage and we're in the car on the way to Kailua.

These first impressions of Hawaii—how precious they are. How can they be captured—not in words, they are not quick enough. The purity of the white suits, laundered as only the Japanese can launder—the grace of the fluted hills—the romance of the coconuts palms curved against the flawless sky. The quiet soft roads lined with flowers and then the bungalow set at one side of a smooth green lawn, hibiscus flowers everywhere, the dull thud of coconuts as they fall and a soft scented breeze.

30 May 1940

And I learn the routine of another household. Am introduced to the exquisite amber glass cups and saucers. We drink our vegetable and fruit juices first, made through a juice extractor, and then breakfast—zweibach, cottage cheese, marmalade and first of all papaya. When the Lord gave the people of Hawaii papaya he gave them a great gift. It is nectar that melts like chilled honey in one's mouth. And somehow Grace and Len just fit into it all. Dear Grace! Her English is perfect, and yet a little, and very little, Americanism has crept in. Her movements are slow and full of grace. The whole house shakes when I thump across the floor in my bare feet but Grace's Japanese slippers just 'pit pat' melodiously. A game of croquet on the lawn in the afternoon. I get beaten badly. We read a bit, play Chinese chequers and strum Hawaiian tunes on the piano, Talk of those at home in New Zealand, drink iced orange juice and at 9.30 drift off to bed. Life is very, very good in Hawaii.

June 1940

Honolulu, Waikiki, Pearl Harbor

3 June 1940

A right busy day sewing. A necessity more than a pleasure. Have got a bit thinner and skirts are falling off me. America has made me smarten up and shorten frocks, and underskirts are too long. Have a lot of fun with the electric machine. To the library—children come and go exchanging books and making notes. Chinese children and Japanese children who are now Americans. It seems that every child reads in Honolulu. Japanese children they say are American citizens unless registered to the Japanese consul within two weeks after birth thus doing away with the vexed problem of dual citizenship. But I notice that both Chinese and Japanese children spend so many hours a day at their own national schools as well as at the American one. I heard today a diminutive Japanese boy haranguing on the virtues of the Mikado. They have some interesting advanced ideas on education here. For instance Parent-Teacher Associations. There are about 60 local units having a total paid up membership of 12,385 parents and teachers, the month's due being 15 cents. Practised the Hula with Thelma in the evening. She is teaching me to Hula to Manuela Boy. Must remember to get Manuela Boy for the gramophone when I get home. The Hula comprises suitable actions to the song—not obvious ones but all blending into the snake-like motions of the dance. My actions are not snake-like—never felt so clumsy in all my life.

6 June 1940

It is strange in this lovely land that I have lost my powers to describe and express. I could draw more telling pictures in the dirt and ugliness of Rotherham. It is because here it is expressed for one—there is no need—nay it is impossible to add to perfection. One's soul is soaked with beauty, one is satiated with a luxurious 'kitten-like' content. We visited Berta today for lunch and take our water melon and our corn on the cob and sit outside. Berta is delightful—a Russian to whom Communistic Russia is a lovely dream. Ring up Dole Pineapple Company and they advise me to take a taxi to their premises. Take a taxi, and I can <u>see</u> the gigantic pineapple that tops their building! Does no-one ever walk? It is the world's largest pineapple that stands on top of the building—it is used as an emergency tank for storing water. Their pineapples are grown on 25,000 acres of land on two islands. They employ 7,000 people on the plantations and 6,000 in the cannery (and no Union). We get to where the girls are filling the cans with sliced, cubed and squashed pineapple. About a dozen men do nothing but sharpen knives. The cafeteria comes next and a kitchen where staff may bring their own dinner and keep it hot in ovens. Then to the greatest machine of all. In goes the whole pineapple and out pops (1) a barrel-shaped piece of pineapple all ready for slicing, cored and peeled, (2) the core all squashed up for juice and (3) the skin scraped to the bone. And what of the waste? There just isn't any. The skin is dried and made into bran for cattle consumption and out of something else (goodness knows what) calcium citrate with its derivative, citric acid.

9 June 1940

Today we saw that epic Grapes of Wrath. One does not feel the happier for seeing it. It is too strong. It carries too much of a message. Did it get its message home to the crowd at Waikiki? One thinks not. After all they are here to play. They are not all people to whom a round of pleasure is the daily round. Some are workers to whom Honolulu is a brief dream. One would not wipe the laughter from the young girl who flirts with the nearly naked figure under the striped umbrella. We dine in the evening at the Tavern, sitting on the terrace for our meal on the edge of the sands with the blue waves lapping almost to our feet. The sun sets but it gets no cooler, still the same soft warmth. Down for a swim after supper. Somehow the moon is not silvery here it is golden and I swam in the golden path it made on the water.

12 June 1940

At Mrs. P.'s flat in Hibiscus Drive. It is a dream flat of soft cushions and a silver-tongued wireless. Here I meet Agnes L. whom we call Narvik in deference to her Norwegian birth. A sculptor and a blonde who eats a mere pittance and is fashionably thin. She is an amazingly self-possessed person capable of supreme indifference and intense interest. Fortunately she seemed to have sufficient money to let her be supremely aloof to the rest of the world. Dear Mr. P. is a communist to a degree, fiercely Russian. He talks ceaselessly of those fascinating things called 'stooges' of the Government, the idle middlemen, parasites, suckers—and yet when I come to think of it, what work does he do himself? I'm not criticising my host, it is no business of mine, but he has an agency for an encyclopaedia, and in Honolulu, the playground of the world! Met Peter R, a fair-haired Jew, whose folks are 'army'. We swam in and out of the warm sea and surfed as far out as I dared but oh the coral hurts one 'on the beach at Waikiki'. The sky is so blue and the sand so cream. One wonders how Mr. P. can even spare a thought for Russia. How few I spare for New Zealand. Sometimes it seems that I am in a hashish dream—something has crept into me that has dulled my thinking into a delicious languor. I see only the beauty.

19 June 1940

Pick up Len, Grace's husband. He's had a hard gruelling day. It seems that the sugar and pineapple plantations have a sort of community settlement for workers. Presumably they have every advantage—recreation grounds, good sanitation, rent-free homes, free water and electricity, medical and hospital attention without charge; and yet trouble arises. Personally I don't like these 'settlements' however perfectly run. They tend to give their organiser an exalted idea of importance. The young ones feel this too. They feel 'patronised' and these troubles arise. For instance the young ones like to have their friends without restrictions at any hour but the plantation owners demand that the gates be shut at a certain time. To 'Mice and Men' at Waikiki. Book by the same author as Grapes of Wrath—a strong picture but slightly depressing. The 'Niagara'[34] has been torpedoed and I'm booked to go home on her. First thoughts 'Hurrah now I won't have to go' but when sanity returns realise it is rather serious. Shipping Co. won't transfer my ticket to the 'Matson'. I can pay full single fare to New Zealand and collect on my 'Niagara' ticket when I get there, if I can! Frankly all I've got in the world is my ticket and about £8. Must get going on this.

22 June 1940

The day is perfect as are all the days in Hawaii. The breakers dash against Waimanalo beach—camping parties are awakening and getting busy with the frying pan. We call at Joe Fatts for a quick 'coc'. Found out the four industries of Hawaii—Pineapple, Sugar, Tourists and Sons-in-Law. At Pearl Harbour most of the Fleet is missing but there are grey battleships against the blue sky. Along the road are weird and wonderful cactus plants. Strange how cactus flourishes with luxuriant vegetation so close. Soldiers guard all the important bridges. Go to the Pan-Pacific dinner. A good lecture on relativity or something or other. I know it was good lecture—it must have been because I didn't understand a word of it. It is no use pretending, it was highly technical and just beyond me. Americans don't pretend as much as we do, if they don't understand a thing they say so straight out.

24 June 1940

Parked in the shipping company's indefinitely and gazed at the vivid picture of the sea in the 'Matson' offices. There is a beautiful but vacant blonde as receptionist. Still vague as to how I'm to get home. Perhaps if I come back in a day or two—meanwhile the immigration office won't extend my permit to stay. Fortunately there's only two things I can do—either stay or go. One office won't let me stay and the other won't let me go! At night to a lecture on the war in China. First of all the local dignitaries speak. One can even pick up the different dialects. Chinese they might be but they still 'er… er' like any other speaker. Then the speaker for the evening. He spoke in Chinese but there were plentiful lantern slides of pitiful scenes of desolation. He was a man of forceful voice and presence. One didn't need to translate his words. The hall was full. When the Chinese attend a lecture they bring the whole family. One wonders exactly what their thoughts are as they view the smoking ruins of a town that might have been their home.

26 June 1940

Go in early again to wrestle with the shipping company. The Matson Co. has interviewed someone and they'll take me on my ticket and my £8. Met Mrs. B, who is an old High School girl, so we have lots in common. The house is really lovely. Quite a number of New Zealand women there and were they fiercely English! Never would they sink their personality into anything American—they just enjoyed living there that's all. All were knitting socks for the soldiers. A silent little Japanese maid in her national dress brings in the dinner. Into town to fix up about shipping in general—De Freest Co. stung me for 6 dollars for storing my cases. Everywhere one goes there is the whirr of sewing machines, be it a Japanese fruit shop, a fancy shop or a meat shop. This then is the secret of the cheap clothing in Hawaii. Child labour is not considered a problem at all. An eight hour day is considered the basic working day but if so those machines go at surprisingly late hours.

July 1940

Pago Pago, Suva, Auckland

1 July 1940

Today I said goodbye to Honolulu. No one can ever forget a Honolulu farewell. The last dinner at the Capitol Market—a huge tuna sandwich, coffee and strawberry shortcake. A last look round the shops and a last dutiful wait for the traffic signals—no one here would dream of disobeying. And then at six o' clock the boat. It was a glorious confusing medley of leis, chatter and tears. I pick up a lei and dropped it in the water for by doing this, and this only, does one ensures coming back.

2 July 1940

Life has begun on the 'Monterey'. A dear little cabin mate who paints—an art teacher in Chicago. She speaks for all the world like Jane Ace! Make friends with Dr. and Mrs. D. and little David. Sensible people and yet how these American children's complexes are analysed. What used to evoke a good old-fashioned 'smacked bottom' now causes long discussions of child psychology, repressions and such. The pretty little girls at the table—it appears that they are Australian of poor parents. A fairy godmother Aunt in America gave them a year or more's holiday. She had one taught hair-dressing and the other commercial work. She had their teeth fixed and bought them pretty and abundant clothes. The other one at table is a man. Not a very satisfactory man. He moons about a lot by himself and seems incapable of behaving naturally. He counters the most innocent remark by a sarcasm. A great number of navy men going down to the base at Pago. They inform me in confidence that the U.S. Navy is 'punk' but they're building it up as quickly as they can.

5 July 1940

Today we crossed the Line. The whistle blows and we all rush to the side to look. What we expect to see I don't know. All issued with a certificate to prove we really sailed the seas. Enjoy Kono coffee for breakfast and think I prefer its flavour to the ordinary kind. The silent man silenter than ever. The girls and I come to the conclusion he is slightly seasick, been given a very recent shock by some woman or is on a secret mission.

6 July 1940

A rainbow welcomes us at Pago Pago—strangely enough this is pronounced Pango Pango. A rainbow and a market where bright beads and baskets, outrigger canoes and coconuts are for sale. In the native village are round grass huts hiding in amongst the trees—or rather I should say there is a round grass roof held up by pillars. When it rains hard grass mats are let down but ordinary family life is definitely not a private affair. The cooking place is public—just a group of stones. A young girl, presumably with no knowledge of English, stirring candy in a kerosene tin. America has taught them that much! Realised that when it was finished it would be coconut ice! Friendly little kiddies, all smiles and white teeth, their little brown bodies encased in faded cotton frocks in the case of girls and for the boys just a piece of cloth round their waists. Some of the kiddies have evidence of skin disease, some sore eyes and some are distinctly mulatto with blue eyes, but only a few. A little girl picks a hibiscus for my hair and tucks it in shyly. She carries my purse and camera carefully. Her brother strides sturdily along beside us picking up shells, carefully washing them and handing them to me. They laugh all the time. A baby looks at us solemnly from up a papaya tree sitting in a fork like a little koala bear. Surely they must climb like monkeys from babyhood? Soft showers come and pass, melting imperceptibly into the trees and huts. The bananas hang full and yellow in great bunches.

We give the little boy and girl a quarter and they melt away to smile into the face of some other tourist. But they are not really commercialised yet. I give them another two or three years before the foreigners with cameras and tripods spoil them. But the missionaries are here. Rival churches hold a service. The women squat on the ground nursing their babies. It is said the services last for hours—the very hymns sound pagan. They are just a soft native chant in a minor key. We attend a concert and when over they give us bananas—no one asks us to buy. They are fat yellow bananas that taste so different to the shop variety. It would seem that Pago is a half-way house between Honolulu and our Maoris. They have the Hawaiian leis and a suspicion of a hula but their songs are more of their Maori strain and their dances restrained. The Pago version of the traditional longshoreman still lounge about the wharf. They smile expansively over their ample tummies where the piece of cloth holds on miraculously, and just lounge. One wonders if they have a Union and a Band! We pull out and Pago fades away into a mist and we drift down to dinner.

8 July 1940

There is a peculiar tension in the air. The New Zealanders get together in a huddle. They might not call at Auckland! Will they dump us at Suva to get home as best we can? It is funny but none of us have any money. We are all getting home with our last cent. I could always sell my typewriter. The mighty Manson line must decide whether Auckland is safe. Feel slightly resentful about all this precaution. The poor old 'Niagara' just sailed as a matter of course. What excitement her going down must have caused at home. It is a long time since I have thought of home and yet it is so near—it is only days away now.

WE GO TO AUCKLAND. The notice has appeared on the board and the New Zealanders breathe again. The silent man gets off at Suva. We are not sorry. He volunteered the information last night that he is going to Fiji to study native head-dress and to our surprise this morning thanked us for our company at the table and said he'd enjoyed his trip.   Evidently he thought us legitimate prey! But what expression does his face assume when he doesn't enjoy a trip! Never have I shown my passport so many times as I have in Fiji. It's British territory and well we know it. A camouflaged tank greets us and all the familiar signs of war. The Americans are all excited and chattery—they have been designated as 'aliens'. I become slightly patronising—if they only knew how I revolted against being an 'alien' in American territory! A native guard does sentry duty outside the wharf gates. How Gilbert and Sullivan would have revelled in him. His bearskin is replaced by a shock of the fuzziest hair I have ever seen. To the waist he is correctly military with a khaki shirt, a dull green official and useful-looking belt and a knapsack but below the waist he wears a green skirt scalloped in large points—the scallops flap against his ample brown legs that end in a pair of feet—the largest and broadest I have ever seen! Here tortoise shell is popular, inset with silver. I buy a long string of beads for *6d*. Two Fijian women in their pink frocks lie languidly on the ground. 'They *6d* to you' one says beaming. She turns to the other, 'She nice, she not American'.

Surely there is no place quite like Suva with its 'strange intrusion of India'. The exotic charm of a Pacific Isle mingled with the age-old wisdom and mysticism of the East. In the post office we send postcards to our friends via Tin-Can Island. We buy silk stockings at the Store for 4/11 per pair. We watch the sun set behind dark hills—I have watched many sunsets.

10 July 1940

The next stop is home. Today I have told Rex about New Zealand. I have talked about it deliberately to make it more real to me. Almost I am frightened of it as something strange. I am trying to 'feel' the air which in every land, in every town, is different. I believe I <u>am</u> frightened. I am frightened of what is ahead—the years that will come. I have loved these last eighteen months so, they have filled my whole being to repletion and even before I went I looked forward and lived for them until they came. And now they are gone. It is foolish but I feel tonight like some futile aimless thing, frightened not of what life will bring but what it will not bring.

11 July 1940

I am almost inclined to tear up yesterday. I'm excited today—my heart is going in absurd little pats and leaps. There'll be Mother and Daddy at the wharf. Not at the wharf for it's wartime but they'll come as close as they can. I'll see them long before I reach them and they'll grow nearer and nearer as once they grew further away. And when I kiss them they'll be real. Little Mum won't just be someone 'like Auntie Lizzie' she'll be real again. And Daddy will say 'Well pet' and his dear kind eyes will be just the same. Tonight we danced a tango and then gathered round the piano. I brought out my Maori songs and did a long poi[35]. It is getting colder. I have learned so much while away, solved such a lot of problems but then on the other hand I have new things to wonder about. Why, for instance, do people who travel, rush to gaze soulfully at the pictures in the Louvre and National Gallery when at home they never so much as set foot in their local gallery?

13 July 1940

This morning at 7 we drew into Auckland Harbour. It is a bright clear day exactly the same as when I left. I'll see the family soon. How can anyone sit and calmly eat breakfast? Drank a cup of tea and on deck again. At last we wait in the lounge. No one can leave the ship yet. Up the gangway comes someone from shore. It is Mr. Wild! I'm the first, the very first, to have someone to meet me. I'm the first, indeed the only one just then to get off. We go out under the amazed and indignant gaze of the others.

How long the wharf seems. I can see them on the other side of the gate—and then we're all mixed up. Daddy, Mother, a basket of coral and an outrigger canoe. Daddy has said 'Well pet' just as I knew he would. Mrs Wild is there and Mr. and Mrs. Lowe and my two dears are just the same as they were when I left.

This then is the diary of one Gwynne Irene Peacock who returned this 13th day of July 1940.

Height 5ft 2ins.

Weight 9 stones 5lbs (131 lbs) !!!!!

Distinguishing marks: Not even the gold filling. Lost it yesterday eating an olive.

She has travelled the world under the benign protection of the great British Empire as represented by His Excellency Viscount Galway. Has returned to her native land with the sum of 25 cents in her purse, complete with five suitcases, one portable typewriter, one camera and one travelling rug and it had been FUN ALL THE WAY.